Introduction to AutoCAD 2008
2D and 3D Design

Alf Yarwood

Authorised Author

ELSEVIER

AMSTERDAM • BOSTON • HEIDELBERG • LONDON • NEW YORK
OXFORD • PARIS • SAN DIEGO • SAN FRANCISCO
SINGAPORE • SYDNEY • TOKYO

Newnes is an imprint of Elsevier

Newnes

Newnes is an imprint of Elsevier
Linacre House, Jordan Hill, Oxford, OX2 8DP
30 Corporate Drive, Burlington, MA 01803

First edition 2007

Notice
No responsibility is assumed by the publisher for any injury and/or damage to persons
or property as a matter of products liability, negligence or otherwise, or from any use or
operation of any methods, products, instructions or ideas contained in the material herein.
Because of rapid advances in the medical sciences, in particular, independent verification
of diagnoses and drug dosages should be made

British Library Cataloguing in Publication Data
A catalogue record for this book is available from the British Library

Library of Congress Cataloging-in-Publication Data
A catalog record for this book is available from the Library of Congress

ISBN: 978-0-75-068512-2

For information on all Newnes publications
visit our web site at http://books.elsevier.com

Typeset by Integra Software Services Pvt. Ltd, Pondicherry, India
www.integra-india.com

Printed and bound in Italy

07   08   09   10   11   11   10   9   8   7   6   5   4   3   2   1

Introduction to AutoCAD 2008

Contents

Preface

The purpose of writing this book is to produce a text suitable for those in Further and/or Higher Education who are required to learn how to use the CAD software package AutoCAD® 2008. Students taking examinations based on computer-aided design will find the contents of the book of great assistance. The book is also suitable for those in industry who wish to learn how to construct technical drawings with the aid of AutoCAD 2008 and those who, having used previous releases of AutoCAD, wish to update their skills in the use of AutoCAD.

The chapters dealing with two-dimensional (2D) drawing will also be suitable for those who wish to learn how to use AutoCAD LT 2008, the 2D version of this latest release of AutoCAD.

Many readers using AutoCAD 2002, 2004, 2005, 2006 or 2007 will find the book's contents largely suitable for use with those versions of AutoCAD, although AutoCAD 2008 has enhancements over AutoCAD 2002, 2004, 2005, 2006 and 2007 (see Chapter 21).

The contents of the book are basically a graded course of work, consisting of chapters giving explanations and examples of methods of constructions, followed by exercises which allow the reader to practise what has been learned in each chapter. The first 12 chapters are concerned with constructing technical drawings in 2D. These are followed by chapters detailing the construction of three-dimensional (3D) solid drawings and rendering. The two final chapters describe the Internet tools of AutoCAD 2008 and the place of AutoCAD in the design process. The book finishes with three appendices: printing and plotting; a list of tools with their abbreviations; a list of some of the set variables upon which AutoCAD 2008 is based.

AutoCAD 2008 is very complex computer-aided design (CAD) software package. A book of this size cannot possibly cover the complexities of all the methods for constructing 2D and 3D drawings available when working with AutoCAD 2008. However, it is hoped that by the time the reader has worked through the contents of the book, they will be sufficiently skilled with the methods of producing drawing with the software, will be able to go on to more advanced constructions with its use, and will have gained an interest in the more advanced possibilities available when using AutoCAD.

Alf Yarwood
Salisbury 2007

Registered Trademarks

Autodesk® and AutoCAD® are registered in the US Patent and Trademark Office by Autodesk Inc.
Windows® is a registered trademark of the Microsoft Corporation.

Alf Yarwood is an Autodesk authorised author and a member of the Autodesk Advanced Developer Network.

PART I

2D Design

CHAPTER I

Introducing AutoCAD 2008

Aim of this chapter

The contents of this chapter are designed to introduce features of the AutoCAD 2008 window and methods of operating AutoCAD 2008.

Opening AutoCAD 2008

AutoCAD 2008 is designed to work in a Windows operating system. In general, to open AutoCAD 2008, either *double-click* on the **AutoCAD 2008** shortcut in the Windows desktop (Fig. 1.1), or *right-click* on the icon, followed by a *left-click* on **Open** in the menu which then appears (Fig. 1.2).

Fig. 1.1 The **AutoCAD 2008** shortcut icon on the Windows desktop

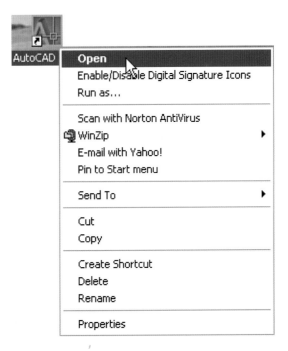

Fig. 1.2 The *right-click* menu which appears from the shortcut icon

When working in education or in industry, computers may be configured to allow other methods of opening AutoCAD, such as a list appearing on the computer in use when the computer is switched on, from which the operator can select the program they wish to use.

When AutoCAD 2008 is opened a window appears, depending upon whether a **3D Modeling, Classic AutoCAD** or a **2D Drafting & Annotation** workspace has been used previously. In this example the **2D Drafting & Annotation** workspace is shown and includes the drop-down menu from which a choice of the AutoCAD workspace to be opened can be made (Fig. 1.3). This **2D Drafting & Annotation** workspace shows:

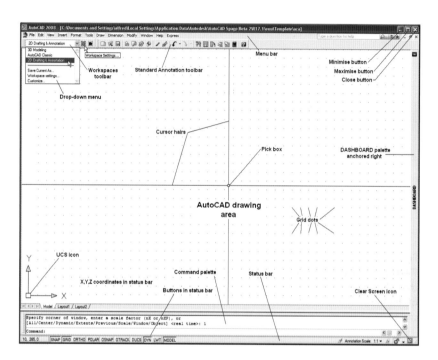

Fig. 1.3 The AutoCAD 2008
2D Drafting & Annotation
workspace with its various parts

Standard Annotation toolbar (Fig. 1.4) *docked* at the top of the Auto-CAD window under the **Menu bar**.

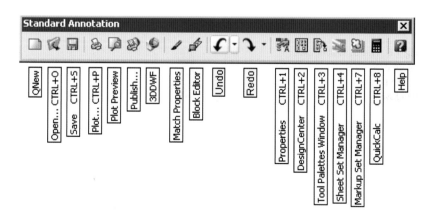

Fig. 1.4 The tools in the
Standard Annotation toolbar

Workspaces toolbar (Fig. 1.5) to the left of **Standard Annotation**.

Fig. 1.5 The **Workspace Settings** dialog appearing when the **Workspace Settings...** icon of the **Workspaces** toolbar is *clicked*

Command palette can be *dragged* from its position at the bottom of the AutoCAD window into the AutoCAD drawing area, when it can be seen as a palette (Fig. 1.6). As with all palettes, an **AutoHide** icon and a *right-click* menu is included:

Fig. 1.6 The command palette when *dragged* from its position at the bottom of the AutoCAD window

DASHBOARD palette showing a number of **Control panels**. In Fig. 1.7 the names of the tools in the **2D Draw** control panel are included.

Menu bar and menus: The **menu bar** is situated under the **title bar** and contains names of menus from which commands can be selected. Fig. 1.8 shows the **View** drop-down menu which appears with a *left-click* on the name. *Left-click* **3D Views** in the drop-down menu and a submenu appears, from which other sub-menus can be selected if required.

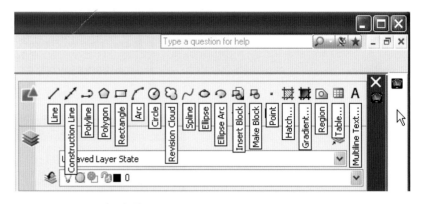

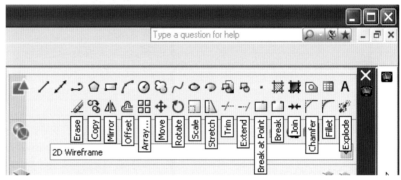

Fig. 1.7 The tools in the **2D Draw** control panel

The mouse as a digitiser

Many operators working in AutoCAD will use a two-button mouse as the digitiser. There are other digitisers which may be used – pucks with tablets, a three-button mouse etc. Fig. 1.9 shows a mouse which has two buttons and a wheel.

To operate this mouse pressing the **Pick button** is a *left-click*. Pressing the **Return** button is a *right-click*. Pressing the **Return** button usually has the same result as pressing the **Enter** key of the keyboard.

When the **wheel** is pressed drawings in the AutoCAD screen can be panned. Moving the wheel forward enlarges (zooms in) the drawing on screen. Moving the wheel backwards reduces the size of a drawing.

The pick box at the intersection of the cursor hairs moves with the cursor hairs in response to movements of the mouse. The AutoCAD window as shown in Fig. 1.3 includes cursor hairs which stretch across the drawing in both horizontal and vertical directions. Some operators prefer cursors hairs to be shorter. The length of the cursor hairs can be adjusted in the **Display** sub-menu of the **Options** dialog (page 10).

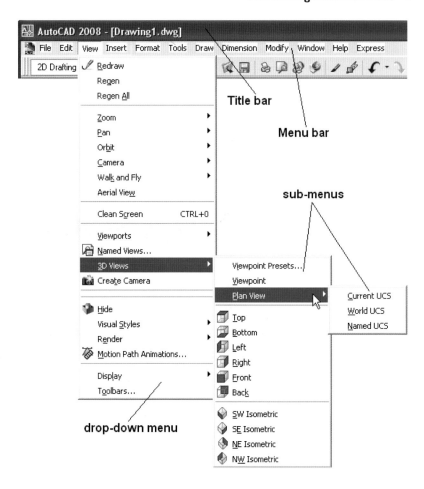

Fig. 1.8 Menus and sub-menus

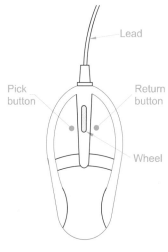

Fig. 1.9 A two-button mouse

Palettes

A palette has already been shown – the **Command** palette. Two palettes which may be frequently used are the **DesignCenter** palette and the **Properties** palette. These can be called to screen from icons in the **Standard Annotation** toolbar. The icon for the **DesignCenter** is shown in Fig. 1.10.

DesignCenter palette: Fig. 1.11 shows the palette showing the **Block** drawings of electronics circuit symbols from an AutoCAD directory **DesignCenter** from which the drawing file **Basic Electronics** has been selected. An electronics symbol drawing can be *dragged* from the **DesignCenter** for inclusion in a drawing under construction.

Properties palette: Fig. 1.12 shows the **Properties** palette, also called from the **Standard Annotation** toolbar, in which the general and

Fig. 1.10 A *left-click* on the **DesignCenter** icon brings the **DesignCenter** palette to screen

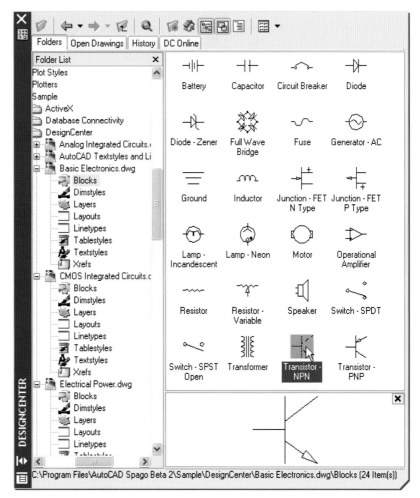

Fig. 1.11 The **DesignCenter** palette

geometrical features of a selected polyline are shown. The polyline can be changed by the *entering* of new figures in parts of the palette.

The DASHBOARD palette

Click on **Tools** in the menu bar and from the drop-down menu which appears *click* **Dashboard**. The **DASHBOARD** palette appears (Fig. 1.13). *Right-click* in the title bar of the palette and a popup menu appears. *Click* on **Control panels** and *click* against names which appear in the sub-menu. Parts of the **DASHBOARD** disappear leaving only those control panels selected from the popup list. This can be reduced in size by *dragging* at corners or edges, or hidden by *clicking* on the **Auto-hide** icon, or moved by *dragging* on the **Move** icon.

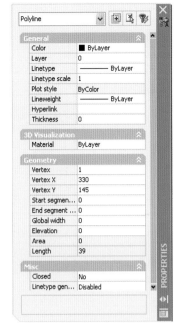

Fig. 1.12 The **Properties** palette

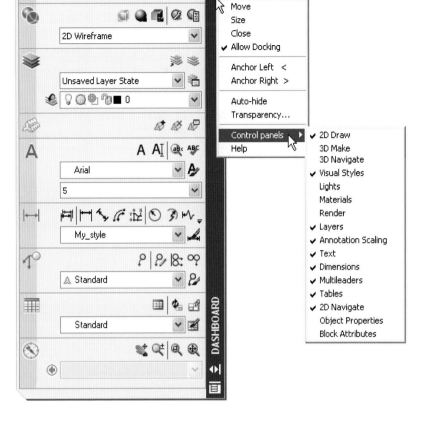

Fig. 1.13 The **DASHBOARD** palette

Notes

1. Throughout this book tools will be shown as selected from the **DASHBOARD** control panels. It will be seen in Chapter 3 that tools can be 'called' in a variety of ways but, in the main, tools will be selected from the control panels in the **DASHBOARD**.
2. For more details about the **DASHBOARD**, see page 18.

Dialogs

Dialogs are an important feature of AutoCAD 2008. Settings can be made in many of the dialogs, files can be saved and opened, and changes can be made to variables.

Examples of dialogs are shown in Figs 1.14 and 1.15. The first example is taken from the **Select File** dialog (Fig. 1.14), opened with a *click* on **Open...** in the **File** drop-down menu (Fig. 1.16). The second example shows part of the **Options** dialog (Fig. 1.15) in which many settings can be made to allow operators the choice of their methods of constructing

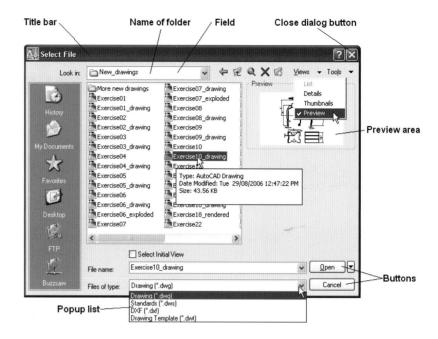

Fig. 1.14 The **Select File** dialog

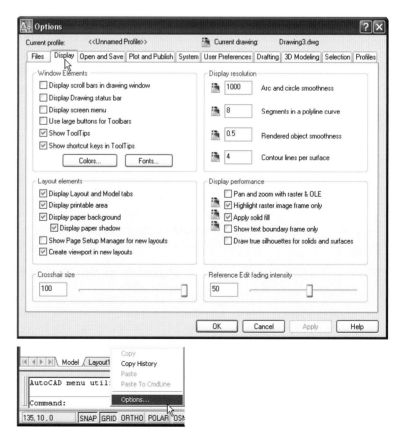

Fig. 1.15 Part of the **Options** dialog

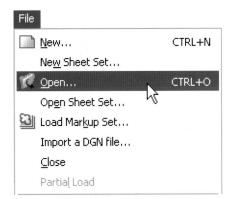

Fig. 1.16 Opening the **Select File** dialog from the **File** drop-down menu

drawings. The **Options** dialog can be opened with a *click* on **Options...** in the *right-click* menu opened in the command window.

Note the following parts in the dialog many of which are common to other AutoCAD dialogs:

Title bar: showing the name of the dialog.
Close dialog button: common to other dialogs.
Popup list: a *left-click* on the arrow to the right of the field brings down a popup list which lists selections available in the dialog.
Buttons: a *click* on the **Open** button brings the selected drawing on screen. A *click* on the **Cancel** button, closes the dialog.
Preview area: available in some dialogs – shows a miniature of the selected drawing or other features, only part of which is shown in Fig. 1.14.

Note the following in the **Options** dialog:

Tabs: a *click* on any of the tabs in the dialog brings a sub-dialog on screen.
Check boxes: a tick appearing in a check box indicates the function described against the box is on. No tick and the function is off. A *click* in a check box toggles between the feature being off or on.
Radio buttons: a black dot in a radio button indicates the feature described is on. No dot and the feature is off.
Slider: a slider pointer can be *dragged* to change sizes of the feature controlled by the slider.

Buttons in the status bar

A number of buttons in the status bar can be used for toggling (turning on/off) various functions when operating within AutoCAD 2008 (Fig. 1.17). A *click* on a button turns that function on, if it is off, a *click* on a button when it is off turns the function back on. Similar results can be obtained by using function keys of the computer keyboard (keys **F1** to **F10**).

SNAP: also toggled using the **F9** key. When snap on, the cursor under mouse control can only be moved in jumps from one snap point to another. See also page 14.

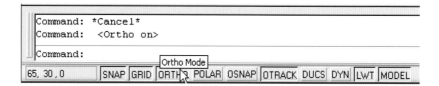

Fig. 1.17 The buttons in the status bar

GRID: also toggled using the **F7** key. When set on, a series of grid points appears in the drawing area. See also page 14.

ORTHO: also toggled using the **F8** key. When on, lines, etc. can only be drawn vertically or horizontally.

POLAR: also toggled using the **F10** key. When set on, a small tip appears showing the direction and length of lines, etc. in degrees and units.

OSNAP: also toggled using the **F3** key. When set on, an osnap icon appears at the cursor pick box. See also page 45.

OTRACK: when set on, lines, etc. can be drawn at exact coordinate points and precise angles.

DUCS: Dynamic UCS. Also toggled by the **F6** key. Used when constructing **3D** solid models.

DYN: Dynamic Input. When set on, the **x, y** coordinates and prompts show when the cursor hairs are moved.

LWT: when set on, lineweights show on screen. When set off, lineweights only show in plotted/printed drawings.

Maximise Viewport: when in **Paper Space** a button can toggle **Model Space** and **Paper Space** and a new button appears for toggling between **Maximizing** and **Minimizing** the workspace.

Note the square light-blue button at the right-hand end of the status bar – the **Clean Screen** button. *Left-click* this button and a screen clear of all but the menu bar and the command palette appears. When in the **Clean Screen** workspace another *click* on the button and the screen reverts to its original state.

Note

When constructing drawings in AutoCAD 2008 it is advisable to toggle between **Snap, Ortho, Osnap** and the other functions in order to make constructing easier.

The AutoCAD coordinate system

In the AutoCAD 2D coordinate system, units are measured horizontally in terms of X and vertically in terms of Y. A 2D point can be determined in terms of X, Y (in this book referred to as *x, y*). $x,y = 0,0$ is the **origin** of the system. The coordinate point $x,y = 100,50$ is 100 units to the right of the origin and 50 units above the origin. The point $x,y = -100,-50$ is 100 units to the left of the origin and 50 points below the origin. Fig. 1.18 shows some 2D coordinate points in the AutoCAD window.

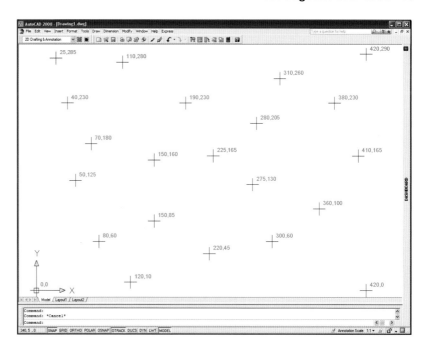

Fig. 1.18 The 2D coordinate
points in the AutoCAD
coordinate system

3D coordinates include a third coordinate (Z), in which positive Z units are towards the operator as if coming out of the monitor screen and negative Z units going away from the operator as if towards the interior of the screen. 3D coordinates are stated in terms of *x,y,z. x,y,z* = 100,50,50 is 100 units to the right of the origin, 50 units above the origin and 50 units towards the operator. A 3D model drawing as if resting on the surface of a monitor is shown in Fig. 1.19.

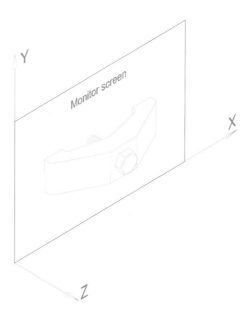

Fig. 1.19 A 3D model drawing
showing the X, Y and Z
coordinate directions

Drawing templates

Drawing templates are files with an extension **.dwt**. Templates are files which have been saved with predetermined settings – such as **Grid** spacing, **Snap** spacing, etc. Templates can be opened from the **Select template** dialog (see Fig. 1.20) called by *clicking* **New...** in the **File** drop-down menu. An example of a template file being opened is shown in Fig. 1.20. In this example the template will be opened in Paper Space and is complete with a title block and borders.

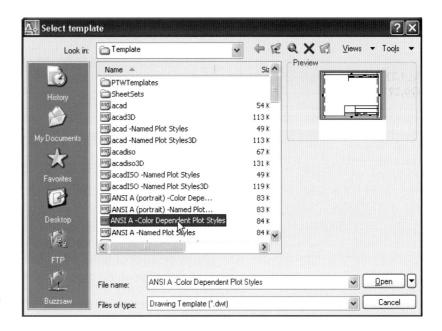

Fig. 1.20 A template selected for opening in the **Select template** dialog

When AutoCAD 2008 is used in European countries, the **acadiso.dwt** template automatically appears on screen. Throughout this book drawings will usually be constructed in an adaptation of the **acadiso.dwt** template. To adapt this template:

1. In the command palette *enter* (type) **grid** followed by a *right-click* (or by pressing the **Enter** key). Then *enter* **10** in response to the prompt which appears, followed by a *right-click* (Fig. 1.21).

```
Command: grid
Specify grid spacing(X) or [ON/OFF/Snap/Major/aDaptive/Limits/Follow/Aspect] <0>: 10
Command: |
```

Fig. 1.21 Setting **Grid** to **10**

2. In the command palette *enter* **snap** followed by *right-click*. Then *enter* **5** followed by a *right-click* (Fig. 1.22).

```
Command: snap
Specify snap spacing or [ON/OFF/Aspect/Style/Type] <0>: 5
Command:
```

Fig. 1.22 Setting **Snap** to **5**

3. In the command palette *enter* **limits**, followed by a *right-click. Right-click* again. Then *enter* **420,297** and *right-click* (Fig. 1.23).

```
Command: limits
Reset Model space limits:
Specify lower left corner or [ON/OFF] <0,0>:
Specify upper right corner <420,297>:

Command:
```

Fig. 1.23 Setting **Limits** to **420,297**

4. In the command window *enter* **zoom** and *right-click*. Then in response to the line of prompts which appears *enter* **a** (for All) and *right-click* (Fig. 1.24).

```
Command: zoom
Specify corner of window, enter a scale factor (nX or nXP), or
[All/Center/Dynamic/Extents/Previous/Scale/Window/Object] <real time>: a
Regenerating model.
Command:
```

Fig. 1.24 **Zooming** to **All**

5. In the command palette *enter* **units** and *right-click*. The **Drawing Units** dialog appears (Fig. 1.25). In the **Precision** popup list of the **Length** area of the dialog, *click* on **0** and then *click* the **OK** button. Note the change in the coordinate units showing in the status bar.

6. *Click* **File** in the menu bar and *click* **Save As...** in the drop-down menu which appears. The **Save Drawing As** dialog appears. In the **Files of type** popup list select **AutoCAD Drawing Template (*.dwt)**. The templates already in AutoCAD are displayed in the dialog. *Click* on **acadiso.dwt**, followed by another *click* on the Save button.

Notes

1. Now when AutoCAD is opened the template saved as **acadiso.dwt** automatically loads with **Grid** set to **10, Snap** set to **5, Limits** set to **420,297** (size of an A3 sheet in millimetres) and with the drawing area zoomed to these limits, with **Units** set to **0**.

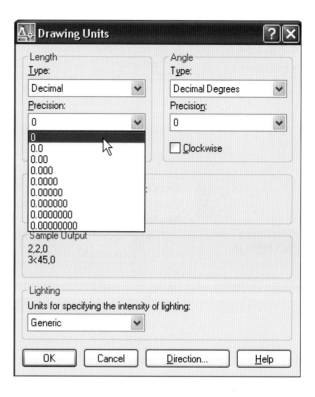

Fig. 1.25 Setting **Units** to **0**

2. However if there are multiple users to the computer, it is advisable to save your template to another file name – I have used **my_template.dwt**.

3. Other features will be added to the template in future chapters.

Method of showing entries in the command palette

Throughout the book, where necessary, details *entered* in the command palette will be shown as follows:

At the command line:

Command: *enter* **zoom** *right-click*
Specify corner of window, enter a scale factor (nX or nXP), or
 [All/Center/Dynamic/Extents/Previous/Scale/Window/Object]
 <real time>: *enter* **a** (All) *right-click*
Regenerating model.
Command:

Note

In later examples this may be shortened to:

Command: *enter* **z** *right-click*
[prompts]: *enter* **a** *right-click*
Command:

Fig. 1.26 Tool icons and a flyout in the **DASHBOARD** palette

Notes

1. In the above *enter* means type the given letter, word or words at the **Command:** prompt.
2. *Right-click* means press the **Return** (right) button of the mouse or press the **Return** key of the keyboard.

Tools and tool icons

An important feature of Windows applications are icons and tooltips. In AutoCAD 2008, tools are shown as icons in toolbars or in the **DASHBOARD** palette. When the cursor is placed over a tool icon a tooltip shows with the name of the tool as shown in the tooltips in the **Draw** and **Modify** toolbars (Fig. 1.7).

If a small arrow is included at the bottom right-hand corner of a tool icon, when the cursor is placed over the icon and the *pick* button of the mouse depressed and held, a flyout appears which includes other tool icons (Fig. 1.26). The example given in this illustration shows a flyout from the **2D Draw** control panel.

Another AutoCAD workspace

Click the arrow to the right of the **Workspaces** toolbar. In the menu which appears *click* **AutoCAD Classic** (Fig. 1.27). The **AutoCAD Classic** window appears (Fig. 1.28). This includes the **Draw** toolbar *docked* against

Fig 1.27 Selecting **AutoCAD Classic** from the **Workspaces** popup list

the left-hand side of the window and the **Modify** toolbar *docked* against the right-hand side of the window with other toolbars *docked* against the top of the window.

Other workspaces can be designed as the operator wishes. One in particular which may appeal to some operators is to *click* the **Clear Screen** icon at the bottom-right corner of the AutoCAD window (Fig. 1.29). This allows more working space. The **DASHBOARD** can be added or tools can be called by *entering* names or abbreviations in the command palette.

Fig. 1.28 The **AutoCAD Classic** window

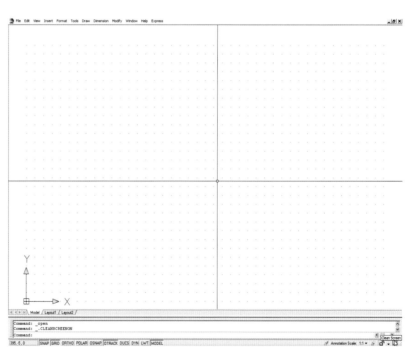

Fig. 1.29 The AutoCAD window after the **Clear Screen** icon has been selected

The DASHBOARD

The **DASHBOARD** includes a number of new control panels over those in AutoCAD 2007. Fig. 1.30 shows the complete list of control panels in the *right-click* popup list from the title bar.

Fig. 1.30 The *right-click* popup list from the **DASHBOARD** showing all the control panel names

Note the other features in the *right-click* popup list:

Allow Docking: When on (tick against the words), the **DASHBOARD** can be *docked* against the left- or right-hand sides of the AutoCAD window with a *click* on either **Anchor Left<** or **Anchor Right>**. Fig. 1.3 on page 4 shows the AutoCAD 2008 window with the **DASH-BOARD** anchored (*docked*) against the right-hand edge of the window. When anchored on either side, a *click* on the title bar (which turns a different colour when anchored) brings the **DASHBOARD** out on screen allowing tools to be selected from any of the control panels.

Transparency: A *click* on this command brings a dialog on screen allowing the **DASHBOARD** to be set in various degrees of transparency allowing drawing details on screen to be seen behind the **DASH-BOARD** (Fig. 1.31).

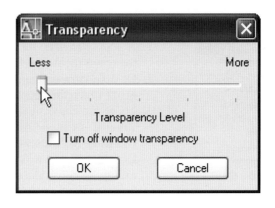

Fig. 1.31 The **Transparency** dialog

Larger Working area

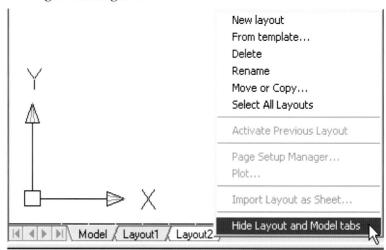

Fig. 1.32 The *right-click* menu from a tab

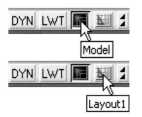

Fig. 1.33 The **Model** and **Layout** buttons in the status bar

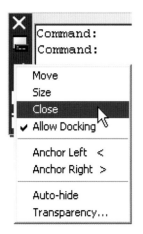

Fig. 1.34 Closing the **Command** palette

If desired the AutoCAD window drawing area can be further increased from that shown in Fig. 1.29 by taking the following two actions:

1. *Right-click* on either the **Model** or a **Layout** tab and, in the menu which appears, select **Hide Model and Layout** tabs (Fig. 1.32). The tabs disappear from the screen. However **Model** and **Paper** can then be selected from the buttons in the status bar (Fig. 1.33) which appears when the tabs are hidden.
2. The command window is really a palette which can be *dragged* from its normal position at the bottom of the AutoCAD window. A *right-click* in its title bar brings up a menu (Fig. 1.34). Select **Close** from the menu and the command palette disappears from the screen after which a warning window appears stating that the palette can be restored by pressing the **Ctrl + 9** keys.

The result of these two actions is to create a larger area for constructing drawings.

Revision notes

1. A *double-click* on the **AutoCAD 2008** shortcut in the Windows desktop opens the AutoCAD window.
2. Or *right-click* on the shortcut, followed by a *left-click* on **Open** in the menu which then appears.
3. There are three main workspaces in which drawings can be constructed – **Classic AutoCAD**, the **3D Modeling** workspace and **2D Drafting & Annotation**. From now on this part of the book (**Part I**), which deals with the construction of 2D drawings, will show examples constructed mainly in the **2D Drafting & Annotation** workspace.

4. A *left-click* on a menu name in the menu bar brings a drop-down menu on screen. In drop-down menus:
   (a) A small outward pointing arrow against a name means that a submenu will appear with a *click* on the name.
   (b) Three dots (**...**) following a name means that a *click* on the name will bring a dialog on screen.
5. All constructions in this book involve the use of a mouse as the digitiser. When a mouse is the digitiser:
   (a) A *left-click* means pressing the left-hand button (the **Pick**) button.
   (b) A *right-click* means pressing the right-hand button (the **Return** button.
   (c) A *double-click* means pressing the left-hand button twice is quick succession.
   (d) *Dragging* means moving the mouse until the cursor is over an item on screen, holding the left-hand button down and moving the mouse. The item moves in sympathy with the mouse movement.
   (e) To *pick* has a similar meaning to a *left-click*.
6. Palettes are a particular feature of AutoCAD 2008. The **Command** palette, the **DesignCenter** palette and the **Properties** palette will be in frequent use.
7. Tools are shown as icons in the control panels.
8. When a tool is *picked* a tooltip describing the tool appears.
9. Dialogs allow opening and saving of files and the setting of parameters.
10. A number of *right-click* menus are used in AutoCAD 2008.
11. A number of buttons in the status bar can be used to toggle features such as snap and grid. Function keys of the keyboard can also be used for toggling most of these functions.
12. The AutoCAD coordinate system determines the position in units of any point in the drawing area (**Classic AutoCAD** and **2D Drafting & Annotation**) and any point in 3D space (**3D Modeling**).
14. Drawings are usually constructed in templates with predetermined settings. Some templates include borders and title blocks.

CHAPTER 2

Introducing drawing

Aims of this chapter

The contents of this chapter are designed to introduce:

1. The construction of 2D drawing in the **2D Drafting & Annotation** workspace.
2. The drawing of simple outlines using the **Line, Circle** and **Polyline** tools from the **Draw** toolbar or the **2D Draw** control panel.
3. Drawing to snap points.
4. Drawing to absolute coordinate points.
5. Drawing to relative coordinate points.
6. Drawing using the 'tracking' method.
7. The use of the **Erase, Undo** and **Redo** tools.

The 2D Drafting & Annotation workspace

Illustrations throughout this chapter will be shown using the **2D Drafting & Annotation** workspace. However the methods of construction will be the same if the reader wishes to work in other workspaces. If the **2D Draw** control panel is on screen, tools can be selected from the panel. In this chapter most illustrations will show tools selected from the **2D Draw** control panel and some illustrations will show tools selected from the **Draw** toolbar. Whether working with the **2D Draw** control panel or the **Draw** toolbar, the sequences and prompts which appear at the command line will be the same.

Drawing with the Line tool

First example – Line tool (Fig. 2.3)

1. Open AutoCAD. The drawing area will show the settings of the **acadiso.dwt** template – **Limits** set to **420,297**, **Grid** set to **10, Snap** set to **5** and **Units** set to **0**.

2. *Left-click* on the **Line** tool in the **2D Draw** control panel (Fig. 2.1).

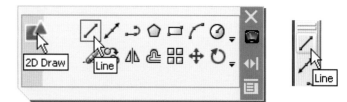

Fig. 2.1 The **Line** tool from the
2D Draw control panel or from
the **Draw** toolbar

Note

(a) The tooltip which appears when the tool icon is *clicked*.
(b) The prompt **Command:_line Specify first point:** which appears
in the command window at the command line (Fig. 2.2).

Fig. 2.2 The prompt appearing at
the command line in the command
palette when **Line** is 'called'

```
Command:
Command:
Command: _line Specify first point:
```

3. Make sure **Snap** is on by either pressing the **F9** key or the **SNAP** button in the status bar. **<Snap on>** will show in the command palette.
4. Move the mouse around the drawing area. The cursor's pick box will
jump from point to point at 5 unit intervals. The position of the pick
box will show as coordinate numbers in the status bar (left-hand end).
5. Move the mouse until the coordinate numbers show **60,240,0** and press
the **Pick** button of the mouse (*left-click*).
6. Move the mouse until the coordinate numbers show **260,240,0** and
left-click.
7. Move the mouse until the coordinate numbers show **260,110,0** and
left-click.
8. Move the mouse until the coordinate numbers show **60,110,0** and *left-
click*.
9. Move the mouse until the coordinate numbers show **60,240,0** and *left-
click*. Then press the **Return** button of the mouse (*right-click*).

Fig. 2.3 appears in the drawing area.

Second example – Line tool (Fig. 2.6)

1. Clear the drawing from the screen with a *click* on the **Close** drawing button (Fig. 2.4). Make sure it is not the AutoCAD 2008 window button.
2. The warning window (Fig. 2.5) appears in the centre of the screen.
Click its **No** button.

Fig. 2.3 First example – **Line** tool

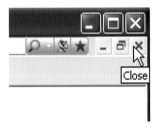

Fig. 2.4 The **Close** drawing button

Fig. 2.5 The **AutoCAD** warning window

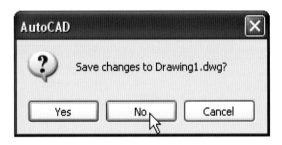

3. *Left-click* on **New...** in the **File** drop-down menu and from the **Select template** dialog which appears *double-click* on **acadiso.dwt**.

4. *Left-click* on the **Line** tool icon and *enter* figures as follows at each prompt of the command line sequence:

Command:_line Specify first point: *enter* **80,235** *right-click*
Specify next point or [Undo]: *enter* **275,235** *right-click*
Specify next point or [Undo]: *enter* **295,210** *right-click*

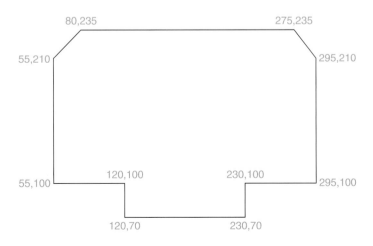

Fig. 2.6 Second example – **Line** tool

Specify next point or [Close/Undo]: *enter* **295,100** *right-click*
Specify next point or [Close/Undo]: *enter* **230,100** *right-click*
Specify next point or [Close/Undo]: *enter* **230,70** *right-click*
Specify next point or [Close/Undo]: *enter* **120,70** *right-click*
Specify next point or [Close/Undo]: *enter* **120,100** *right-click*
Specify next point or [Close/Undo]: *enter* **55,100** *right-click*
Specify next point or [Close/Undo]: *enter* **55,210** *right-click*
Specify next point or [Close/Undo]: *enter* **c** (Close) *right-click*
Command:

The result is as shown in Fig. 2.6.

Third example – Line tool (Fig. 2.7)

1. Close the drawing and open a new **acadiso.dwt** window.
2. *Left-click* on the **Line** tool icon and *enter* figures as follows at each prompt of the command line sequence:

Command:_line Specify first point: *enter* **60,210** *right-click*
Specify next point or [Undo]: *enter* **@50,0** *right-click*
Specify next point or [Undo]: *enter* **@0,20** *right-click*
Specify next point or [Close/Undo]: *enter* **@130,0** *right-click*
Specify next point or [Close/Undo]: *enter* **@0,−20** *right-click*
Specify next point or [Close/Undo]: *enter* **@50,0** *right-click*
Specify next point or [Close/Undo]: *enter* **@0,−105** *right-click*
Specify next point or [Close/Undo]: *enter* **@−50,0** *right-click*
Specify next point or [Close/Undo]: *enter* **@0,−20** *right-click*
Specify next point or [Close/Undo]: *enter* **@−130,0** *right-click*
Specify next point or [Close/Undo]: *enter* **@0,20** *right-click*
Specify next point or [Close/Undo]: *enter* **@−50,0** *right-click*
Specify next point or [Close/Undo]: *enter* **c** (Close) *right-click*
Command:

The result is as shown in Fig. 2.7.

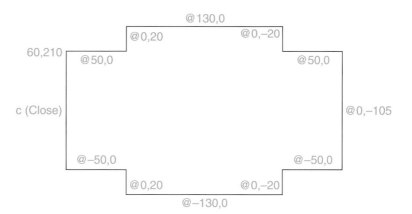

Fig. 2.7 Third example – **Line**
tool

Notes

1. The figures typed at the keyboard determining the corners of the out-lines in the above examples are two-dimensional (2D) **x, y** coordinate points. When working in 2D, coordinates are expressed in terms of two numbers separated by a comma.
2. Coordinate points can be shown as positive or negative numbers.
3. The method of constructing an outline as shown in the first two examples is known as the **absolute coordinate entry** method, where the **x, y** coordinates of each corner of the outlines are *entered* at the command line as required.
4. The method of constructing an outline as in the third example is known as the **relative coordinate entry** method – coordinate points are *entered* relative to the previous entry. In relative coordinate entry, the @ symbol is *entered before* each set of coordinates with the following rules in mind:

+ve x entry is to the right
−ve x entry is to the left
+ve y entry is upwards
−ve y entry is downwards.

5. The next example (the fourth) shows how lines at angles can be drawn taking advantage of the relative coordinate entry method. Angles in AutoCAD are measured in 360 degrees in a counter-clockwise (anti-clockwise) direction (Fig. 2.8). The < symbol precedes the angle.

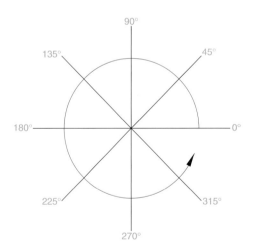

Fig. 2.8 The counter-clockwise direction of measuring angles in AutoCAD

Fourth example – Line tool (Fig. 2.9)

1. Close the drawing and open a new acadiso.dwt window.
2. *Left-click* on the **Line** tool icon and *enter* figures as follows at each prompt of the command line sequence:

Command:_line Specify first point: 70,230
Specify next point: @220,0

Specify next point: @0,−70
Specify next point or [Undo]: @115 < 225
Specify next point or [Undo]: @−60,0
Specify next point or [Close/Undo]: @115 < 135
Specify next point or [Close/Undo]: @0,70
Specify next point or [Close/Undo]: c (Close)
Command:

The result is as shown in Fig. 2.9.

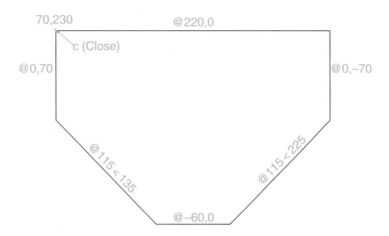

Fig. 2.9 Fourth example – **Line tool**

Fifth example – Line tool (Fig. 2.10)

Another method of constructing accurate drawings is by using a method known as **tracking**. When **Line** is in use, as each **Specify next point:** appears at the command line, a *rubber-banded* line appears from the last point *entered*. *Drag* the rubber-band line in any direction and *enter* a number at the keyboard, followed by a *right-click*. The line is drawn in the *dragged* direction of a length in units equal to the *entered* number.

In this example because all lines are drawn in either the vertical or the horizontal direction, either press the **F8** key or *click* the **ORTHO** button in the status bar.

1. Close the drawing and open a new **acadiso.dwt** window.
2. *Left-click* on the **Line** tool icon and *enter* figures as follows at each prompt of the command line sequence:

   Command:_line Specify first point: *enter* **65,220** *right-click*
   Specify next point: *drag* to right *enter* **240** *right-click*
   Specify next point: *drag* down *enter* **145** *right-click*
   Specify next point or [Undo]: *drag* left *enter* **65** *right-click*
   Specify next point or [Undo]: *drag* upwards *enter* **25** *right-click*
   Specify next point or [Close/Undo]: *drag* left *enter* **120** *right-click*

Specify next point or [Close/Undo]: *drag* upwards *enter* **25** *right-click*
Specify next point or [Close/Undo]: *drag* left *enter* **55** *right-click*
Specify next point or [Close/Undo]: c (Close) *right-click*
Command:

The result is as shown in Fig. 2.10.

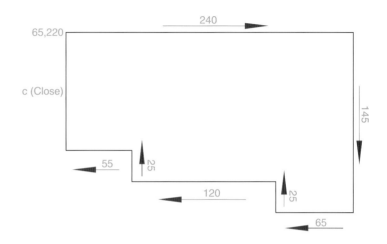

Fig. 2.10 Fifth example – **Line** tool

Drawing with the Circle tool

First example – Circle tool (Fig. 2.13)

1. Close the drawing just completed and open the **acadiso.dwt** screen.
2. *Left-click* on the **Circle** tool icon in the **2D Draw** control panel (Fig. 2.11).

Fig. 2.11 The **Circle** tool from the **2D Draw** control panel or from the **Draw** toolbar

3. *Enter* numbers against the prompts appearing in the command window as shown in Fig. 2.12, followed by *right-clicks*. The circle (Fig. 2.13) appears on screen.

Fig. 2.12 First example – **Circle**. The command line prompts when **Circle** is called

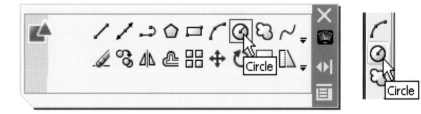

```
Command: _circle Specify center point for circle or [3P/2P/Ttr (tan tan
radius)]: 180,160
Specify radius of circle or [Diameter]: 55
Command:
```

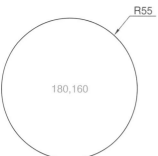

R55

180,160

Fig. 2.13 First example – **Circle** tool

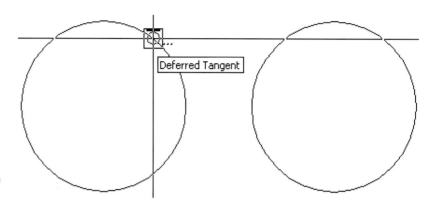

Deferred Tangent

Fig. 2.14 Second example – **Circle** tool – the two circles of radius 50

Second example – Circle tool (Fig. 2.14)

1. Close the drawing and open the **acadiso.dwt** screen.
2. *Left-click* on the **Circle** tool icon and construct two circles as shown in the drawing Fig. 2.14 in the positions and radii shown in Fig. 2.15.

3. *Click* the **Circle** tool again and against the first prompt *enter* **t** (the abbreviation for the prompt **tan tan radius**), followed by a *right-click*.

> **Command_circle Specify center point for circle or [3P/2P/Ttr (tan tan radius]:** *enter* **t** *right-click*
> **Specify point on object for first tangent of circle:** *pick*
> **Specify point on object for second tangent of circle:** *pick*
> **Specify radius of circle (50):** *enter* **40** *right-click*
> **Command:**

The radius **40** circle tangential to the two circles already drawn then appears (Fig. 2.15).

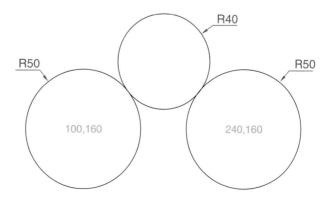

R40

R50

R50

100,160

240,160

Fig. 2.15 Second example – **Circle** tool. The radius-40 circle tangential to the radius-50 circles

Notes

1. When a point on either circle is picked the **Deferred Tangent** tip appears. This tip will only appear when the **OSNAP** button is set on with a *click* on its button in the status bar, or by pressing the **F3** key of the keyboard.
2. Circles can be drawn through 3 points or 2 points *entered* at the command line in response to prompts brought to the command line by using **3P** and **2P** in answer to the circle command line prompts.

The Erase tool

If an error has been made when using any of the AutoCAD 2008 tools, the object or objects which have been incorrectly drawn can be deleted with the **Erase** tool. The **Erase** tool icon can be selected from the **2D Draw** control panel (Fig. 2.16) or by *entering* **e** at the command line.

Fig. 2.16 The **Erase** tool icon from the **2D Draw** control panel or from the **Modify** toolbar

First example – Erase (Fig. 2.18)

1. With **Line** construct the outline in Fig. 2.17.

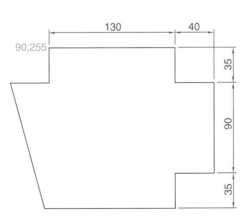

Fig. 2.17 First example – **Erase**. An incorrect outline

2. Assuming two lines of the outline have been incorrectly drawn, *left-click* on the **Erase** tool icon. The command line shows:

Command:_erase
Select objects: *pick* one of the lines

Select objects: *pick* the other line
Select objects: *right-click*
Command:

And the two lines are deleted (right-hand drawing of Fig. 2.18).

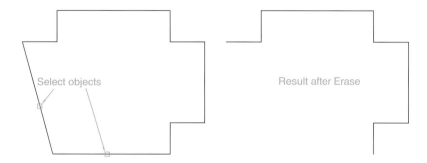

Fig. 2.18 First example – **Erase**

Second example – Erase (Fig. 2.19)

The two lines could also have been deleted by the following method:

1. *Left-click* the **Erase** tool icon. The command line shows:

Command:_erase
Select objects: *enter* c (Crossing)
Specify first corner: *pick* **Specify opposite corner:** *pick* **2 found**
Select objects: *right-click*
Command:

And the two lines are deleted as in the right-hand drawing in Fig. 2.18.

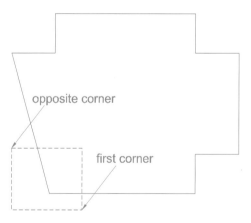

opposite corner

first corner

Fig. 2.19 Second example – **Erase**

Undo and Redo tools

Two other tools of value when errors have been made are the **Undo** and **Redo** tools. To undo the last action taken by any tool when constructing a drawing, either *left-click* the **Undo** tool in the **Standard Annotation**

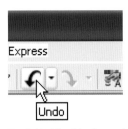

Fig. 2.20 The **Undo** tool in the
Standard Annotation toolbar

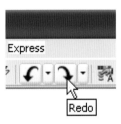

Fig. 2.21 The **Redo** tool in the
Standard Annotation toolbar

Fig. 2.22 The **Polyline** tool icon
in the **2D Draw** control panel

toolbar (Fig. 2.20) or type **u** at the command line. No matter which
method is adopted the error is deleted from the drawing.

Everything done during a session in constructing a drawing can be
undone by repeated *clicking* on the **Undo** tool icon or by *entering* **u**'s at
the command line.

To bring back objects that have just been removed by the use of
Undo's *left-click* the **Redo** tool icon in the **Standard Annotation** toolbar
(Fig. 2.21) or *enter* **redo** at the command line.

Drawing with the Polyline tool

When drawing lines with the **Line** tool, each line drawn is an object in its
own right. A rectangle drawn with the **Line** tool is four objects. A rectangle
drawn with the **Polyline** tool is a single object. Lines of different thickness,
arcs, arrows and circles can all be drawn using this tool as will be shown in
the examples describing constructions using the **Polyline** tool. Constructions resulting from using the tool are known as **polylines** or **plines**.

The **Polyline** tool can be called from the **2D Draw** control panel
(Fig. 2.22) or from the **Draw** toolbar.

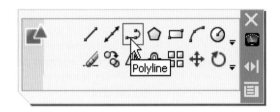

First example – Polyline tool (Fig. 2.23)

Note

In this example *enter* and *right-click* have not been included.

Left-click the **Polyline** tool (Fig. 2.22). The command line shows:

Command:_pline Specify start point: 30,250
Current line width is 0
Specify next point or [Arc/Halfwidth/Length/Undo/Width]: 230,250
Specify next point or [Arc/Close/Halfwidth/Length/Undo/Width]:
 230,120
Specify next point or [Arc/Close/Halfwidth/Length/Undo/Width]:
 30,120
Specify next point or [Arc/Close/Halfwidth/Length/Undo/Width]:
 c (Close)
Command:

Notes

1. Note the prompts – **Arc** for constructing pline arcs; **Close** to close an
 outline; **Halfwidth** to halve the width of a wide pline; **Length** to *enter*

30,250   230,250

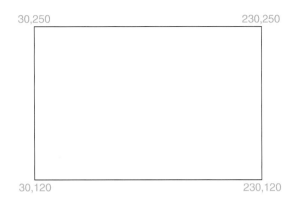

30,120   230,120

Fig. 2.23 First example – **Polyline** tool

the required length of apline; **Undo** to undo the last pline constructed; **Close** to close an outline.

2. Only the capital letter(s) of a prompt needs to be *entered* in upper or lower case to make that prompt effective.

3. Other prompts will appear when the **Polyline** tool is in use as will be shown in later examples.

Second example – Polyline tool (Fig. 2.24)

This will be a long sequence, but it is typical of a reasonably complex drawing using the **Polyline** tool. In the following sequences, when aprompt line is to be repeated, the prompts in square brackets ([ ]) will be replaced by **[prompts]**.

Left-click the **Polyline** tool icon. The command line shows:

Command:_pline Specify start point: 40,250
Current line width is 0
Specify next point or [Arc/Halfwidth/Length/Undo/Width]: w (Width)
Specify starting width <0>: 5
Specify ending width <5>: *right-click*
Specify next point or [Arc/Close/Halfwidth/Length/Undo/Width]:
    160,250
Specify next point or [prompts]: h (Halfwidth)
Specify starting half-width <2.5>: 1

40,250   160,250   260,250

                                                  260,180

Fig. 2.24 Second example – **Polyline** tool

40,120   160,120   260,120

Specify ending half-width <1>: *right-click*
Specify next point or [prompts]: 260,250
Specify next point or [prompts]: 260,180
Specify next point or [prompts]: w (Width)
Specify starting width <1>: 10
Specify ending width <10>: *right-click*
Specify next point or [prompts]: 260,120
Specify next point or [prompts]: h (Halfwidth)
Specify starting half-width <5>: 2
Specify ending half-width <2>: *right-click*
Specify next point or [prompts]: 160,120
Specify next point or [prompts]: w (Width)
Specify starting width <4>: 20
Specify ending width <20>: *right-click*
Specify next point or [prompts]: 40,120
Specify starting width <20>: 5
Specify ending width <5>: *right-click*
Specify next point or [prompts]: c (Close)
Command:

Third example – Polyline tool (Fig. 2.25)

Left-click the **Polyline** tool icon. The command line shows:

Command:_pline Specify start point: 50,220
Current line width is 0
[prompts]: w (Width)
Specify starting width <0>: 0.5
Specify ending width <0.5>: *right-click*
Specify next point or [prompts]: 120,220
Specify next point or [prompts]: a (Arc)
Specify endpoint of arc or [prompts]: s (second pt)
Specify second point on arc: 150,200
Specify end point of arc: 180,220
Specify end point of arc or [prompts]: l (Line)
Specify next point or [prompts]: 250,220
Specify next point or [prompts]: 250,190
Specify next point or [prompts]: a (Arc)

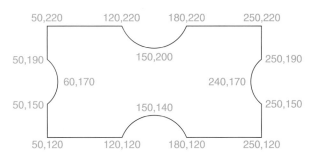

Fig. 2.25 Third example –
Polyline tool

Specify endpoint of arc or [prompts]: s (second pt)
Specify second point on arc: 240,170
Specify end point of arc: 250,150
Specify end point of arc or [prompts]: l (Line)
Specify next point or [prompts]: 250,150
Specify next point or [prompts]: 250,120

And so on until the outline in Fig. 2.25 is completed.

Fourth example – Polyline tool (Fig. 2.26)

Left-click the **Polyline** tool icon. The command line shows:

Command:_pline Specify start point: 80,170
Current line width is 0
Specify next point or [prompts]: w (Width)
Specify starting width <0>: 1
Specify ending width <1>: *right-click*
Specify next point or [prompts]: a (Arc)
Specify endpoint of arc or [prompts]: s (second pt)
Specify second point on arc: 160,250
Specify end point of arc: 240,170
Specify end point of arc or [prompts]: cl (CLose)
Command:

And the circle in Fig. 2.26 is formed.

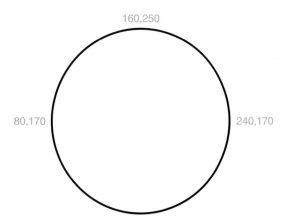

Fig. 2.26 Fourth example –
Polyline tool

Fifth example – Polyline tool (Fig. 2.27)

Left-click the **Polyline** tool icon. The command line shows:

Command:_pline Specify start point: 60,180
Current line width is 0
Specify next point or [prompts]: w (Width)

Specify starting width <0>: 1
Specify ending width <1>: *right-click*
Specify next point or [prompts]: 190,180
Specify next point or [prompts]: w (Width)
Specify starting width <1>: 20
Specify ending width <20>: 0
Specify next point or [prompts]: 265,180
Specify next point or [prompts]: *right-click*
Command:

And the arrow in Fig. 2.27 is formed.

Fig. 2.27 Fifth example – **Polyline** tool

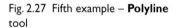
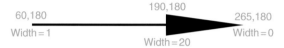

60,180
Width = 1

190,180
Width = 20

265,180
Width = 0

Revision notes

The following terms have been used in this chapter:

Left-click – press the left-hand button of the mouse.
Click – same meaning as *left-click*.
Double-click – press the left-hand button of the mouse twice.
Right-click – press the left-hand button of the mouse; it has the same result as pressing the **Return** key of the keyboard.
Drag – move the cursor on to an object and, holding down the right-hand button of the mouse, pull the object to a new position.
Enter – type the letters or numbers which follow at the keyboard.
Pick – move the cursor on to an item on screen and press the *left-hand* button of the mouse.
Return – press the **Enter** key of the keyboard. This key may also be marked with a left-facing arrow. In most cases (but not always) it has the same result as a *right-click*.
Dialog – a window appearing in the AutoCAD window in which settings may be made.
Drop-down menu – a menu appearing when one of the names in the menu bars is *clicked*.
Tooltip – the name of a tool appearing when the cursor is placed over a tool icon from a toolbar.
Prompts – text appearing in the command window when a tool is selected which advise the operator as to which operation is required.

Methods of coordinate entry – Three methods of coordinate entry have been used in this chapter:

1. **Absolute method** – the coordinates of points on an outline are *entered* at the command line in response to prompts.
2. **Relative method** – the distances in coordinate units are *entered* preceded by @ from the last point which has been determined on an

outline. Angles which are measured in a counter-clockwise direction are preceded by >.

3. **Tracking** – the rubber band of the tool is *dragged* in the direction in which the line is to be drawn and its distance in units is *entered* at the command line followed by a *right-click*.

Line and Polyline tools – an outline drawn using the **Line** tool consists of a number of objects equal to the number of lines in the outline. An outline drawn using the **Polyline** is a single object.

Exercises

1. Using the **Line** tool construct the rectangle in Fig. 2.28.

Fig. 2.28 Exercise 1

2. Construct the outline in Fig. 2.29 using the **Line** tool. The coordinate points of each corner of the rectangle will need to be calculated from the lengths of the lines between the corners.

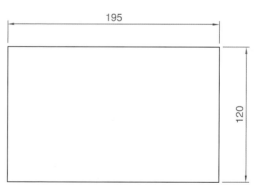

Fig. 2.29 Exercise 2

3. Using the **Line** tool, construct the outline in Fig. 2.30.
4. Using the **Circle** tool, construct the two circles of radius 50 and 30. Then, using the **Ttr** prompt, add the circle of radius 25 (Fig. 2.31).

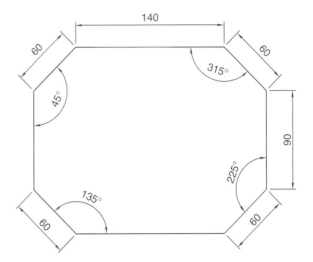

Fig. 2.30 Exercise 3

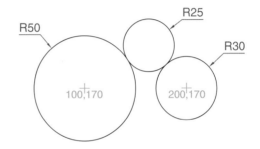

Fig. 2.31 Exercise 4

5. In an **acadiso.dwt** screen and using the **Circle** and **Line** tools, construct the line and the circle of radius 40 as given in Fig. 2.32. Then, using the **Ttr** prompt, add the circle of radius 25.

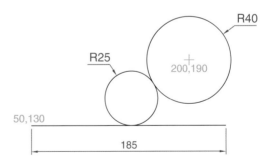

Fig. 2.32 Exercise 5

6. Using the **Line** tool construct the two lines at the length and angle as given in Fig. 2.33. Then with the **Ttr** prompt of the **Circle** tool, add the circle as shown.

7. Using the **Polyline** tool, construct the outline given in Fig. 2.34.

8. Construct the outline in Fig. 2.35 using the **Polyline** tool.

9. With the **Polyline** tool construct the arrows shown in Fig. 2.36.

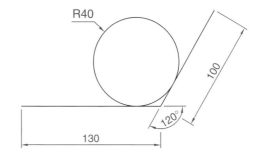

Fig. 2.33 Exercise 6

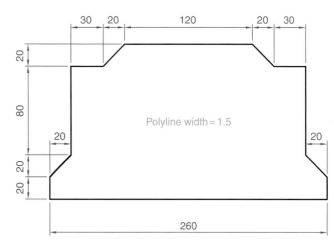

Fig. 2.34 Exercise 7

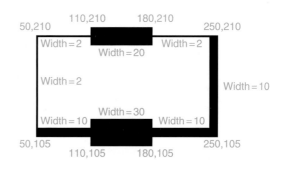

Fig. 2.35 Exercise 8

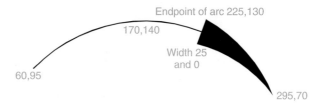

Fig. 2.36 Exercise 9

CHAPTER 3

Draw tools, Osnap and AutoSnap

Fig. 3.1 The tool names in the **Draw** drop-down menu

Aims of this chapter

1. To describe the use of the **Arc, Ellipse, Polygon and Rectangle** tools from the **Draw** toolbar.
2. To describe the uses of the **Polyline Edit** (pedit) tool.
3. To introduce the **AutoSnap** system and its uses.
4. To introduce the **Object Snap** (osnap) system and its uses.
5. To introduce the **Dynamic Input (DYN)** system and its uses.

Introduction

The majority of tools in AutoCAD 2008 can be called into use in any one of the following five ways:

1. With a *click* on the tool's icon in the **DASHBOARD** palette.
2. With a *click* on the tool's name in a toolbar.
3. By *clicking* on the tool's name in an appropriate drop-down menu. Fig. 3.1 shows the tool names displayed in the **Draw** drop-down menu.
4. By *entering* an abbreviation for the tool name at the command line in the Command palette. For example the abbreviation for the **Line** tool is l, for the **Polyline** tool it is **pl** and for the **Circle** tool it is **c**.
5. By *entering* the full name of the tool at the command line.

In practice operators constructing drawings in AutoCAD 2008 may well use a combination of these five methods.

The Arc tool

In AutoCAD 2008, arcs can be constructed using any three of the following characteristics of an arc: its **Start** point; a point on the arc (**Second** point); its **Center**; its **End**; its **Radius; Length** of the arc; **Direction** in which the arc is to be constructed? **Angle** between lines of the arc.

In the examples which follow, *entering* initials for these characteristics in response to prompts at the command line when the **Arc** tool is called allows arcs to be constructed in a variety of ways.

To call the **Arc** tool *click* on its tool icon in the **2D Draw** control panel (Fig. 3.2), or *click* on **Arc** in the **Draw** drop-down menu. A sub-menu

Fig. 3.2 The **Arc** tool icon in the
2D Draw control panel

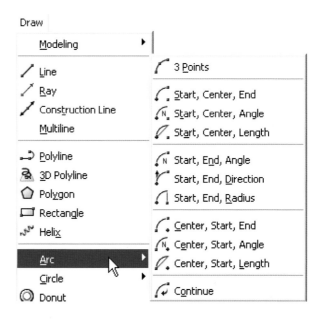

Fig. 3.3 The **Arc** sub-menu of the
Draw drop-down menu

shows the possible methods of constructing arcs (Fig. 3.3). The abbreviation for calling the **Arc** tool is **a**.

First example – Arc tool (Fig. 3.4)

Left-click the **Arc** tool icon. The command line shows:

> **Command:_arc Specify start point of arc or [Center]:** 100,220
> **Specify second point of arc or [Center/End]:** 55,250
> **Specify end point of arc:** 10,220
> **Command:**

Second example – Arc tool (Fig. 3.4)

> **Command:** *right-click* brings back the **Arc** sequence
> **ARC Specify start point of arc or [Center]:** c (Center)
> **Specify center point of arc:** 200,190
> **Specify start point of arc:** 260,215
> **Specify end point of arc or [Angle/chord Length]:** 140,215
> **Command:**

Third example – Arc tool (Fig. 3.4)

Command: *right-click* brings back the **Arc** sequence
ARC Specify start point of arc or [Center]: 420,210
Specify second point of arc or [Center/End]: e (End)
Specify end point of arc: 320,210
Specify center point of arc or [Angle/Direction/Radius]: r (Radius)
Specify radius of arc: 75
Command:

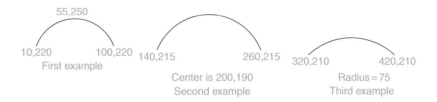

Fig. 3.4 Examples – **Arc** tool

The Ellipse tool

Ellipses can be regarded as what is seen when a circle is viewed from directly in front of the circle and the circle rotated through an angle about its horizontal diameter. Ellipses are measured in terms of two axes – a **major axis** and a **minor axis**, the major axis being the diameter of the circle, the minor axis being the height of the ellipse after the circle has been rotated through an angle (Fig. 3.5).

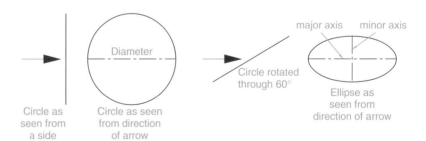

Fig. 3.5 An ellipse can be regarded as viewing a rotated circle

To call the **Ellipse** tool, *click on* its tool icon in the **2D Draw** control panel (Fig. 3.6) or *click* on its name in the **Draw** drop-down menu. The abbreviation for calling the **Ellipse** tool is **el**.

Fig. 3.6 The **Ellipse** tool icon in the **2D Draw** control panel

First example – Ellipse (Fig. 3.7)

Left-click the **Ellipse** tool icon. The command line shows:

Command:_ellipse
Specify axis endpoint of elliptical arc or [Center]: 30,190
Specify other endpoint of axis: 150,190
Specify distance to other axis or [Rotation]: 25
Command:

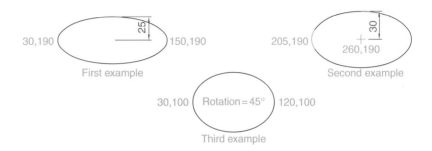

Fig. 3.7 Examples – **Ellipse**

Second example – Ellipse (Fig. 3.7)

In this second example, the coordinates of the centre of the ellipse (the point where the two axes intersect) are *entered*, followed by *entering* coordinates for the end of the major axis, followed by *entering* the units for the end of the minor axis.

Command: *right-click*
ELLIPSE
Specify axis endpoint of elliptical arc or [Center]: c
Specify center of ellipse: 260,190
Specify endpoint of axis: 205,190
Specify distance to other axis or [Rotation]: 30
Command:

Third example – Ellipse (Fig. 3.7)

In this third example, after setting the positions of the ends of the major axis, the angle of rotation of the circle from which an ellipse can be obtained is *entered*.

Command: *right-click*
ELLIPSE
Specify axis endpoint of elliptical arc or [Center]: 30,100
Specify other endpoint of axis: 120,100
Specify distance to other axis or [Rotation]: r (Rotation)
Specify rotation around major axis: 45
Command:

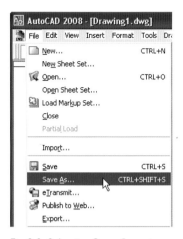

Fig. 3.8 Selecting **Save As...** in
the **File** drop-down menu

Fig. 3.9 The **Save Drawing As**
dialog

Saving drawings

Before going further it is as well to know how to save the drawings constructed when answering examples and exercises in this book. When a
drawing has been constructed, *left-click* on **File** in the menu bar and on
Save As... in the drop-down menu (Fig. 3.8). The **Save Drawing As** dialog appears (Fig. 3.9).

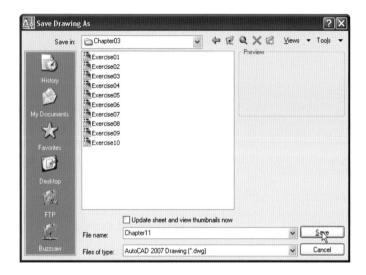

Unless you are the only person to use the computer on which the drawing has been constructed, it is best to save work to a floppy disk, usually
held in the drive **A:**. To save a drawing to a floppy in drive **A:**

1. Place a floppy disk in drive **A:**.
2. In the **Save in:** field of the dialog, *click the* arrow to the right of the
   field and from the popup list select **3½ Floppy [A:]**.
3. In the **File name:** field of the dialog type a suitable name. The file
   name extension **.dwg** does not need to be typed because it will automatically be added to the file name.
4. *Left-click* the **Save** button of the dialog. The drawing will be saved to
   the floppy with the file name extension **.dwg** – the AutoCAD file name
   extension.

Osnap, AutoSnap and Dynamic Input

In previous chapters several methods of constructing accurate drawings
have been described – using **Snap**; absolute coordinate entry; relative
coordinate entry and tracking.

Other methods of ensuring accuracy between parts of constructions are
by making use of **Object Snaps (Osnaps), AutoSnap** and **Dynamic
Input (DYN)**.

Snap, Grid, Osnap and DYN can be set from the buttons in the status bar or by pressing the keys F3 (Osnap), F7 (Grid), F9 (Snap) and F12 (DYN).

Object Snaps (Osnaps)

Osnaps allow objects to be added to a drawing at precise positions in relation to other objects already on screen. With osnaps, objects can be added to the end points, mid points, to intersections of objects, to centres and quadrants of circles and so on. Osnaps also override snap points even when snap is set on.

To set Osnaps, at the command line:

Command: *enter* os

And the Drafting Settings dialog appears. *Click* the Object Snap tab in the upper part of the dialog and *click* in each of the check boxes (the small squares opposite the osnap names). See Fig. 3.10.

When osnaps are set ON, as outlines are constructed using osnaps, osnap icons and their tooltips appear as indicated in Fig. 3.11.

It is sometimes advisable not to have Osnaps set on in the Drafting Settings dialog, but to set Osnap off and use osnap abbreviations at the command line when using tools. The following examples show the use of some of these abbreviations.

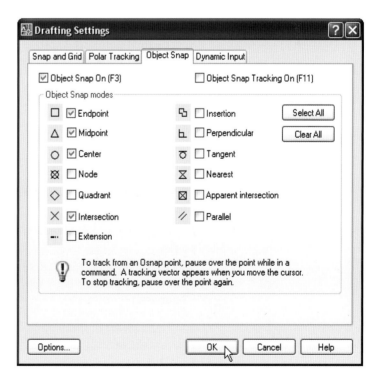

Fig. 3.10 The **Drafting Settings** dialog with some **Osnaps** set on

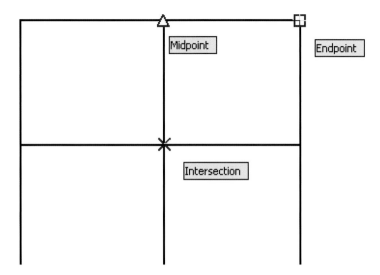

Fig. 3.11 Three osnap icons and their tooltips

First example – Osnap abbreviations (Fig. 3.12)

Call the **Polyline** tool:

> **Command:_pline**
> **Specify start point:** 50,230
> **[prompts]:** w (Width)
> **Specify starting width:** 1
> **Specify ending width <1>:** *right-click*
> **Specify next point:** 260,230
> **Specify next point:** *right-click*
> **Command:** *right-click*
> **PLINE**
> **Specify start point:** end **of** *pick* the right-hand end of the pline
> **Specify next point:** 50,120
> **Specify next point:** *right-click*
> **Command:** *right-click*
> **PLINE**
> **Specify start point:** mid **of** *pick* near the middle of first pline
> **Specify next point:** 155,120
> **Specify next point:** *right-click*
> **Command:** *right-click*
> **PLINE**
> **Specify start point:** int **of** *pick* the plines at their intersection
> **Specify start point:** *right-click*
> **Command:**

The result is shown in Fig. 3.12. In this illustration the osnap tooltips are shown as they appear when each object is added to the outline.

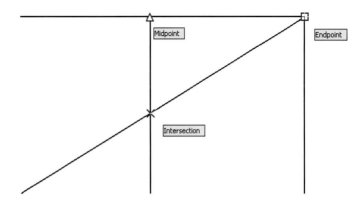

Fig. 3.12 First example – **Osnaps**

Second example – Osnap abbreviations (Fig. 3.13)

Call the **Circle** tool:

> **Command:_circle**
> **Specify center point for circle:** 180,170
> **Specify radius of circle:** 60
> **Command:** *enter* **l** (Line) *right-click*
> **Specify first point:** enter **qua** *right-click*
> **of** *pick* near the upper quadrant of the circle
> **Specify next point:** *enter* **cen** *right-click*
> **of** *pick* near the centre of the circle
> **Specify next point:** *enter* **qua** *right-click*
> **of** *pick* near right-hand side of circle
> **Specify next point:** *right-click*
> **Command:**

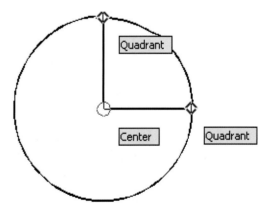

Fig. 3.13 Second example –
Osnaps

Note

With osnaps off, the following abbreviations can be used:

> **end** endpoint
> **int** intersection

> **qua** quadrant
> **ext** extension
> **mid** midpoint
> **cen** centre
> **nea** nearest

Using AutoSnap

AutoSnap is similar to **Osnap**. To set **AutoSnap**, *right-click* in the command window and from the menu which appears *click* **Options...** The **Options** dialog appears. *Click* the **Drafting** tab in the upper part of the dialog and set the check boxes against the **AutoSnap Settings** on (tick in boxes). These settings are shown in Figs 3.14 and 3.15.

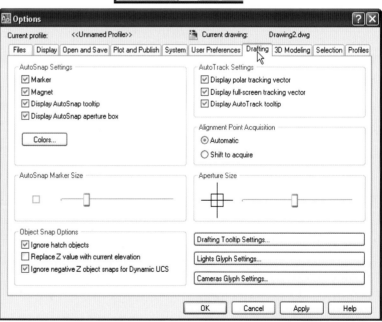

Fig. 3.14 Setting **AutoSnap** in the **Options** dialog

With **AutoSnap** set, each time an object is added to a drawing the AutoSnap features appear as indicated in Fig. 3.16.

Part of a drawing showing the features of a number of **AutoSnap** points is given in Fig. 3.17.

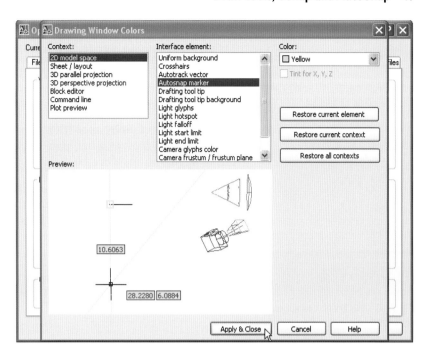

Fig. 3.15 Setting the colours of the parts of the **AutoSnap** features

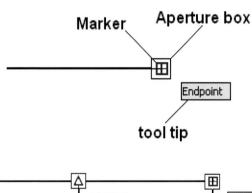

Fig. 3.16 The features of **AutoSnap**

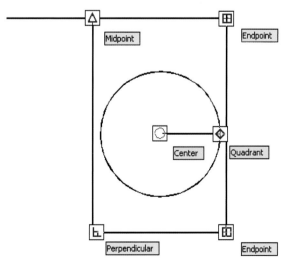

Fig. 3.17 A number of **AutoSnap** features

Note

OSNAP must be set ON for the **AutoSnap** features to show when constructing a drawing with their aid.

Dynamic Input

When **DYN** is set on by either pressing the **F12** key or with a *click* on the **DYN** button in the status bar, dimensions, coordinate positions and commands appear as tips when no tool is in action (Fig. 3.18).

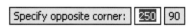

Fig. 3.18 The **DYN** tips appearing when no tool is in action and the cursor is moved

With a tool in action, as the cursor hairs are moved in response to movement of the mouse, **DYN** tips showing the coordinate figures for the point of the cursor hairs will show (Fig. 3.19), together with other details. To see the drop-down menu giving the prompts available with **DYN** press the down key of the keyboard and *click* the prompt to be used. Fig. 3.19 shows the **Arc** prompt as being the next to be used.

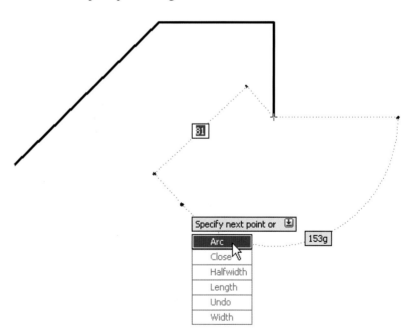

Fig. 3.19 Coordinate tips when **DYN** is in action

Notes on the use of DYN

1. A *click* on the **Clean Screen** icon at the bottom right-hand corner of the AutoCAD 2008 window produces an uncluttered workspace area with only the menu bar (Fig. 3.20). The command palette can also be cleared from screen by *entering* **commandlinehide** at the command line. To bring it back press the keys **Ctrl+9**. Some operators may well prefer working in such a larger than normal workspace. All the tool names or abbreviations can be *entered* at the keyboard. Thus working with **DYN** set on can be of benefit to those who prefer doing so.

2. Settings for **DYN** can be made in the **Drafting Settings** dialog (Fig. 3.21), brought to screen by *entering* **ds** at the command line.

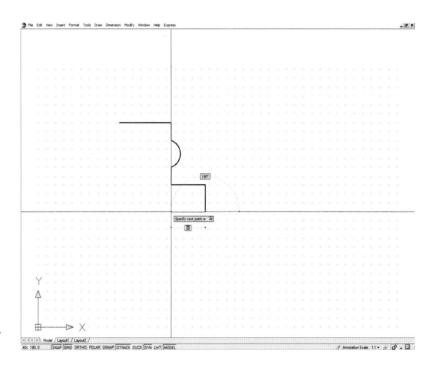

Fig. 3.20 Example of using **DYN –**
Polyline

An example of using DYN (Fig. 3.22)

This is a simple example of how **DYN** can be used to construct drawings in a **Clean Screen** workspace.

1. Turn **DYN** on with a *click* on its button in the status bar.
2. Turn **OSNAP** off with a *click* at the status bar.
3. *Click* the **Clean Screen** button at the bottom-right of the AutoCAD 2008 screen.
4. *Enter* **commandlinehide** to hide the command palette.
5. *Enter* **pl** (for **Polyline**) at the keyboard followed by pressing *Return*.
6. *Enter* **100,100** *Return*.

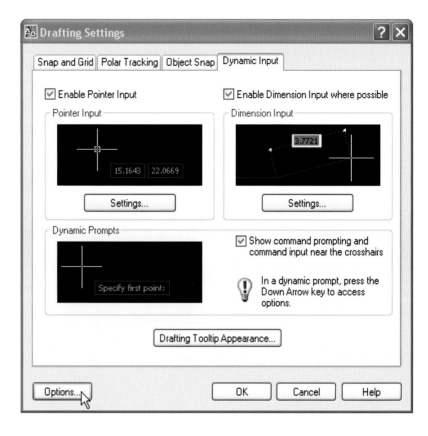

Fig. 3.21 Settings for **DYN** can be made in the **Drafting Settings** dialog

7. *Enter* **250,0** *Return*.
8. *Enter* **0,135** *Return*.
9. *Enter* **−250,0** *Return*.
10. *Enter* **0,−50** *Return*.
11. *Enter* **80,0** *Return*.
12. *Enter* **0,−35** *Return*.
13. Enter **−80,0** *Return*.
14. *Enter* **c** *Return*.
15. *Enter* **pe** (for **Polyline Edit**) *Return*.
16. Press the **down arrow** key of the keyboard.
17. In the menu which appears *click* **Width** *Return*.
18. *Click* on the pline just drawn and *enter* **2** *Return*.

The result is shown in Fig. 3.22.

Examples of using other Draw tools

First example – Polygon tool (Fig. 3.25)

1. Call the **Polygon** tool – either with a *click* on its tool icon in the **2D Draw** control panel (Fig. 3.23), by *entering* **pol** or **polygon** at the

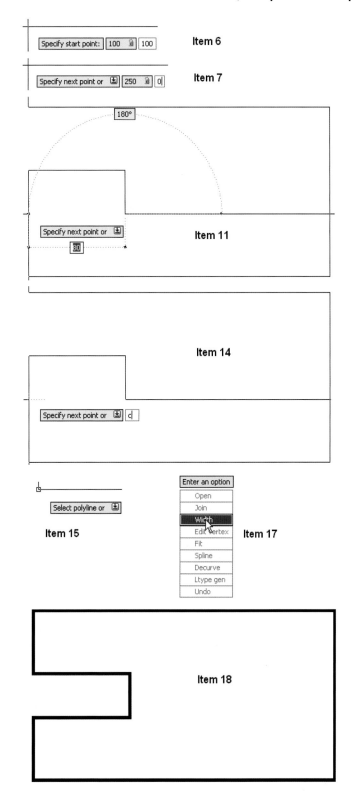

Fig. 3.22 An example of using **DYN** – stages in constructing the pline

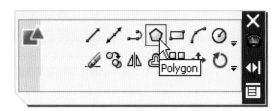

Fig. 3.23 The **Polygon** tool icon in the **2D Draw** control panel

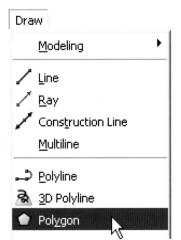

Fig. 3.24 Calling the **Polygon** tool from the **Draw** drop-down menu

command line. Or it can be called from the **Draw** drop-down menu (Fig. 3.24). The command line shows:

Command:_polygon Enter number of sides <4>: 6
Specify center of polygon or [Edge]: 60,210
Enter an option [Inscribed in circle/Circumscribed about circle]
 <I>: *right-click* (accept Inscribed)
Specify radius of circle: 60
Command:

2. In the same manner construct a **5**-sided polygon of centre **200,210** and of radius **60**.
3. Then, construct an **8**-sided polygon of centre **330,210** and radius **60**.
4. Repeat to construct a **9**-sided polygon circumscribed about a circle of radius **60** and centre **60,80**.
5. Construct yet another polygon with **10** sides of radius **60** and of centre **200,80**.
6. Finally another polygon circumscribing a circle of radius **60**, of centre **330,80** and sides **12**.

The result is shown in Fig. 3.25.

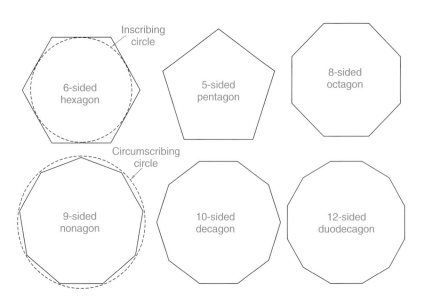

Fig. 3.25 First example – **Polygon** tool

Second example – Rectangle tool (Fig. 3.27)

Call the **Rectangle** tool – either, with a *click* on its tool icon in the **2D Draw** control panel (Fig. 3.26), or by *entering* **rec** or **rectangle** at the command line. The tool can be called from the **Draw** drop-down menu. The command line shows:

Fig. 3.26 The **Rectangle** tool icon in the **2D Draw** control panel

Command:_rectang
Specify first corner point or [Chamfer/Elevation/Fillet/Thickness/Width]: 25,240
Specify other corner point or [Area/Dimensions/Rotation]: 160,160
Command:

Third example – Rectangle tool (Fig. 3.27)

Command:_rectang
[prompts]: c (Chamfer)
Specify first chamfer distance for rectangles <0>: 15
Specify first chamfer distance for rectangles <15>: *right-click*
Specify first corner point: 200,240
Specify other corner point: 300,160
Command:

Fourth example – Rectangle tool (Fig. 3.27)

Command:_rectang
Specify first corner point or [Chamfer/Elevation/Fillet/Thickness/Width]: w (Width)
Specify line width for rectangles <0>: 4
Specify first corner point or [Chamfer/Elevation/Fillet/Thickness/Width]: c (Chamfer)
Specify first chamfer distance for rectangles <0>: 10
Specify second chamfer distance for rectangles <10>: 15
Specify first corner point or [Chamfer/Elevation/Fillet/Thickness/Width]: 200,120
Specify other corner poi nt or [Area/Dimensions/Rotation]: 315,25
Command:

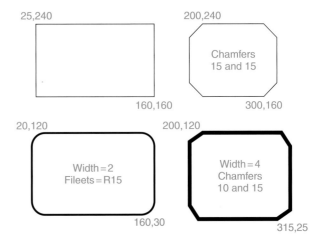

Fig. 3.27 Examples – **Rectangle** tool

The Polyline Edit tool

Polyline Edit or **Pedit** is a valuable tool for editing plines.

First example – Polyline Edit (Figs 3.28 and 3.30)

1. With the **Polyline** tool construct the outlines **1** to **6** of Fig. 3.28.

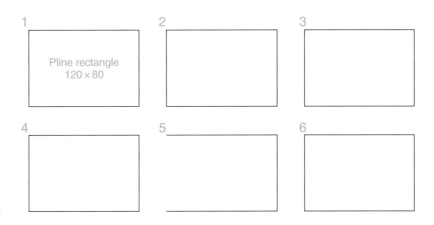

Fig. 3.28 Examples – **Edit Polyline** – the plines to be edited

2. Call the **Edit Polyline** tool – either from the **Modify** drop-down menu (Fig. 3.29), or by *entering* **pe** or **pedit** at the command line. The command line shows:

Command: *enter* pe
PEDIT Select polyline or [Multiple]: *pick* pline **2**
Enter an option [Open/Join/Width/Edit vertex/Fit/Spline/Decurve/ Ltype gen/Undo]: w (Width)
Specify new width for all segments: 2

Enter an option [Open/Join/Width/Edit vertex/Fit/Spline/ Decurve/ Ltype gen/Undo]: *right-click*
Command:

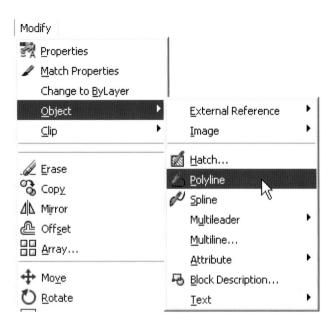

Fig. 3.29 Calling **Edit Polyline** from the **Modify** drop-down menu

3. Repeat with pline 3 and pedit to Width = 10.
4. Repeat with pline 4 and *enter* **s** (Spline) in response to the prompt line:

Enter an option [Open/Join/Width/Edit vertex/Fit/Spline/Decurve/ Ltype gen/Undo]:

5. Repeat with pline **5** and *enter* **j** (Join) in response to the prompt line:

Enter an option [Open/Join/Width/Edit vertex/Fit/Spline/Decurve/ Ltype gen/Undo]:

The result is shown in pline **6**. The resulting examples are shown in Fig. 3.30.

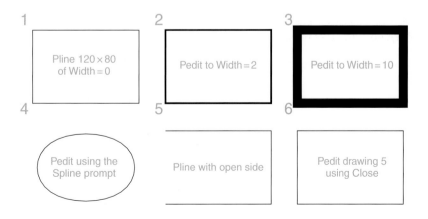

Fig. 3.30 Examples – **Edit Polyline**

Example – Multiple Polyline Edit (Fig. 3.31)

1. With the **Polyline** tool construct the left-hand outlines of Fig. 3.31.
2. Call the **Edit Polyline** tool. The command line shows:

> **Command:** *enter* pe
> **PEDIT Select polyline or [Multiple]:** m (Multiple)
> **Select objects:** *pick* any one of the lines or arcs of the left-hand outlines
>   of Fig. 3.31 **1 found**
> **Select objects:** *pick* another line or arc **1 found 2 total**

> Continue selecting lines and arcs as shown by the *pick* boxes of the left-
> hand drawing of Fig. 3.31 until the command line shows:

> **Select objects:** *pick* another line or arc **1 found 24 total**
> **Select objects:** *right-click*
> **[prompts]:** w (Width)
> **Specify new width for all segments:** 2
> **[prom pts]:** *right-click*
> **Command:**

The result is shown in the right-hand drawing of Fig. 3.31.

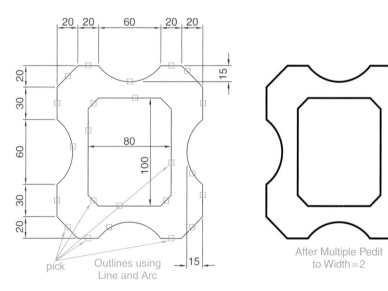

Fig. 3.31 Example – **Multiple Polyline Edit**

Transparent commands

When any tool is in operation it can be interrupted by prefixing the interrupting command with an apostrophe ('). This is particularly useful when
wishing to zoom when constructing a drawing (see page 65). As an example when the **Line** tool is being used:

> **Command:_line**
> **Specify first point:** 100,120

> **Specify next point:** 190,120
> **Specify next point:** *enter'z* (Zoom)
> **>> Specify corner of window or [prompts]:** *pick*
> **>>>>Specify opposite corner:** *pick*
> **Resuming line command.**
> **Specify next point:**

And so on. The transparent command method can be used with any tool.

The set variable PELLIPSE

Many of the operations performed in AutoCAD are carried out under the settings of **set variables**. Some of the numerous set variables available in AutoCAD 2008 will be described in later pages. The variable **PELLIPSE** controls whether ellipses are drawn as splines or as polylines. It is set as follows:

> **Command:** *enter* **pellipse** *right-click*
> **Enter new value for PELLIPSE <0>:** *enter* **1** *right-click*
> **Command:**

And now when ellipses are drawn they are plines. If the variable is set to **0**, the ellipses will be splines. The value of changing ellipses to plines is that they can then be edited using the **Polyline Edit** tool.

Revision notes

The following terms have been used in this chapter:

Field – a part of a window or of a dialog in which numbers or letters are *entered* or can be read from.

Popup list – a list brought in screen with a *click* on the arrow often found at the right-hand end of a field.

Object – a part of a drawing which can be treated as a single object. For example a line constructed with the **Line** tool is an object; a rectangle constructed with the **Polyline** tool is an obj ect; an arc constructed with the **Arc** tool is an object. It will be seen in Chapter 9 that several objects can be formed into a single object.

Toolbar – a collection of tool icons all of which have similar functions. For example in the **Classic AutoCAD** workspace the **Draw** toolbar contains tool icons for those tools which are used for drawing and the **Modify** toolbar contains tool icons of those tools used for modifying parts of drawings.

DASHBOARD palette – when working in either the **Classic AutoCAD** workspace, in the **3D Modeling** workspace, or in the My **Workspace** workspace, tool icons are held in the **DASHBOARD** palette.

Command line – a line in the command palette which commences with the word 'Command:'.

Snap, Grid and **Osnap** can be toggled with *clicks* on their respective buttons in the status bar. These functions can also be set with function keys: **Snap – F9; Grid – F7; Osnap – F3**.

Osnaps ensure accurate positioning of objects in drawings.

AutoSnap can also be used for ensuring accurate positioning of objects in relation to other objects in a drawing.

Osnap must be set **ON** before **AutoSnap** can be used.

Osnap abbreviations can be used at the command line rather than setting it **ON** in the **Drafting Settings** dialog.

DYN – Dynamic input. Allows constructions in an enlarged workspace, without having to use the command palette.

Notes on tools

1. Polygons constructed with the **Polygon** tool are regular polygons – the edges of the polygons are all the same length and the angles are of the same degrees.
2. Polygons constructed with the **Polygon** tool are plines, so they can be acted upon with the **Edit Polyline** tool.
3. The easiest method of calling the **Edit Polyline** tool is to *enter* **pe** at the command line.
4. The **Multiple** prompt of the **pedit** tool saves considerable time when editing a number of objects in a drawing.
5. Transparent commands can be used to interrupt tools in operation by preceding the interrupting tool name with an apostrophe (').
6. Ellipses drawn when the variable **PELLIPSE** is set to **0** are splines, when **PELLIPSE** is set to **1**, ellipses are polylines. When ellipses are in polyline form they can be modified using the **pedit** tool.

Exercises

1. Using the **Line** and **Arc** tools, construct the outline given in Fig. 3.32.
2. With the **Line** and **Arc** tools, construct the outline in Fig. 3.33.

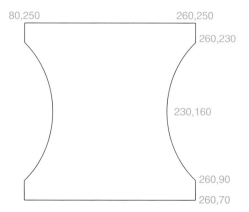

Fig. 3.32 Exercise 1

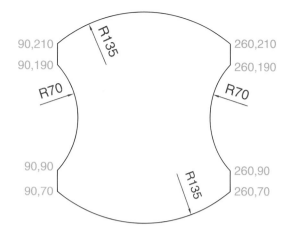

Fig. 3.33 Exercise 2

3. Using the **Ellipse** and **Arc** tools, construct the drawing in Fig. 3.34.

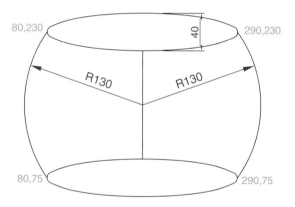

Fig. 3.34 Exercise 3

4. With the **Line, Circle** and **Ellipse** tools, construct Fig. 3.35.

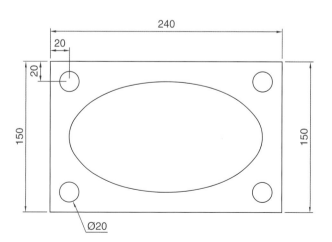

Fig. 3.35 Exercise 4

5. With the **Ellipse** tool, construct the drawing in Fig. 3.36.

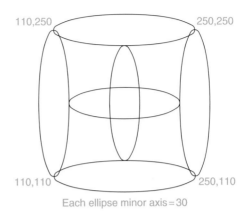

Fig. 3.36 Exercise 5

6. Fig. 3.37 shows a rectangle in the form of a square with hexagons along each edge. Using the **Dimensions** prompt of the **Rectangle** tool construct the square. Then, using the **Edge** prompt of the **Polygon** tool, add the four hexagons. Use the **Osnap endpoint** to ensure the polygons are in their exact positions.

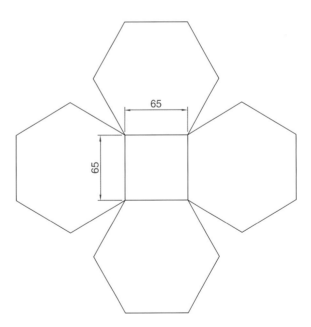

Fig. 3.37 Exercise 6

7. Fig. 3.38 shows seven hexagons with edges touching. Construct the inner hexagon using the **Polygon** tool, then with the aid of the **Edge** prompt of the tool, add the other six hexagons.

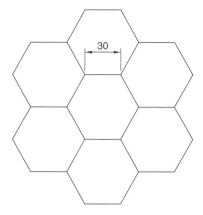

Fig. 3.38 Exercise 7

8. Fig. 3.39 was constructed using only the Rectangle tool. Make an exact copy of the drawing using only the Rectangle tool.

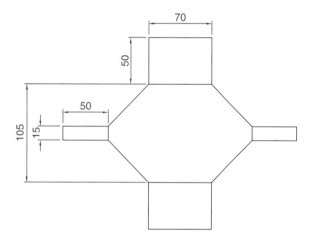

Fig. 3.39 Exercise 8

9. Construct the drawing in Fig. 3.40 using the **Line** and Arc tools. Then, with the aid of the **Multiple prompt of** the **Edit Polyline** tool, change the outlines into plines of **Width = 1**.

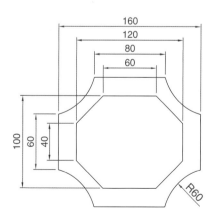

Fig. 3.40 Exercise 9

10. Construct Fig. 3.41 using the **Line** and **Arc** tools. Then change all widths of lines and arcs to a width of **2** with **Polyline Edit**.

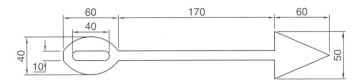

Fig. 3.41 Exercise 10

11. Construct the two outlines in Fig. 3.42 using the **Rectangle** and **Line** tools and then with **Edit Polyline** change the parts of the drawing to plines of widths as shown in Fig. 3.42.

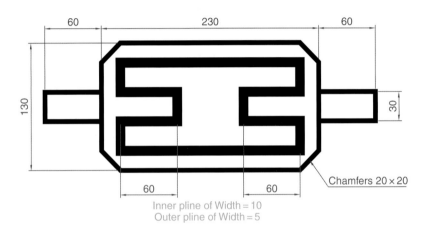

Fig. 3.42 Exercise 11

CHAPTER 4

Zoom, Pan and templates

Aims of this chapter

1. To demonstrate the value of the **Zoom** tools.
2. To introduce the **Pan** tool.
3. To describe the value of using the **Aerial View** window in conjunction with the **Zoom** and **Pan** tools.
4. To update the **acadiso.dwt** template.
5. To describe the construction and saving of drawing templates.

Introduction

The use of the **Zoom** tools allows not only the close inspection of the most minute areas of a drawing in the AutoCAD 2008 drawing area, but also the construction of very small details accurately in a drawing.

The **Zoom** tools can be called from the **Zoom** sub-menu of the **View** drop-down menu (Fig. 4.1). However by far the easiest and

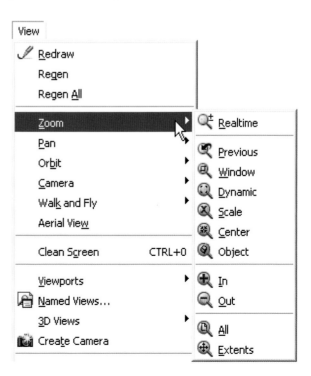

Fig. 4.1 Calling the **Zoom** tools from the **Zoom** sub-menu of the **View** drop-down menu

quickest method of calling **Zoom** is to *enter* **z** at the command line as follows:

> **Command:** *enter* **z** *right-click*
> **ZOOM Specify corner of window, enter a scale factor (nX or nXP) or [All/Center/Dynamic/Extents/Previous/Scale/Window/Object] <real time>:**

This allows the different zooms:

Realtime – selects parts of a drawing within a window
All – the screen reverts to the limits of the template.
Center – the drawing centres itself around a *picked* point.
Dynamic – a broken line surrounds the drawing which can be changed in size and repositioned to part of the drawing.
Extents – the drawing fills the AutoCAD drawing area.
Previous – the screen reverts to its previous zoom.
Scale – entering a number or a decimal fraction scales the drawing.
Window – the parts of the drawing within a *picked* window appears on screen. The effect is the same as using **Realtime**.
Object – *pick* any object on screen and the object zooms.

The operator will probably be using **Realtime, Window** and **Previous** zooms most frequently.

Note the following illustrations: Fig. 4.2 – drawing which has been constructed, Fig. 4.3 – a **Zoom Window** of part of the drawing allowing it to be checked for accuracy and Fig. 4.4 – a **Zoom Extents**.

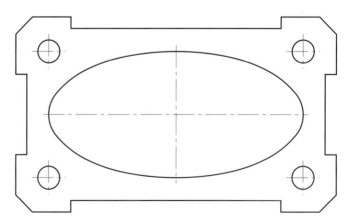

Fig. 4.2 A drawing constructed using the **Polyline** tool

It will be found that the **Zoom** tools are among those most frequently used when working in AutoCAD 2008.

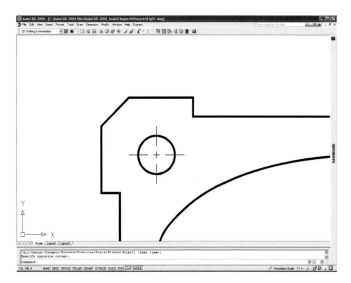

Fig. 4.3 A **Zoom Window** of part of the drawing in Fig. 4.2

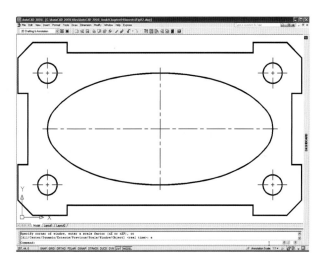

Fig. 4.4 A **Zoom Extents** of the drawing in Fig. 4.2

The Aerial View window

Left-click on **Aerial View** from the **View** drop-down menu and the **Aerial View** window appears – usually in the bottom right-hand corner of the AutoCAD 2008 window (Fig. 4.6). The **Aerial View** window shows the whole of a drawing with that part which is within the **Limits** of the drawing template being used bounded with a thick black line.

The **Aerial View** window is of value when dealing with large drawings – it allows that part of the window on screen to be shown in relation to other parts of the drawing. Fig. 4.5 shows the three-view orthographic projection of a small bench vice shown in Figs 4.6 and 4.7.

The area of the drawing within a **Zoom** window in the drawing area is bounded by a thick black line in the **Aerial View** window.

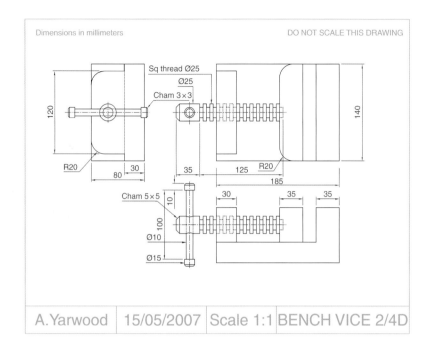

Fig. 4.5 The drawing used to illustrate Figs 4.6 and 4.7

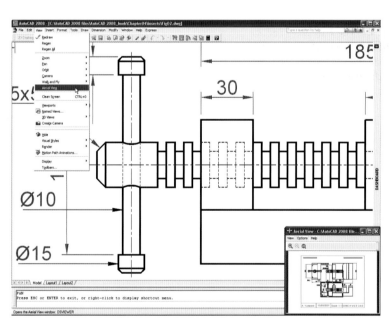

Fig. 4.6 A **Zoom Window** of the drawing in Fig. 4.5 with its surrounding zoom rectangle showing in the **Aerial View** window

The Pan tool

The **Pan** tools can be called from the **Pan** sub-menu of the **View** drop-down menu (Fig. 4.7) or by *entering* **p** at the command line. When the tool is called, the cursor on screen changes to a hand icon. *Dragging* the hand across screen under mouse movement allows various parts of the drawing not on screen to be viewed. As the *dragging* takes place, the black rectangle in the **Aerial View** window moves in sympathy (see Fig. 4.7). The **Pan** tool allows any part of the drawing to be viewed and/or modified. When that part of the drawing which is required is on screen a *right-click* calls up the menu as shown in Fig. 4.7, from which either the tool can be exited, or other tools can be called.

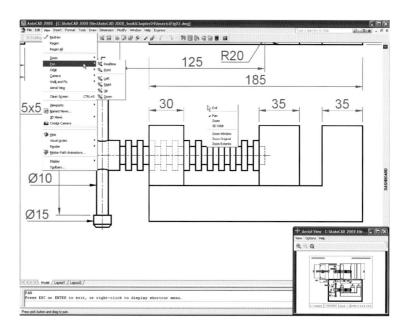

Fig. 4.7 The **Pan** tool in action showing a part of the drawing, while the whole drawing is shown in the **Aerial View** window

Notes

1. If using a mouse with a wheel both zooms and pans can be performed with the aid of the wheel. See page 7.
2. The **Zoom** tools are important in that they allow even the smallest parts of drawings to be examined and, if necessary, amended or modified.
3. The zoom tools can be called from the **Zoom** sub-menu of the **View** drop-down menu or by *entering* **zoom** at the command line. But easiest of all is to *enter* **z** at the command line followed by a *right-click*.
4. Similarly the easiest method of calling the **Pan** tool is to *enter* **p** at the command line followed by a *right-click*.
5. When constructing large drawings, the **Pan** tool and the **Aerial View** window are of value for allowing work to be carried out in any part of a drawing, while showing the whole drawing in the **Aerial View** window.

Drawing templates

In Chapters 1–3, drawings were constructed in the template **acadiso.dwt** which loaded when AutoCAD 2008 was opened. Now the default **acadiso** template is amended with **Limits** set to **420,297** (coordinates within which a drawing can be constructed), **Grid** set to **10, Snap** set to **5**, and the drawing area **Zoomed** to **All**.

Throughout this book most drawings will be based on an **A3** sheet, which measures 420 units by 297 units (the same as the **Limits**).

Note

As mentioned on page 16 if there are multiple users to the computer on which drawings are being constructed, it is as well to save the template being used to another file name or, if thought necessary, to a floppy disk. A file name **My_template.dwt**, as suggested earlier, or a name such as **book_template** can be given.

Adding features to the template

Four other features will now be added to our template:

1. **Text style** – set in the **Text Style** dialog.
2. **Dimension style** – set in the **Dimension Style Manager** dialog.
3. **Shortcutmenu variable** – set to **0**.
4. **Layers** – set in the **Layer Properties Manager** dialog.

Setting Text

1. At the command line:

   Command: *enter* **st** (Style) *right-click*

2. The **Text style** dialog appears (Fig. 4.8). In the dialog, *enter* **5** in the **Height** field. Then *left-click* on **Arial** in the **Font name** popup list. **Arial** font letters appear in the **Preview** area of the dialog.
3. *Left-click* the **New** button and *enter* **Arial** in the **New Text Style** sub-dialog which appears (Fig. 4.9) and *click* the **OK** button.
4. *Left-click* the **Set Current** button of the **Text Style** dialog.
5. *Left-click* the **Close** button of the dialog.

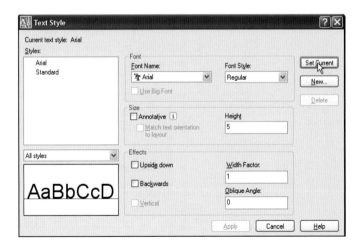

Fig. 4.8 The **Text Style** dialog

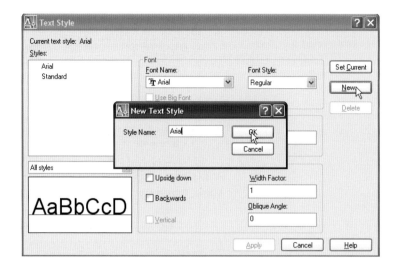

Fig. 4.9 The **New Text Style**
sub-dialog

Setting Dimension style

Settings for dimensions require making *entries* in a number of sub-dialogs in the **Dimension Style Manager**. To set the dimensions style:

1. At the command line:

    Command: *enter* **d** *right-click*

And the **Dimension Style Manager** dialog appears (Fig. 4.10).

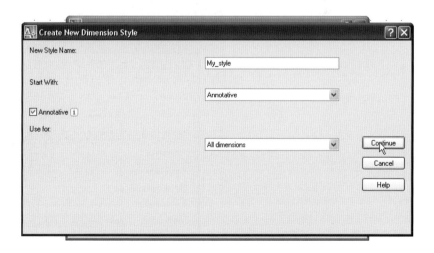

Fig. 4.10 The **Dimension Style Manager** dialog

2. In the dialog, *click* the **New...** button. In the **Create New Dimension Style** sub-dialog which appears, *enter* **My_style** in the **New Style Name** field, followed by a *click* on the sub-dialog's **Continue** button.
3. The **New Dimension Style** sub-dialog appears (Fig. 4.11). In the dialog make settings as shown. Then *click* the **OK** button of that dialog.

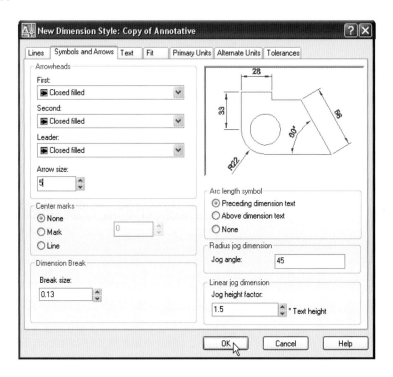

Fig. 4.11 Setting symbols and arrows in the **New Dimension Style** sub-dialog

4. The original **Dimension Style Manager** reappears. *Click* its **Modify** button.
5. In the **Modify Dimension Style** sub-dialog which appears (Fig. 4.12), *click* the **Text** tab at the top of the dialog. Then *click* the arrow to the

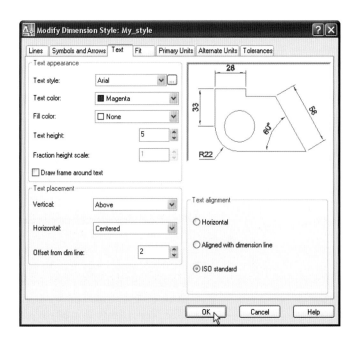

Fig. 4.12 Setting text style and height in the **Text** sub-dialog

right of the **Text Style** field and select **Arial** from the popup list. *Enter* a height of **5** in the **Text height** field and **2** in the **Offset from dim line** field.

6. Then *click* the **Primary Units** tab and set the units **Precision** in both **Linear** and **Angular Dimensions** to **0**, that is no units after decimal point. *Click* the sub-dialog's **OK** button (Fig. 4.13). The **Dimension Style Manager** dialog reappears showing dimensions, as they will appear in a drawing, in the **Preview of: My_style** box. *Click* the **Set Current** button (Fig. 4.14), followed by another *click* on the **Close** button.

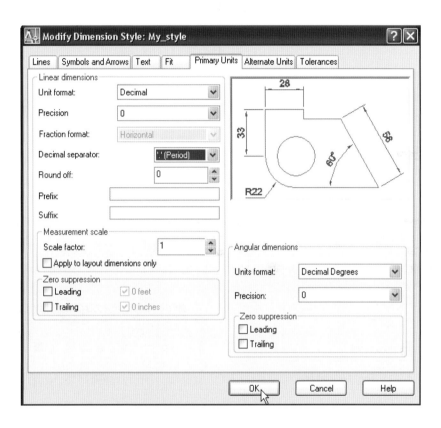

Fig. 4.13 Setting units in the **Primary Units** sub-dialog

Setting the shortcutmenu variable

Call the line tool, draw a few lines and then *right-click*. The *right-click* menu shown in Fig. 4.15 may well appear. The menu will also appear when any tool is called. Some operators prefer using this menu when constructing drawings. To stop this menu appearing:

Command: *enter* **shortcutmenu** *right-click*
Enter new value for SHORTCUTMENU <12>: 0
Command:

And the menu will no longer appear when a tool is in action.

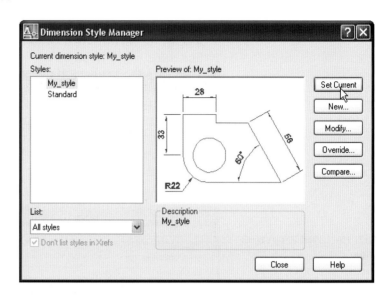

Fig. 4.14 *Click* the **Set Current** button

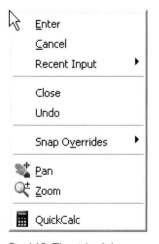

Fig. 4.15 The *right-click* menu

Fig. 4.16 The **Layer Properties Manager** icon in the **Layers** control panel

Setting Layers (see also page 127)

1. *Left-click* on the **Layer Properties Manager** tool icon in the **Layers** control panel (Fig. 4.16).

The **Layer Properties Manager** dialog appears on screen (Fig. 4.17).

2. *Click* the **New Layer** icon. **Layer1** appears in the layer list. Overwrite the name **Layer1** *entering* **Centre**.

3. Repeat step **2** four times and make four more layers titled **Construction, Dimensions, Hidden** and **Text**.

4. *Click* against one of the squares under the **Color** column of the dialog. The **Select Color** dialog appears (Fig. 4.18). *Double-click* on one of the colours in the **Index Color** squares. The selected colour appears

against the layer name in which the square was selected. Repeat until all five new layers have a colour.

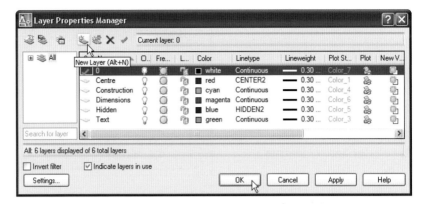

Fig. 4.17 The **Layer Properties Manager** dialog

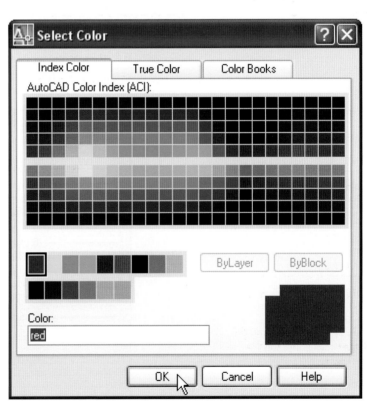

Fig. 4.18 The **Select Color** dialog

5. *Click* on the linetype **Continuous** against the layer name **Centre**. The **Select Linetype** dialog appears (Fig. 4.19). *Click* its **Load...** button and from the **Load or Reload Linetypes** dialog *double-click* **CENTER2**. The dialog disappears and the name appears in the **Select Linetype** dialog. *Click* the **OK** button and the linetype **CENTER2** appears against the layer **Centre**.

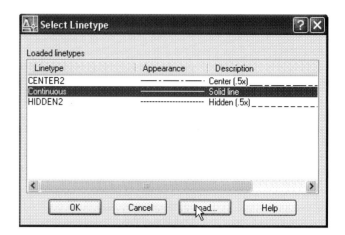

Fig. 4.19 The **Select Linetype** dialog

6. Repeat with layer **Hidden**, load the linetype **HIDDEN2** and make the linetype against this layer **HIDDEN2**.
7. *Click* on the any of the lineweights in the **Layer Properties Manager**. This brings up the **Lineweight** dialog (Fig. 4.20). Select the lineweight **0.3**. Repeat the same for all the other layers. Then *click* the **Close** button of the **Layer Properties Manager**.

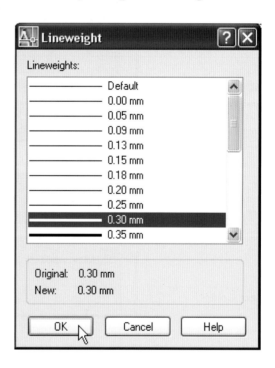

Fig. 4.20 The **Lineweight** dialog

Saving the template file

1. *Left-click* **Save As...** in the **File** drop-down menu.
2. In the **Save Drawing As** dialog which comes on screen (Fig. 4.21), *click* the arrow to the right of the **Files of type** field and in the popup

list associated with the field *click* on **AutoCAD Drawing Template (*.dwt)**. The list of template files in the **AutoCAD 2008/Template** directory appears in the file list.

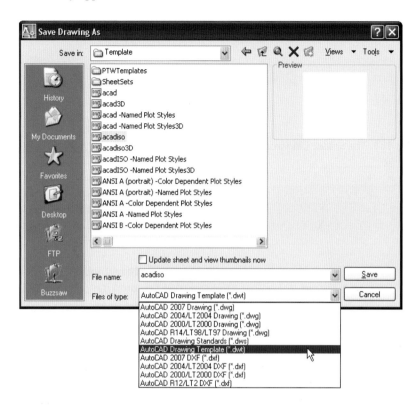

Fig. 4.21 Saving the template to the name **acadiso.dwt**

3. *Click* on **acadiso** in the file list, followed by a *click* on the **Save** button.
4. A **Template Description** dialog appears. Make *entries* as indicated in Fig. 4.22, making sure that **Metric** is chosen from the popup list.

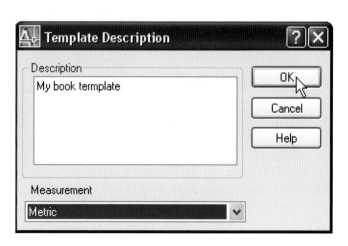

Fig. 4.22 The **Template Description** dialog

The template can now be saved to be opened for the construction of drawings as needed.

When AutoCAD 2008 is opened the template **acadiso.dwt** fills the drawing area.

Note

Please remember that if there are multiple users to the computer it is advisable to save the template to a name of your own choice.

Another template

A template A3_template.dwt – Fig. 4.25

In the **Select Template** dialog a *click* on any of the file names causes a preview of the template to appear in the **Preview** box of the dialog, unless the template is free of information – as is **acadiso.dwt**. To construct another template which includes a title block and other information based on the **acadiso.dwt** template:

1. In an **acadiso.dwt** template construct the required border, title block, etc.
2. *Click* the **Layout1** tab (Fig. 4.23). The screen changes to a **Paper Space** setting.

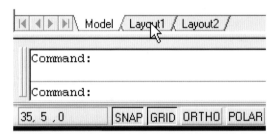

Fig. 4.23 The **Layout1** tab

3. *Click* the **Maximize Viewport** icon in the status bar (Fig. 4.24).

Fig. 4.24 The **Maximize Viewport** icon in the status bar

4. **Zoom** to **Extents**.
5. It is suggested this template be saved as a **Paper Space** template with the name **A3_template.dwt**.

Fig. 4.25 The **A3_template.dwt**

Notes

1. The outline for this template is a pline from **0,290** to **420,290** to **420,0** to **0,0** to **290,0** and of width **0.5**.
2. The upper line of the title block is a pline from **0,20** to **420,20**.
3. **Pspace** is two-dimensional.
4. Further uses for **Layouts** and **Pspace** are given in Chapter 11.

Revision notes

1. The **Zoom** tools are important in that they allow even the smallest parts of drawings to be examined and, if necessary, amended or modified.
2. The zoom tools can be called from the **Zoom** sub-menu of the **View** drop-down menu, or by *entering* **z** or **zoom** at the command line. The easiest is to *enter* **z** at the command line followed by a *right-click*.
3. There are five methods of calling tools for use – selecting a tool icon from a toolbar; selecting a tool icon from the **DASHBOARD** palette; *entering* the name of a tool in full at the command line; *entering* an abbreviation for a tool; selecting from a drop-down menu.
4. When constructing large drawings, the **Pan** tool and the **Aerial View** window are of value for allowing work to be carried out in any part of a drawing, while showing the whole drawing in the **Aerial View** window.

5. An A3 sheet of paper is 420 mm × 297 mm. If a drawing constructed in the template **acadiso.dwt** is printed/plotted full size (scale 1:1), each unit in the drawing will be 1 mm in the print/plot.

6. When limits are set it is essential to call **Zoom** followed by **a** (All) to ensure that the limits of the drawing area are as set.

7. If the *right-click* menu appears when using tools, the menu can be aborted if required by setting the **SHORTCUTMENU** variable to **0**.

CHAPTER 5

The Modify tools

Aim of this chapter

To describe the uses of tools for modifying parts of drawings.

Introduction

The **Modify** tools are among the most frequently used of AutoCAD 2008. Their tool icons are found in the **Modify** drop-down menu (Fig. 5.1), or in the **Modify** toolbar in the **2D Classic AutoCAD** work-space, or in the lower set of tool icons in the **2D Draw** control panel (Fig. 5.2).

Using the **Erase** tool was described in Chapter 2. Examples of tools other than the **Explode** follow. See also Chapter 9 for **Explode**.

The Copy tool

Example – Copy (Fig. 5.5)

1. Construct Fig. 5.3 using **Polyline**. Do not include the dimensions.
2. Call the **Copy** tool – either *left-click* on its tool icon in the **Modify** toolbar, or *pick* **Copy** from the **Modify** tools in the **2D Draw** control panel (Fig. 5.4), or *enter* **cp** or **copy** at the command line.

The command line shows:

Command: _copy
Select objects: *pick* the cross **1 found**
Select objects: *right-click*
Current settings: Copy mode = Multiple
Specify base point or [Displacement/mOde] <Displacement>: O (mOde)
Enter a copy mode option [Single/Multiple] <Multiple>: s
Specify base point or [Displacement/mOde/Multiple] <Displacement>: *pick*
Specify second point or <use first point as displacement>: *pick*

The result is given in Fig. 5.5.

Fig. 5.1 The **Modify** tools in the **Modify** drop-down menu

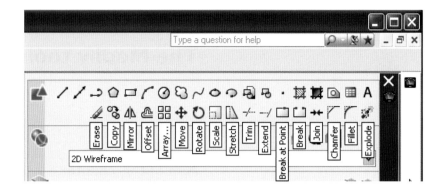

Fig. 5.2 The **Modify** tools in the **2D Draw** control panel

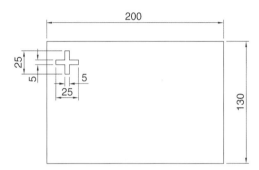

Fig. 5.3 Example – **Copy Object** – outlines

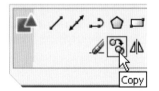

Fig. 5.4 The **Copy** tool icon from the **2D Draw control panel**

Fig. 5.5 First example – **Copy**

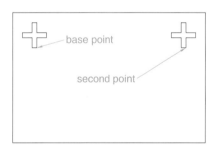

Example – Multiple copy (Fig. 5.6)

1. Erase the copied object.
2. Call the **Copy** tool. The command line shows:

> **Command: _copy**
> **Select objects:** *pick* the cross **1 found**
> **Select objects:** *right-click*
> **Current settings: Copy mode = Single**
> **Specify base point or [Displacement/mOde/Multiple] <Displace-**
>   **ment>:** o (mOde)
> **Enter a copy mode option [Single/Multiple] <Single>:** m
> **Specify base point or [Displacement/mOde] <Displacement>:** *pick*
> **Specify second point or <use first point as displacement>:** *pick*
> **Specify second point or [Exit/Undo] <Exit>:** *pick*
> **Specify second point or [Exit/Undo] <Exit>:** *pick*

Specify second point or [Exit/Undo] <Exit>: e (Exit)
Command

The result is shown in Fig. 5.6.

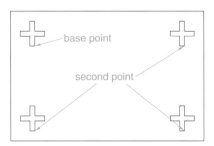

Fig. 5.6 Example – **Copy –**
Multiple

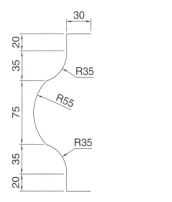

Fig. 5.7 The **Mirror** tool icon
from the **2D Draw** control panel

The Mirror tool

First example – Mirror (Fig. 5.9)

1. Construct the outline in Fig. 5.8 using **Line** and **Arc**.
2. Call the **Mirror** tool – *left-click* on its tool icon in the **2D Draw** control panel (Fig. 5.7), or *pick* the **Mirror** tool icon from the **Modify** toolbar, or *pick* **Mirror** from the **Modify** drop-down menu, or *enter* **mi** or **mirror** at the command line. The command line shows:

Command:_mirror
Select objects: *pick* first corner **Specify opposite corner:** *pick* **7 found**
Select objects: *right-click*
Specify first point of mirror line: end **of** *pick*
Specify second point of mirror line: end **of** *pick*
Erase source objects [Yes/No] <N>: *right-click*
Command:

The result is shown in Fig. 5.9.

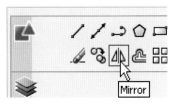

Fig. 5.8 First example – **Mirror** –
outline

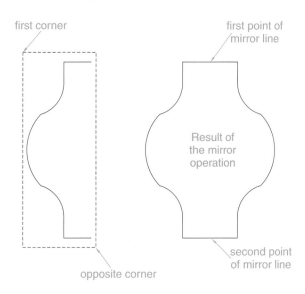

Fig. 5.9 First example – **Mirror**

Second example – Mirror (Fig. 5.10)

1. Construct the outline of the dimensioned polyline as shown in the upper drawing of Fig. 5.10.
2. Call **Mirror** and using the tool three times complete the given outline. The two points shown in Fig. 5.10 are to mirror the right-hand side of the outline.

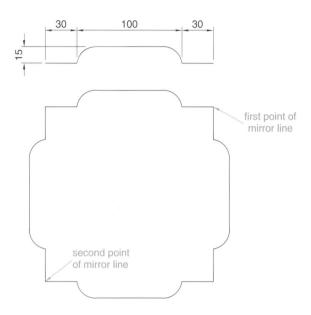

Fig. 5.10 Second example – **Mirror**

Fig. 5.11 Third example – **Mirror**

Third example – Mirror (Fig. 5.11)

If text is involved when using the **Mirror** tool, the set variable **MIRRTEXT** must be set correctly. To set the variable:

> **Command:** mirrtext
> **Enter new value for MIRRTEXT <1>:** 0
> **Command:**

If set to **0** text will mirror without distortion. If set to **1** text will read backwards as indicated in Fig. 5.11.

The Offset tool

Examples – Offset (Fig. 5.14)

1. Construct the four outlines shown in Fig. 5.13.
2. Call the **Offset** tool – *left-click* its tool icon in the **2D Draw** control panel (Fig. 5.12), or *pick* the tool from the **Modify** toolbar, or *pick* the tool name in the **Modify** drop-down menu, or *enter* **o** or **offset** at the command line. The command line shows:

> **Command:_offset**
> **Current settings: Erase source = No Layer = Source OFFSET-**
> **GAPTYPE = 0**

Specify offset distance or [Through/Erase/Layer] <Through>: 10
Select object to offset or [Exit/Undo] <Exit>: *pick* drawing **1**
Specify point on side to offset or [Exit/Multiple/Undo] <Exit>:
  pick inside the rectangle
Select object to offset or [Exit/Undo] <Exit>: e (Exit)
Command:

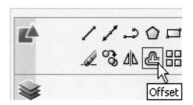

Fig. 5.12 The **Offset** tool from the **2D Draw** control panel

3. Repeat for drawings **2, 3** and **4** in Fig. 5.13 as shown in Fig. 5.14.

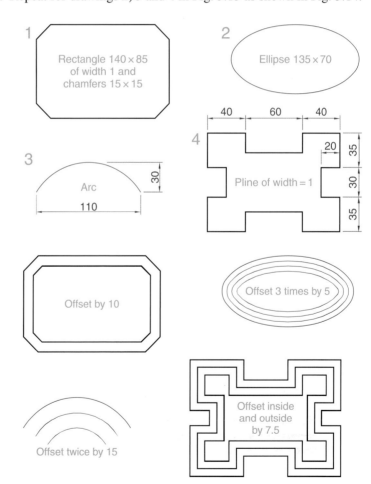

Fig. 5.13 Examples – **Offset** – outlines

Fig. 5.14 Examples – **Offset**

The Array tool

Arrays can be in either a **Rectangular** form or in a **Polar** form as shown in the examples below.

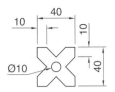

Fig. 5.15 First example – **Array** – drawing to be arrayed

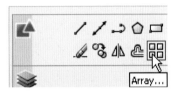

Fig. 5.16 The **Array** tool icon from the **2D Draw** control panel

First example – Rectangular Array (Fig. 5.18)

1. Construct the drawing in Fig. 5.15.
2. Call the **Array** tool – either *left-click* the **Array** tool icon in the **2D Draw** control panel (Fig. 5.16), or *pick* the **Array** tool icon from the **Modify** toolbar, or *pick* **Array...** from the **Modify** drop-down menu, or *enter* **ar** or **array** at the command line. No matter which method is used the **Array** dialog appears (Fig. 5.17).

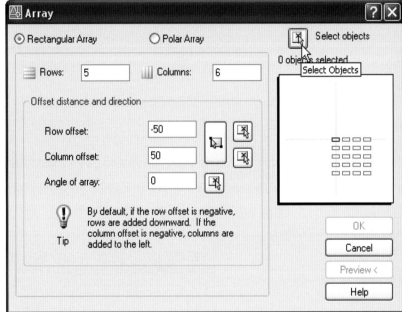

Fig. 5.17 First example – the **Array** dialog

3. Make settings in the dialog:

   Rectangular Array – radio button set on (dot in button)
   Row field – *enter* **5**
   Column field – *enter* **6**
   Row offset field – *enter* −**50** (note the minus sign)
   Column offset field – *enter* **50**

4. *Click* the **Select objects** button and the dialog disappears. *Window* the drawing. The dialog reappears.
5. *Click* the **Preview<** button. The dialog disappears and the array appears with a warning dialog in the centre of the array (Fig. 5.18).
6. If satisfied *click* the **Accept** button. If not, *click* the **Modify** button and make revisions to the **Array** dialog fields.

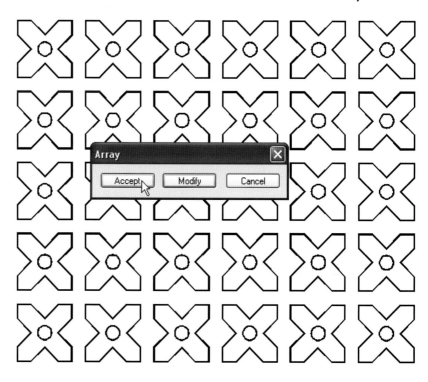

Fig. 5.18 First example – **Array**

Second example – Polar Array (Fig. 5.22)

1. Construct the drawing in Fig. 5.19.
2. Call **Array**. The **Array** dialog appears. Make settings as shown in Fig. 5.20.

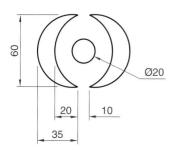

Fig. 5.19 Second example – **Array** – drawing to be arrayed

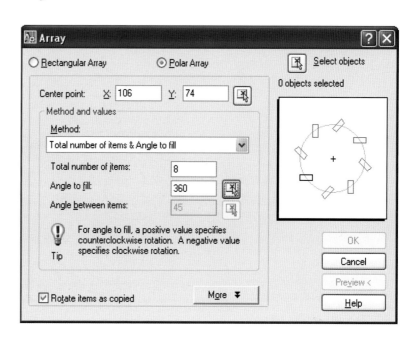

Fig. 5.20 Second example – **Array** – settings in the dialog

3. *Click* the **Select objects** button of the dialog and *window* the drawing. The dialog returns to screen. *Click* the **Pick Center Point** button (Fig. 5.21) and when the dialog disappears, *pick* a centre point for the array.

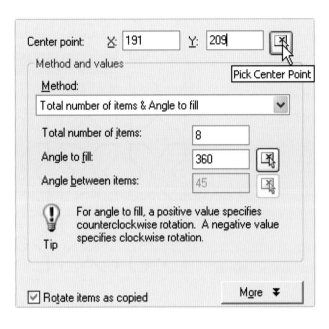

Fig. 5.21 Second example –
Array – the **Pick Center Point** button

4. The dialog reappears. *Click* its **Preview**< button, the array appears with its warning dialog; if satisfied with the result, *click* the **Accept** button of this dialog (Fig. 5.22).

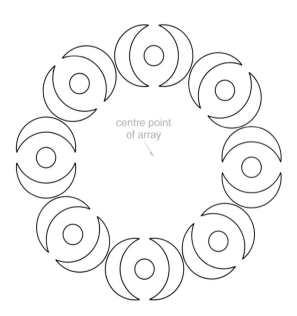

Fig. 5.22 Second example – **Array**

The Move tool

Example – Move (Fig. 5.25)

1. Construct the drawing in Fig. 5.23.

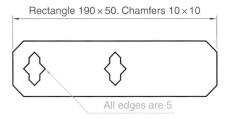

Rectangle 190 × 50. Chamfers 10 × 10

All edges are 5

Fig. 5.23 Example – **Move** –
drawing

2. Call **Move** – either *click* the **Move** tool icon in the **Modify** toolbar, or *pick* **Move** from the **2D Draw** control panel (Fig. 5.24), or *pick* **Move** from the **Modify** drop-down menu, or *pick* the **Move** tool icon from the **Modify** toolbar, or *enter* **m** or **move** at the command line, which shows:

Command:_move
Select objects: *pick* the middle shape in the drawing **1 found**
Select objects: *right-click*
Specify base point or [Displacement] <Displacement>: *pick*
Specify second point or <use first point as displacement>: *pick*
Command:

Fig. 5.24 The **Move** tool icon
from the **2D Draw** control panel

The result is given in Fig. 5.25.

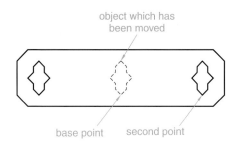

object which has
been moved

base point   second point

Fig. 5.25 Example – **Move**

The Rotate tool

When using the **Rotate** tool remember that the default rotation of objects within AutoCAD 2008 is counterclockwise (anticlockwise).

Example – Rotate (Fig. 5.27)

1. Construct drawing **1** of Fig. 5.27 with **Polyline**. Copy the drawing **1** three times – shown as drawings **2, 3** and **4** in Fig. 5.27.
2. Call **Rotate** – *left-click* its tool icon in the **2D Draw** control panel (Fig. 5.26), or *pick* its tool icon from the **Modify** toolbar, or *pick* **Rotate** from the **Modify** drop-down menu, or *enter* **ro** or **rotate** at the command line. The command line shows:

Command:_rotate
Current positive angle in UCS: ANGDIR = counterclockwise ANGBASE = 0
Select objects: *window* the drawing **3 found**
Select objects: *right-click*
Specify base point: *pick*
Specify rotation angle or [Copy/Reference] <0>: 45
Command:

And the first copy rotates through the specified angle.

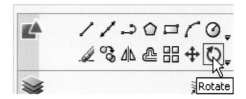

Fig. 5.26 The **Rotate** tool icon from the **2D Draw** control panel

3. Repeat for drawings **3** and **4** rotating through angles as shown in Fig. 5.27.

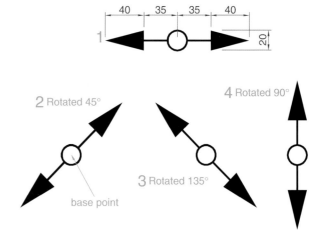

Fig. 5.27 Example – **Rotate**

The Scale tool

Examples – Scale (Fig. 5.29)

1. Using the **Rectangle** and **Polyline** tools, construct drawing **1** of Fig. 5.29. The **Rectangle** fillets are R10. The line width of all parts is **1**. Copy the drawing 3 times to give drawings **2, 3** and **4**.
2. Call **Scale** – *left-click* its tool icon in the **2D Draw** control panel (Fig. 5.28), or *pick* its tool icon in the **Modify** toolbar, or *pick* **Scale** from the **Modify** drop-down-menu, or *enter* **sc** or **scale** at the command line, which then shows:

Command:_scale
Select objects: *window* drawing 2 **5 found**
Select objects: *right-click*
Specify base point: *pick*
Specify scale factor or [Copy/Reference] <1>: 0.75
Command:

Fig. 5.28 The **Scale** tool icon from the **2D Draw** control panel

3. Repeat for the other two drawings **3** and **4** scaling to the scales given with the drawings.

The results are shown in Fig. 5.29.

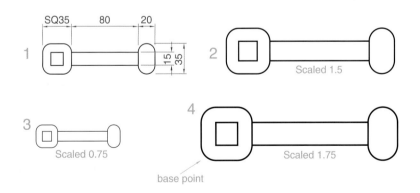

Fig. 5.29 Examples – **Scale**

The Trim tool

This tool is one which will be of frequent use for the construction of drawings.

First example – Trim (Fig. 5.31)

1. Construct the drawing **Original drawing** in Fig. 5.31.
2. Call **Trim** – either *left-click* its tool icon in the **2D Draw** control panel (Fig. 5.30), or *pick* its tool icon in the **Modify** toolbar, or *pick* **Trim** from the **Modify** drop-down menu, or *enter* **tr** or **trim** at the command line, which then shows:

Command:_trim
Current settings: Projection UCS. Edge=None
Select cutting edges: *pick* the left-hand circle **1 found**
Select objects: *right-click*
Select objects to trim or shift-select to extend or [Fence/Project/ Crossing/Edge/eRase//Undo]: *pick* one of the objects
Select objects to trim or shift-select to extend or [Fence/Crossing/ Project/Edge/eRase/Undo]: *pick* the second of the objects
Select objects to trim or shift-select to extend or [Project/Edge/ Undo]: *right-click*
Command:

Fig. 5.30 The **Trim** tool icon
from the **2D Draw** control panel

3. This completes the **First stage** as shown in Fig. 5.31. Repeat the **Trim** sequence for the **Second stage**.
4. The **Third stage** drawing of Fig. 5.31 shows the result of the trims at the left-hand end of the drawing.

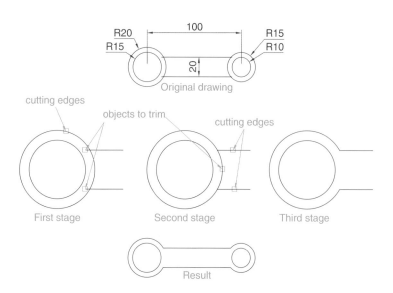

Fig. 5.31 First example – **Trim**

5. Repeat for the right-hand end. The final result is shown in the drawing labelled **Result** in Fig. 5.31.

Second example – Trim (Fig. 5.32)

1. Construct the left-hand drawing of Fig. 5.32.
2. Call **Trim**. The command line shows:

Command:_trim
Current settings: Projection UCS. Edge = None
Select cutting edges...
Select objects or <select all>: *pick* the left-hand arc **1 found**
Select objects: *right-click*
Select objects to trim or shift-select to extend or [Fence/Crossing/
Project/Edge/eRase/Undo]: e (Edge)
Enter an implied edge extension mode [Extend/No extend] <No
extend>: e (Extend)
Select objects to trim: *pick*
Select objects to trim: *pick*
Select objects to trim: *right-click*
Command:

3. Repeat for the other required trims. The result is given in Fig. 5.32.

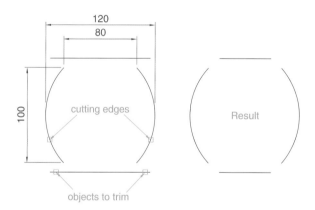

Fig. 5.32 Second example – **Trim**

The Stretch tool

Examples – Stretch (Fig. 5.34)

As its name implies the **Stretch** tool is for stretching drawings or parts of drawings. The action of the tool prevents it from altering the shape of circles in any way. Only **crossing** or **polygonal** windows can be used to determine the part of a drawing which is to be stretched.

1. Construct the drawing labelled **Original** in Fig. 5.34, but do not include the dimensions. Use the **Circle, Arc, Trim** and **Polyline Edit** tools. The resulting outlines are plines of width = **1**. With the **Copy** tool make two copies of the drawing.

Note

In each of the three examples in Fig. 5.34, the broken lines represent the crossing windows required when **Stretch** is used.

2. Call the **Stretch** tool – either *click* on its tool icon in the **2D Draw control panel** (Fig. 5.33), or *left-click* on its tool icon in the **Modify** toolbar, or *pick* its name in the **Modify** drop-down menu, or *enter* **s** or **stretch** at the command line, which shows:

Command:_stretch
Select objects to stretch by crossing-window or crossing-polygon...
Select objects: *enter* **c** *right-click*
Specify first corner: *pick* **Specify opposite corner:** *pick* **1 found**
Select objects: *right-click*
Specify base point or [Displacement] <Displacement>: *pick* beginning of arrow
Specify second point of displacement or <use first point as displacement>: *drag* in the direction of the arrow to the required second point and *right-click*
Command:

Fig. 5.33 The **Stretch** tool icon from the **2D Draw** control panel

Notes

1. When circles are *windowed* with the crossing window no stretching can take place. This is why, in the case of the first example in Fig. 5.34, when the **second point of displacement** was *picked*, there was no result – the outline did not stretch.
2. Care must be taken when using this tool as unwanted stretching can occur.

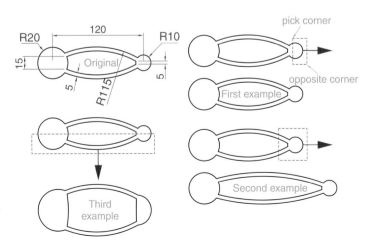

Fig. 5.34 Examples – **Stretch**

The Break tool

Examples – Break (Fig. 5.36)

1. Construct the rectangle, arc and circle shown in Fig. 5.36.
2. Call **Break** – either *click* its tool icon in the **2D Draw** control panel (Fig. 5.35), or *pick* its tool icon in the **Modify** toolbar, or *click* **Break** in the **Modify** drop-down menu, or *enter* **br** or **break** at the command line, which shows the following.

Fig. 5.35 The **Break** tool icon from the **2D Draw** control panel

For drawings 1 and 2

Command:_break Select object *pick* at the point
Specify second break point or [First point]: *pick*
Command:

For drawing 3

Command:_break Select object *pick* at the point
Specify second break point or [First point]: *enter* **f** *right-click*
Specify first break point: *pick*
Specify second break point: *pick*
Command:

The results are shown in Fig. 5.36.

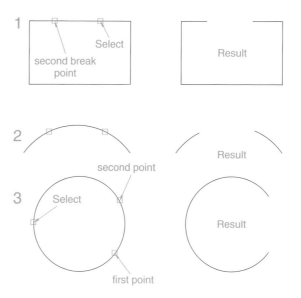

Fig. 5.36 Examples – **Break**

Note

Remember the default rotation of AutoCAD 2008 is counterclockwise. This applies to the use of the **Break** tool also.

The Join tool

The **Join** tool can be used to join plines providing their ends are touching; to join lines which are in line with each other; to join arcs; and to convert arcs to circles.

Examples – Join (Fig. 5.38)

1. Construct a rectangle from four separate plines – drawing **1** of Fig. 5.38; construct two lines – drawing **2** of Fig. 5.38 and an arc – drawing **3** of Fig. 5.38.
2. Call the **Join** tool – either *click* the **Join** tool icon in the **2D Draw** control panel (Fig. 5.37), or *left-click* its tool icon in the **Modify** toolbar, or select **Join** from the **Modify** drop-down menu, or *enter* **join** or **j** at the command line. The command line shows:

Command: _join Select source object:
Select objects to join to source: *pick* a pline **1 found**
Select objects to join to source: *pick* another **1 found, 2 total**
Select objects to join to source: *pick* another **1 found, 3 total**
Select objects to join to source: *right-click*
3 segments added to polyline
Command: *right-click*
JOIN Select source object: *pick one* of the lines
Select lines to join to source: *pick* the other **1 found**
Select lines to join to source: *right-click*
1 line joined to source
Command: *right-click*

Fig. 5.37 The **Join** tool icon from the **2D Draw** control panel

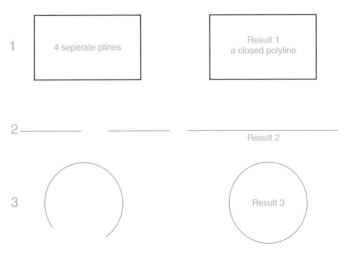

Fig. 5.38 Examples – **Join**

JOIN Select source object: *pick* the arc
Select arcs to join to source or [cLose]: *enter* **l** *right-click*
Arc converted to a circle.
Command:

The results are shown in Fig. 5.38.

The Extend tool

Examples – Extend (Fig. 5.40)

1. Construct plines and a circle as shown in the left-hand drawings of Fig. 5.40.
2. Call **Extend** – either *click* the **Extend** tool in the **2D Draw** control panel (Fig. 5.39), or *click* its tool icon in the **Modify** toolbar, or *pick* **Extend** from the **Modify** drop-down menu, or *enter* **ex** or **extend** at the command line, which then shows:

Command:_extend
Current settings: Projection = UCS Edge = Extend
Select boundary edges...
Select objects or <select all>: *pick* **1 found**
Select objects: *pick*
Select objects: *right-click*
Select object to extend or shift-select to trim or [Fence/Crossing/Project/Edge/Undo]: *pick*

Repeat for each object to be extended. Then:

Select object to extend or shift-select to trim or [Fence/Crossing/Project/Edge/Undo]: *right-click*
Command:

Fig. 5.39 The **Extend** tool icon from the **2D Draw** control panel

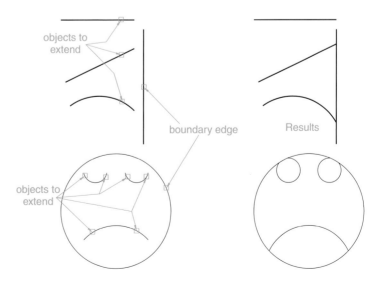

Fig. 5.40 Examples – **Extend**

Note

Observe the similarity of the **Extend** and **No extend** prompts with those of the **Trim** tool.

The Chamfer and Fillet tools

There are similarities in the prompt sequences for these two tools. The major differences are that two settings (**Dist1** and **Dist2**) are required for a chamfer, but only one (**Radius**) for the fillet. The basic prompts for both are given below.

Chamfer

Command:_chamfer
(TRIM mode) Current chamfer Dist1 = 1, Dist2 = 1
Select first line or [Undo/Polyline/Distance/Angle/Trim/mEthod/
    Multiple]: *enter* **d** (Distance) *right-click*
Specify first chamfer distance <1>: 10
Specify second chamfer distance <10>: *right-click*

Fillet

Command:_fillet
Current settings: Mode = TRIM, Radius = 1
Select first object or [Polyline/Radius/Trim/mUltiple]: *enter* **r** (Radius)
    right-click
Specify fillet radius <1>: 15

Examples – Chamfer (Fig. 5.42)

1. Construct three rectangles 100 × 60 using either the **Line** or the **Polyline** tool.
2. Call **Chamfer** – either *click* its tool icon in the **2D Draw** control panel (Fig. 5.41), or *click* on its tool icon in the **Modify** toolbar, or *pick* **Chamfer** from the **Modify** drop-down menu, or *enter* **cha** or **chamfer** at the command line, which then shows:

Command:_chamfer
(TRIM mode) Current chamfer Dist1 = 1, Dist2 = 1
Select first line or [Undo/Polyline/Distance/Angle/Trim/
mEthod/Multiple]: d
Specify first chamfer distance <1>: 10
Specify second chamfer distance <10>: *right-click*
Select first line or [Undo/Polyline/Distance/Angle/Trim/mEthod/
    Multiple]: *pick* the first line for the chamfer
Select second line or shift-select to apply corner: *pick*
Command:

Fig. 5.41 The **Chamfer** tool icon from the **2D Draw** control panel

The other two rectangles are chamfered in a similar manner except that the **No trim** prompt is brought into operation with the bottom left-hand example.

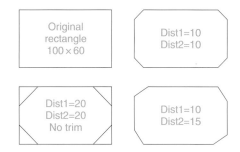

Fig. 5.42 Examples – **Chamfer**

Examples – Fillet (Fig. 5.44)

1. Construct three rectangles as for the **Chamfer** examples.
2. Call Fillet – either *clickits* tool icon in the **2D Draw** control panel (Fig. 5.43), or *pick* its tool icon in the **Modify** toolbar, or *pick* **Fillet** from the **Modify** drop-down menu, or *enter* **f** or **fillet** at the command line, which then shows:

Fig. 5.43 The **Fillet** tool icon from the **2D Draw** control panel

Command:_fillet
Current settings: Mode = TRIM, Radius = 1
Select first object or [Polyline/Radius/Trim/mUltiple]: r (Radius)
Specify fillet radius <1>: 15
Select first object or [Undo/Polyline/Radius/Trim/Multiple]: *pick*
Select second object or shift-select to apply corner: *pick*
Command:

Three examples are given in Fig. 5.44.

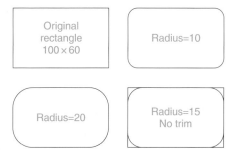

Fig. 5.44 Examples – **Fillet**

Revision notes

1. The **Modify** tools are among the most frequently used tools in Auto-CAD 2008.
2. The abbreviations for the **Modify** tools are:

Copy	**cp** or **co**
Mirror	**mi**
Offset	**o**
Array	**ar**

Move   m
Rotate   ro
Scale   sc
Stretch   s
Trim   tr
Extend   ex
Break   br
Join   j
Chamfer   cha
Fillet   f

3. There are two other tools in the **Modify** toolbar or in the **2D Draw** control panel: **Erase** – some examples were given in Chapter 2 and **Explode** – further details of this tool will be given in Chapter 9.

A note – Selection windows and crossing windows

In the **Options** dialog settings can be made in the **Selection** sub-dialog for **Visual Effects**. A *click* on the **Visual Effect Settings...** button brings up another dialog. If the **Area Selection Effect** settings are set on, a normal window from top left to bottom right will be coloured in a chosen colour (default blue). A crossing window – bottom left to top right – will be coloured red (default colour). Note also that higlighting – **Selection Preview Effect** – allows objects to highlight if this feature is on. These settings are shown in Fig. 5.45.

4. When using **Mirror**, if text is part of the area to be mirrored, the set variable **MIRRTEXT** will require setting – to either **1** or **0**.

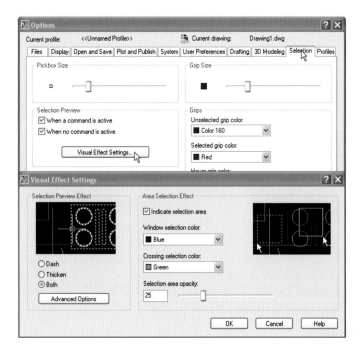

Fig. 5.45 **Visual Effect Settings** sub-dialog of the **Options** dialog

5. When using **Offset**, the **Through** prompt can be answered by *clicking* two points in the drawing area, the distance of the desired offset distance.
6. **Polar Arrays** can be arrays around any angle set in the **Angle of array** field of the **Array** dialog.
7. When using **Scale**, it is advisable to practise the **Reference** prompt.
8. The **Trim** tool in either its **Trim** or its **No trim** modes is among the most useful tools in AutoCAD 2008.
9. When using **Stretch**, circles are unaffected by the stretching.

Exercises

1. Construct the drawing in Fig. 5.46. All parts are plines of width = **0.7** with corners filleted R10. The long strips have been constructed using **Circle, Polyline, Trim** and **Polyline Edit**. Construct one strip and then copy it using **Copy**.

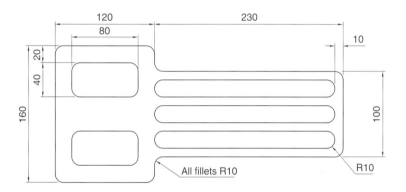

Fig. 5.46 Exercise 1

2. Construct the drawing in Fig. 5.47. All parts of the drawing are plines of width = **0.7**. The setting in the **Array** dialog is to be **180** in the **Angle of array** field.

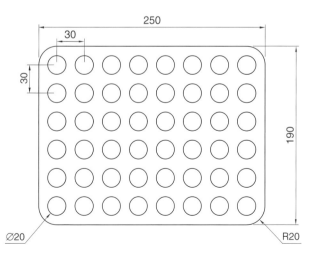

Fig. 5.47 Exercise 2

3. Using the tools **Polyline, Circle, Trim, Polyline Edit, Mirror** and **Fillet** construct the drawing in Fig. 5.48.

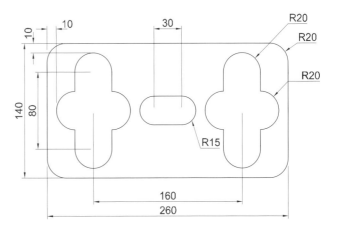

Fig. 5.48 Exercise 3

4. Construct the circles and lines (Fig. 5.49). Using **Offset** and the **Ttr** prompt of the **Circle** tool followed by **Trim**, construct one of the outlines arrayed within the outer circle. Then, with **Polyline Edit**, change the lines and arcs into a pline of width = **0.3**. Finally array the outline twelve times around the centre of the circles (Fig. 5.50).

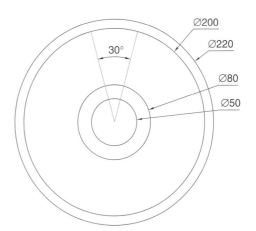

Fig. 5.49 Exercise 4 – circles and lines on which the exercise is based

5. Construct the arrow (Fig. 5.51). Array the arrow around the centre of its circle eight times to produce the right-hand drawing of Fig. 5.51.
6. Construct the left-hand drawing of Fig. 5.52. Then with **Move**, move the central outline to the top left-hand corner of the outer outline. Then with **Copy** make copies to the other corners.

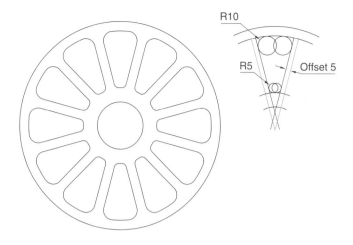

Fig. 5.50 Exercise 4

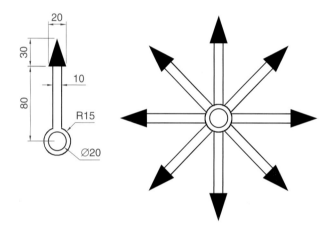

Fig. 5.51 Exercise 5

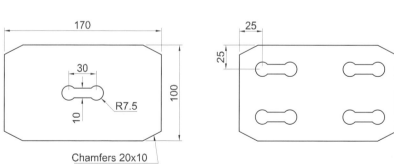

Fig. 5.52 Exercise 6

7. Construct the drawing in Fig. 5.53 and make two copies using **Copy**. With **Rotate** rotate each of the copies to the angles as shown.

8. Construct the dimensioned drawing of Fig. 5.54. With **Copy** copy the drawing. Then with **Scale** scale the drawing to a scale of **0.5**, followed by using **Rotate** to rotate the drawing through an angle as shown. Finally scale the original drawing to a scale of **2:1**.

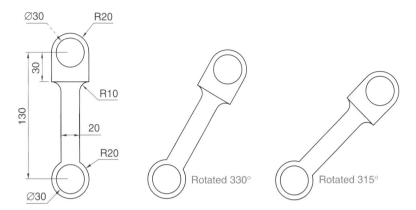

Fig. 5.53 Exercise 7

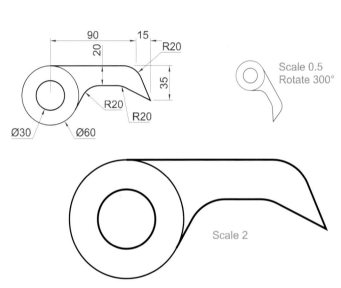

Fig. 5.54 Exercise 8

9. Construct the left-hand drawing of Fig. 5.55. Include the dimensions in your drawing. Then, using the **Stretch** tool, stretch the drawing, including its dimensions to the sizes as shown in the right-hand drawing. The dimensions are said to be **associative** (see Chapter 6).

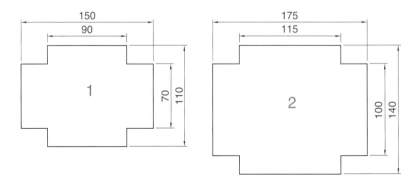

Fig. 5.55 Exercise 9

10. Construct the drawing in Fig. 5.56. All parts of the drawing are plines of width = **0.7**. The setting in the **Array** dialog is to be **180** in the **Angle of array** field.

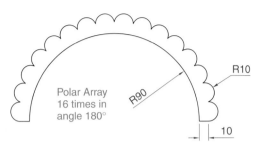

Fig. 5.56 Exercise 10

CHAPTER 6

Dimensions and Text

Aims of this chapter

1. To describe the variety of methods of dimensioning drawings.
2. To describe methods of adding text to drawings.

Introduction

We have already set a dimension style (**My_Style**) in the **acadiso.dwt** template, so we can now commence adding dimensions to drawings using this dimension style.

The Dimension tools

There are several ways in which the dimensions tools can be called.

1. From the **Dimensions** control panel in the **DASHBOARD** (Fig. 6.1).

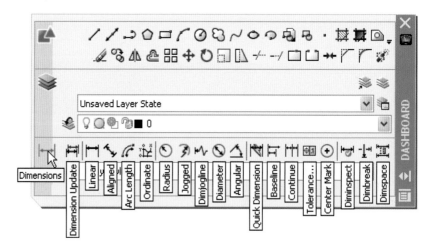

Fig. 6.1 Dimension tools in the **Dimensions** control panel

2. *Click* **Dimension** in the menu bar. Tools can be selected from the drop-down menu which appears.

3. From the **Dimension** toolbar. The toolbar can be called to screen with a *right-click* in any toolbar on screen followed by a *click* on **Dimension** in the popup menu which appears.
4. By *entering* an abbreviation for a dimension tool at the command line.

Any one of these methods can be used when dimensioning a drawing, but some operators may well decide to use a combination of the four methods.

Adding dimensions using the tools

First example – Linear dimension (Fig. 6.3)

1. Construct a rectangle 180 × 110 using the **Polyline** tool.
2. *Left-click* the **Linear** tool icon in the **Dimensions** control panel (Fig. 6.2) or on **Linear** in the **Dimension** toolbar. The command line shows:

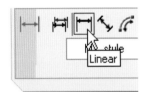

Fig. 6.2 The **Linear** tool icon in the **Dimensions** control panel

Command: _dimlinear
Specify first extension line origin or <select object>: *pick*
Specify second extension line origin: *pick*
Non-associative dimension created.
Specify dimension line location or [Mtext/Text/Angle/Horizontal/ Vertical/Rotated]: *pick*
Dimension text = 180
Command:

Fig. 6.3 shows the 180 dimension. Follow exactly the same procedure for the 110 dimension.

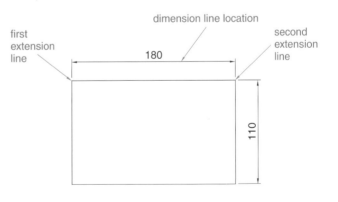

Fig. 6.3 First example – **Linear** dimension

Notes

1. If necessary use **Osnaps** to locate the extension line locations.
2. The prompt **Specify first extension line origin or [select object]:** also allows the line being dimensioned to be *picked*.

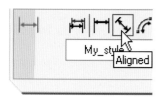

Fig. 6.4 The **Aligned** tool icon in the **Dimensions** control panel

Second example – Aligned dimension (Fig. 6.5)

1. Construct the outline in Fig. 6.5 using the **Line** tool.
2. *Left-click* the **Aligned** tool icon (Fig. 6.4) and dimension the outline. The prompts and replies are similar to the first example.

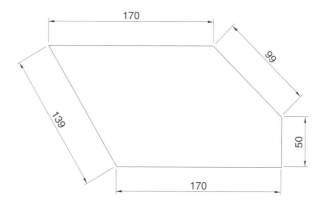

Fig. 6.5 Second example – **Aligned** dimension

Third example – Radius dimension (Fig. 6.7)

1. Construct the outline in Fig. 6.7 using the **Line** and **Fillet** tools.
2. *Left-click* the **Radius** tool icon (Fig. 6.6). The command line shows:

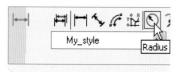

Fig. 6.6 The **Radius** tool icon in the **Dimensions** control panel

> **Command:_dimradius**
> **Select arc or circle:** *pick* one of the arcs
> **Dimension text = 30**
> **Specify dimension line location or [Mtext/Text/Angle]:** *pick*
> **Command:**

3. Continue dimensioning the outline as shown in Fig. 6.7.

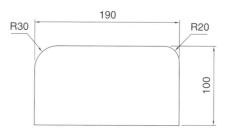

Fig. 6.7 Third example – **Radius** dimension

Notes

1. At the prompt:

   [Mtext/Text/Angle]:
   If a **t** (Text) is *entered*, another number can be *entered*, but remember if the dimension is a radius the letter **R** must be *entered* as a prefix to the new number.

Fig. 6.8 A radius dimension at an angle of 45°

2. If the response is **a** (Angle), and an angle number is *entered* the text for the dimension will appear at an angle. Fig. 6.8 show a radius dimension *entered* at an angle of 45°.
3. If the response is **m** (Mtext), the **Text Formatting** dialog appears together with a box in which new text can be *entered*. See page 120.
4. Dimensions added to a drawing using other tools from the **Dimensions** control panel or from the **Dimension** toolbar should be practised.

Adding dimensions from the command line

From Fig. 6.1 it will be seen that there are some dimension tools which have not been described in examples. Some operators may prefer *entering* dimensions from the command line. This involves abbreviations for the required dimension such as:

For **Linear dimension – hor** (horizontal) or ve (vertical)
For **Aligned dimension – al**
For **Radius dimension – ra**
For **Diameter dimension – d**
For **Angular dimension – an**
For **Dimension Text Edit – te**
For **Quick Leader – l**
And to exit from the dimension commands – **e** (Exit).

First example – hor and ve (Horizontal and vertical) – Fig. 6.10

1. Construct the outline in Fig. 6.9 using the **Line** tool. Its dimensions are shown in Fig. 6.10.

Fig. 6.9 First example – outline to dimension

2. At the command line *enter* **dim**. The command line will show:

Command: *enter* **dim** *right-click*
Dim: *enter* **hor** (horizontal) *right-click*
Specify first extension line origin or <select object>: *pick*
Specify second extension line origin: *pick*
Non-associative dimension created.
Specify dimension line location or [Mtext/Text/Angle]: *pick*
Enter dimension text <50>: *right-click*
Dim: *right-click*

HORIZONTAL
Specify first extension line origin or <select object>: *pick*
Specify second extension line origin: *pick*
Non-associative dimension created.
**Specify dimension line location or [Mtext/Text/Angle/Horizontal/
    Vertical/Rotated]:** *pick*
Enter dimension text <140>: *right-click*
Dim: *right-click*

And the 50 and 140 horizontal dimensions are added to the outline.

3. Continue to add the right-hand 50 dimension. Then when the command line shows:

Dim: *enter* **ve** (vertical) *right-click*
Specify first extension line origin or <select object>: *pick*
Specify second extension line origin: *pick*
**Specify dimension line location or [Mtext/Text/Angle/Horizontal/
    Vertical/Rotated]:** *pick*
Dimension text <20>: *right-click*
Dim: *right-click*
VERTICAL
Specify first extension line origin or <select object>: *pick*
Specify second extension line origin: *pick*
**Specify dimension line location or [Mtext/Text/Angle/Horizontal/
    Vertical/Rotated]:** *pick*
Dimension text <100>: *right-click*
Dim: *enter* **e** (Exit) *right-click*
Command:

The result is shown in Fig. 6.10.

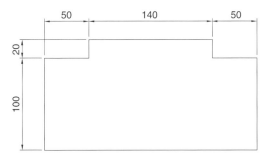

Fig. 6.10 First example – horizontal
and vertical dimensions

Second example – an (Angular) – Fig. 6.12

1. Construct the outline in Fig. 6.11 – a pline of width = **1**.
2. At the command line:

Command: *enter* **dim** *right-click*
Dim: *enter* **an** *right-click*

Select arc, circle, line or <specify vertex>: *pick*
Select second line: *pick*
Specify dimension arc line location or [Mtext/Text/Angle/Quadrant]: *pick*
Enter dimension <90>: *right-click*
Enter text location (or press ENTER): *pick*
Dim:

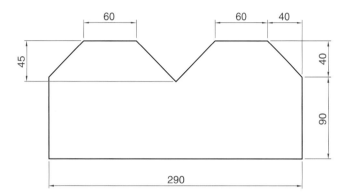

Fig. 6.11 Second example – outline for dimensions

And so on to add the other angular dimensions.
The result is given in Fig. 6.12.

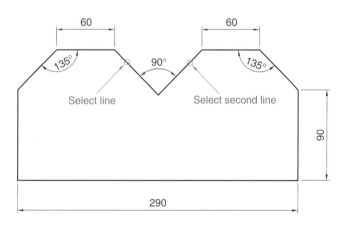

Fig. 6.12 Second example – an (Angle) dimension

Third example – l (Leader) – (Fig. 6.14)

1. Construct the outline in Fig. 6.13.
2. At the command line:

   Command: *enter* **dim** *right-click*
   Dim: *enter* l (Leader) *right-click*
   Leader start: *enter* **nea** (osnap nearest) *right-click* **to** *pick* one of the chamfer lines

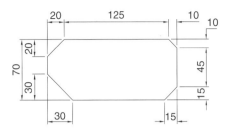

Fig. 6.13 Third example – outline
for dimensioning

> **To point:** *pick*
> **To point:** *pick*
> **To point:** *right-click*
> **Dimension text <0>:** *enter* **CHA 10 × 10** *right-click*
> **Dim:** *right-click*

Continue to add the other leader dimensions – Fig. 6.14.

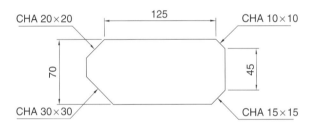

Fig. 6.14 Third example – l
(Leader) dimensions

Fourth example – te (Dimension Text Edit) – (Fig. 6.16)

1. Construct the dimensioned drawing in Fig. 6.15.

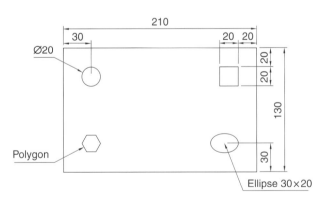

Fig. 6.15 Fourth example –
dimensioned drawing

2. At the command line:

> **Command:** *enter* **dim** *right-click*
> **Dim:** *enter* **te** (tedit) *right-click*
> **Select dimension:** *pick* the dimension to be changed

Specify new location for text or [Left/Right/Center/Home/Angle]:
either *pick* or *enter a* prompt's capital letter
Dim:

The results as given in Fig. 6.16 show dimensions which have been moved: the **210** dimension changed to the left-hand end of the dimension line, the **130** dimension changed to the left-hand end of the dimension line and the **30** dimension position changed.

The Arc Length tool (Fig. 6.18)

1. Construct two arcs of different sizes as in Fig. 6.18.

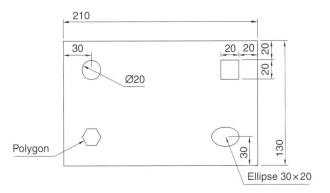

Fig. 6.16 Fourth example –
dimensions amended with **tedit**

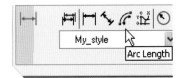

Fig. 6.17 The **Arc Length** tool in
the **Dimensions** control pane

2. Call the **Arc Length** tool with a *click* on its tool icon in the **Dimensions** control panel (Fig. 6.17), or with a *click* on **Arc Length** in the **Dimension** toolbar, or by *entering* **dimarc** at the command line. The command line shows:

Command: _dimarc
Select arc or polyline arc segment: *pick* an arc
Specify arc length dimension location, or [Mtext/Text/Angle/
Partial/Leader]: *pick* a suitable position
Dimension text = 147
Command:

Examples on two arcs are shown in Fig. 6.18.

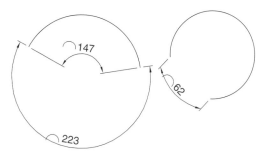

Fig. 6.18 Examples – **Arc Length**
tool

The Jogged tool (Fig. 6.20)

1. Draw a circle and an arc as indicated in Fig. 6.20.
2. Call the **Jogged** tool, either with a *left-click* on its tool icon in the **Dimensions** control panel (Fig. 6.19), or with a *click* on **Jogged** in the **Dimension** toolbar, or by *entering* **jog** at the command line. The command line shows:

Fig. 6.19 The **Jogged** tool icon in the **Dimensions** control panel

Command: _dimjogged
Select arc or circle: *pick* the circle or the arc
Specify center location override: *pick*
Dimension text = 60
Specify dimension line location or [Mtext/Text/Angle]: *pick*
Specify jog location: *pick*
Command:

The results of placing a jogged dimension on a circle and an arc are shown in Fig. 6.20.

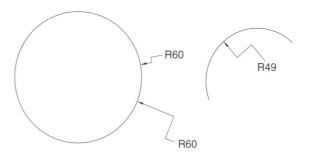

Fig. 6.20 Examples – the **Jogged** tool

Dimension tolerances

Before simple tolerances can be included with dimensions, new settings will need to be made in the **Dimension Style Manager** dialog as follows:

1. Open the dialog. The quickest way of doing this is to *enter* **d** at the command line followed by a *right-click*. This opens up the dialog.
2. *Clickthe* **Modify...** button of the dialog, followed by a *left-click on* the **Primary Units** tab and in the resulting sub-dialog make settings as shown in Fig. 6.21. Note the changes in the preview box of the dialog.

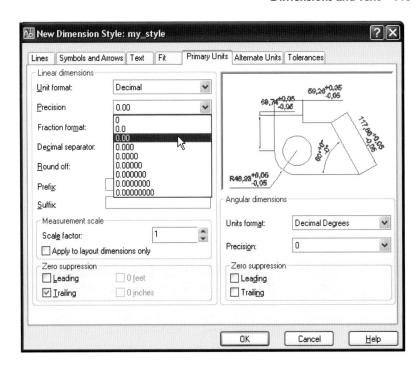

Fig. 6.21 The **Primary Units** sub-dialog of the **Dimension Style Manager**

3. *Click* the **Tolerances** tab and in the resulting sub-dialog, make settings as shown in Fig. 6.22. *Left-click* the **OK** button, then in the main dialog, *click* the **Set Current** button, followed by a *left-click* on the **Close** button.

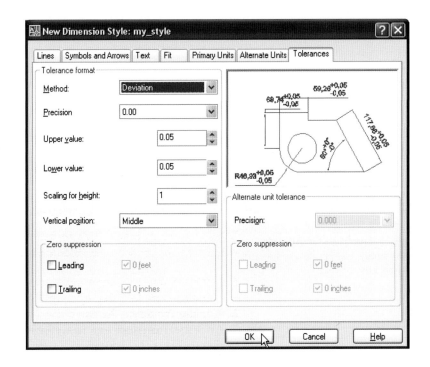

Fig. 6.22 The **Tolerances** sub-dialog of the **Dimension Style manager**

Example – simple tolerances (Fig. 6.24)

1. Construct the outline in Fig. 6.23.

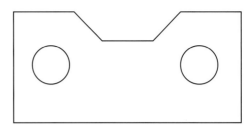

Fig. 6.23 Example – simple
tolerances – outline

2. Dimension the drawing using either tools from the **Dimension** toolbar or by *entering* abbreviations at the command line. Because tolerances have been set in the **Dimension Style Manager** dialog, the toleranced dimensions will automatically be added to the drawing (Fig. 6.24).

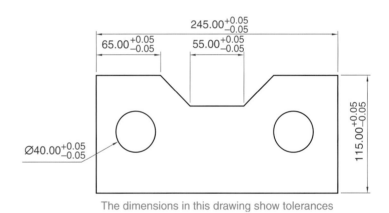

Fig. 6.24 Example – simple
tolerances

The dimensions in this drawing show tolerances

Example – Geometric tolerances (Fig. 6.30)

1. Construct the two rectangles with circles as in Fig. 6.25.

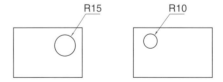

Fig. 6.25 Example – **Geometric
tolerances** – dimensions to be
toleranced

2. Add dimensions to the two circles.
3. *Click* the **Tolerance** tool icon (Fig. 6.26). The **Geometrical Tolerance** dialog (Fig. 6.27) appears.

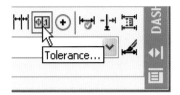

Fig. 6.26 The **Tolerance** tool icon in the **Dimensions** control panel

4. In the dialog *click* the black box under **Sym**. The **Symbol** sub-dialog appears (Fig. 6.27) with a *click* on the top left-hand square.

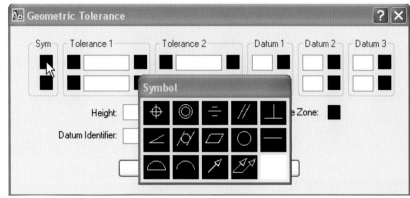

Fig. 6.27 The **Geometric Tolerance** dialog and the **Symbol** sub-dialog

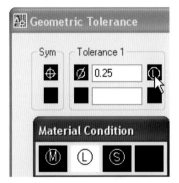

Fig. 6.28 The **Geometric Tolerance** dialog and the **Material Condition** sub-dialog

5. Still in the dialog *click* the left-hand black square under **Tolerance 1**. The **Material Condition** dialog appears (Fig. 6.28). *Click* **L**. The letter appears in the top right-hand square of the dialog.

6. *Enter* **0.05** in the **Tolerance 1** field (Fig. 6.29), followed by a *click* on the dialog's **OK** button. The geometrical tolerance appears. Move it to a position near the **R10** dimension in the drawing (Fig. 6.30).

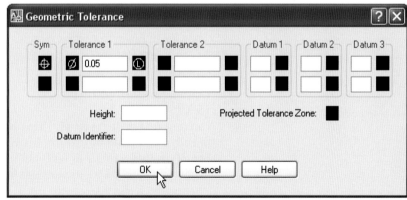

Fig. 6.29 The completed **Geometric Tolerance** dialog

7. Now add a geometrical tolerance to the **15** dimension as shown in Fig. 6.30.

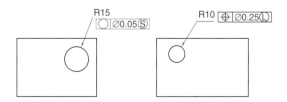

Fig. 6.30 Example – **Geometric tolerances**

The meanings of the symbols

The **Material Condition** letters have the following meanings:

M – maximum amount of material
L – least amount of material
S – size within the limits

Fig. 6.31 shows the meanings of the geometrical symbols.

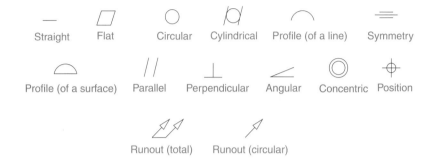

Fig. 6.31 The meanings of the symbols

Text

There are two main methods of adding text to drawings – **Multiline Text** and **Single Line Text**.

Example – Single Line Text (Fig. 6.24)

1. Open the drawing from the example on tolerances – Fig. 6.24.
2. At the command line *enter* **dt** (for Single Line Text) followed by a *right-click*:

> **Command:** *enter* **dt** *right-click*
> **TEXT**
> **Current text style "ARIAL" Text height: 8 Annotative No:**
> **Specify start point of text or [Justify/Style]:** *pick*
> **Specify rotation angle of text <0>:** *right-click*
> **Enter text:** *enter* **The dimensions in this drawing show tolerances**
>   *press* the **Return** key twice
> **Command:**

The result is given in Fig. 6.24 on page 116.

Notes

1. When using **Dynamic Text**, the **Return** key of the keyboard is pressed after the text has been *entered* and **NOT** a *right-click*.
2. At the prompt:

> **Specify start point of text or [Justify/Style]:** *enter* **s** (Style) *right-click*
> **Enter style name or [?] <ARIAL>:** *enter* **?** *right-click*
> **Enter text style(s) to list <*>:** *right-click*

And an **AutoCAD Text Window** (Fig. 6.32) appears listing all the styles which have been selected in the **Text Style** (see page 70).

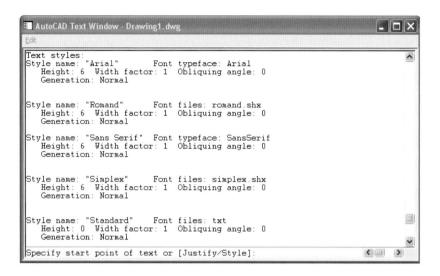

Fig. 6.32 The **AutoCAD Text Window**

3. In order to select the required text style its name must be *entered* at the prompt:

   Enter style name or [?] <ARIAL>: *enter* **Romand** *right-click*

   And the text *entered* will be in the **Romand** style of height **9**. But only if that style was previously selected in the **Text Style** dialog.

4. Fig. 6.33 shows some text styles from the **AutoCAD Text Window**.

This is the TIMES text

This is ROMANC text

This is ROMAND text

This is STANDARD text

This is ITALIC text

This is ARIAL text

Fig. 6.33 Some text styles

5. There are two types of text fonts available in AutoCAD 2008 – the **AutoCAD SHX** fonts and the **Windows True Type** fonts. The **ITALIC, ROMAND, ROMANS** and **STANDARD** styles shown in Fig. 6.33 are AutoCAD text fonts. The **TIMES** and **ARIAL** styles are **Windows True Type** styles. Most of the **True Type** fonts can be *entered* in **Bold, Bold Italic, Italic** or **Regular** styles, but these variations are not possible with the AutoCAD fonts.

6. The **Font name** popup list of the **Text Style** dialog shows that a large number of text styles are available to the AutoCAD 2008 operator. It is

Fig. 6.34 The **Multiline Text** tool icon from the **2D Draw** control panel

advisable to practise using a variety of these fonts to familiarise one-self with the text opportunities available with AutoCAD 2008.

Example – Multiline Text (Fig. 6.35)

1. Either *left-click* on the **Multiline Text** tool icon in the **2D Draw** control panel (Fig. 6.34), or *click* on **Multiline Text...** in the **Draw** toolbar, or *enter* **t** at the command line:

Command:_mtext
Current text style: "ARIAL" Text height: 8 Annotative No:
Specify first corner: *pick*
Specify opposite corner or [Height/Justify/Line spacing/Rotation/
    Style/Width/Columns]: *pick*

As soon as the **opposite corner** is *picked*, the **Text Formatting** dialog appears and the box changes as in Fig. 6.35. Text can now be *entered* as required within the box as indicated in this illustration.
When all the required text has been *entered, left-click* the **OK** button at the top right-hand corner of the **Text Formatting** dialog.

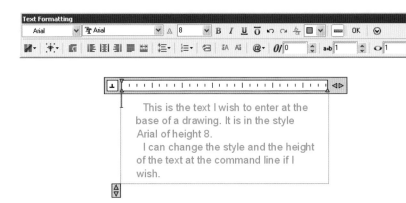

Fig. 6.35 Example – **Multiline Text** *entered* in the text box

2. Changes can be made to various aspects of the text being *entered* by making choices from the various popup lists in the **Text Formatting** dialog. These popups are shown in Fig. 6.36.

Symbols used in text

When text has to be added by *entering* symbols and figures as part of a dimension, the following keyboard entries must be used:

To obtain **Ø75** *enter* **%%c75**;
To obtain **55%** *enter* **55%%%**;
To obtain **±0.05** *enter* **%%p0.05**;
To obtain **90°** *enter* **90%%d**.

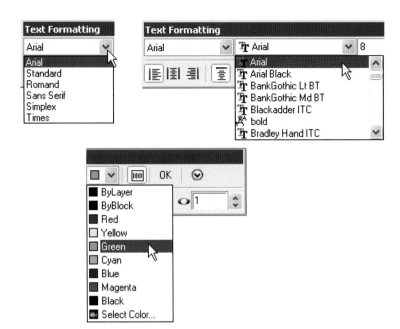

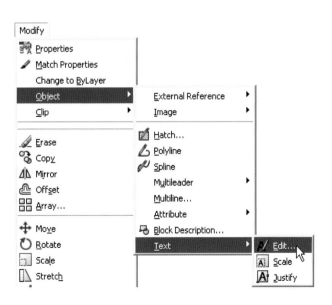

Fig. 6.36 The popups from the
Text Formatting dialog

Checking spelling

There are two methods for the checking of spelling in AutoCAD 2008.

First example – the Spelling tool (Fig. 6.38)

1. *Enter* some badly spelt text as indicated in Fig. 6.38.
2. *Left-click* on **Edit...** from the sub-menu of **Text** in the **Modify** drop-down menu (Fig. 6.37) or *enter* **ddedit** at the command line.

Fig. 6.37 Selecting **Edit...** from
the **Text** sub-menu of the **Modify**
drop-down menu

3. *Left-click* on the text. The text is highlighted. Edit the text as if working in a word-processing application and when satisfied *click* the **Return** key of the keyboard (Fig. 6.38).

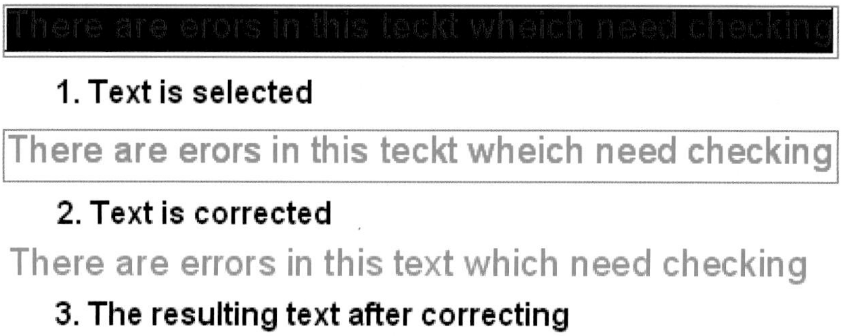

There are erors in this teckt wheich need checking

1. Text is selected

There are erors in this teckt wheich need checking

2. Text is corrected

There are errors in this text which need checking

3. The resulting text after correcting

Fig. 6.38 The three stages in checking spelling using **Text Edit**

Second example – the Spelling tool (Fig. 6.40)

1. *Enter* some badly spelt text as indicated in Fig. 6.40.
2. Either *click* the **Spell Check...** icon in the **Text** control panel (Fig. 6.39) or *enter* **spell** or **sp** at the command line.

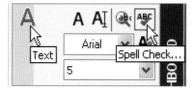

Fig. 6.39 The **Spell Check...** icon in the **Text** control panel

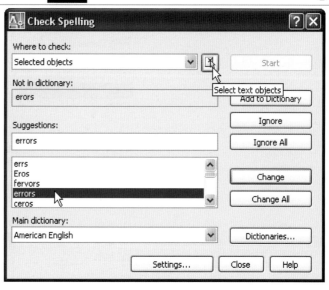

Fig. 6.40 Second example – the **Check Spelling** dialog

Fig. 6.41 The **AutoCAD Message** window showing that spelling check is complete

3. The **Check Spelling** dialog appears (Fig. 6.40). In the **Where to check** field select **Selected objects** from the field's popup list, followed by a *click* on the **Select text Objects** button. *Click* the badly spelt text and *left-click* followed by a *right-click*. The **Check Spelling** dialog appears (Fig. 6.40). Wrongly spelt words appear in the **Not in dictionary** field with words to replace them listed in the **Suggestions** field. Select the appropriate correct spelling as shown. Continue until all text is checked. When completely checked an **AutoCAD Message** window appears (Fig. 6.41).

Revision notes

1. In the **Line and Arrows** sub-dialog of the **Dimension Style Manager** dialog, **Lineweights** were set to **0.3** (page 75). If these lineweights are to show in the drawing area of AutoCAD 2008, the **LWT** button in the status bar must be set **ON**.
2. Dimensions can be added to drawings using the tools from the **Dimensions** control panel, or from the **Dimension** toolbar, or by *entering* **dim**, followed by abbreviations for the tools at the command line.
3. It is usually advisable to use osnaps when locating points on a drawing for dimensioning.
4. The **Style** and **Angle** of the text associated with dimensions can be changed during the dimensioning process.
5. When wishing to add tolerances to dimensions it will probably be necessary to make new settings in the **Dimension Style Manager** dialog.
6. There are two methods for adding text to a drawing – **Single Line Text** and **Multiline Text**.
7. When adding text to a drawing, the **Return** key must be used and not the right-hand mouse button.
8. Text styles can be changed during the process of adding text to drawings.
9. AutoCAD 2008 uses two types of text style – **AutoCAD SHX** fonts and **Windows True Type** fonts.
10. Most **True Type** fonts can be in **bold**, ***bold italic***, *italic* or regular format. **AutoCAD** fonts can only be added in a single format.
11. When using **Multiline Text**, changes can be made by selection from the popup lists in the **Text Formatting** dialog.
12. To obtain the symbols **Ø; ±; °; %** use **%%c; %%p; %%d; %%%** respectively before the figures of the dimension. These symbols can also be selected from the **Symbol** drop-down menu in the **Text Formatting** dialog (Fig. 6.42).
13. Text spelling can be checked with by selecting **Text/Edit...** from the **Modify** drop-down menu, or by selecting **Spell Check...** from the **Text** control panel, or by *entering* **spell** or **sp** at the command line.

Fig. 6.42 The **Symbol** icon in the
Text Formatting dialog

Exercises

1. Open any of the drawings previously saved from working through examples or as answers to exercises and add appropriate dimensions.
2. Construct the drawing in Fig. 6.43 but in place of the given dimensions add dimensions showing tolerances of 0.25 above and below.

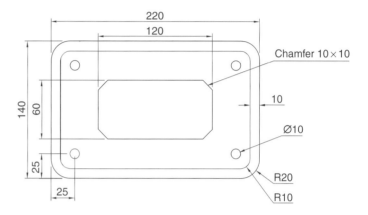

Fig. 6.43 Exercise 2

3. Construct two polygons as in Fig. 6.44 and add all diagonals. Set osnaps **endpoint** and **intersection** and using the lines as in Fig. 6.44

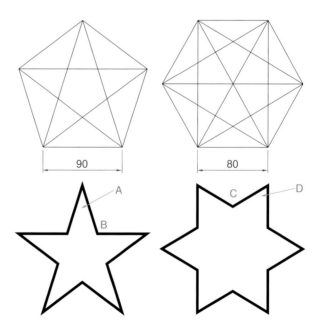

Fig. 6.44 Exercise 3

construct the stars as shown using a polyline of width = **3**. Next erase
all unwanted lines. Dimension the angles labelled **A, B, C** and **D**.

4. Construct and dimension the drawing in Fig. 6.45.

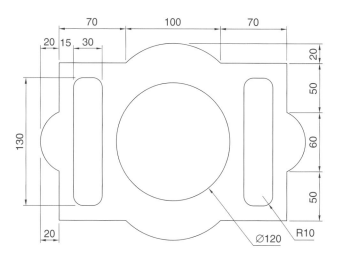

Fig. 6.45 Exercise 4

5. Using the text style **Arial** of height **20** and enclosing the wording within
a pline rectangle of Width = **5** and Fillet = **10**, construct Fig. 6.46.

Fig. 6.46 Exercise 5

CHAPTER 7

Orthographic and isometric

Fig. 7.1 Example – orthographic projection – the solid being drawn

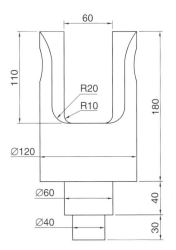

Fig. 7.2 The **front view** of the solid

Aim of this chapter

To introduce methods of constructing drawings of the two types – orthographic projection and isometric drawings.

Orthographic projection

Orthographic projection involves viewing an article being described in a technical drawing from different directions – from the front, from a side, from above, from below or from any other viewing position. Orthographic projection often involves:

1. The drawing of details which are hidden, using hidden detail lines,
2. Sectional views in which the article being drawn is imagined as being cut through and the cut surface drawn,
3. Centre lines through arcs, circles spheres and cylindrical shapes.

An example of an orthographic projection

Taking the solid shown in Fig. 7.1, construct a three-view orthographic projection of the solid:

1. Draw what is seen when the solid is viewed from its left-hand side and regard this as the **front** of the solid. What is drawn will be a **front view** (Fig. 7.2).
2. Draw what is seen when the solid is viewed from the left-hand end of the front view. This produces an **end view**. Fig. 7.3 shows the end view alongside the front view.
3. Draw what is seen when the solid is viewed from above the front view. This produces a **plan**. Fig. 7.4 shows the plan below the front view.
4. Draw centre and hidden detail lines:
    (a) In the **Layers** control panel, *click* the arrow to the right of the **Layers** field to show all layers set in the **acadiso.dwt** template on which the drawing has been constructed (Fig. 7.5).
    (b) *Left-click* the **Centre** layer name in the layers list, making it the current layer. All lines will now be drawn as centre lines.
5. In the three-view drawing add centre lines.
6. Make the **Hidden** layer the current layer and add hidden detail lines.

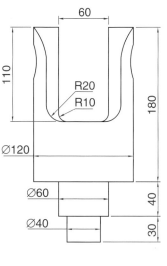

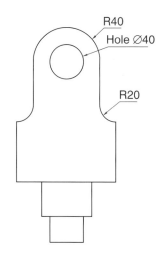

Fig. 7.3 **Front** and **end** views of the solid

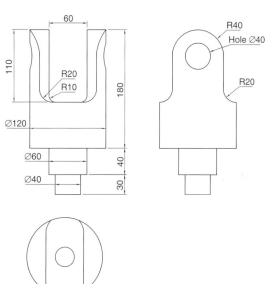

Fig. 7.4 **Front** and **end** views and **plan** of the solid

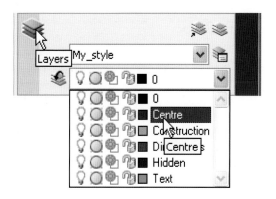

Fig. 7.5 Making the layer **Centre** current

7. Make the **Text** layer current and add border lines and a title block.
8. Make the **Dimensions** layer current and add all dimensions.

The completed drawing is shown in Fig. 7.6.

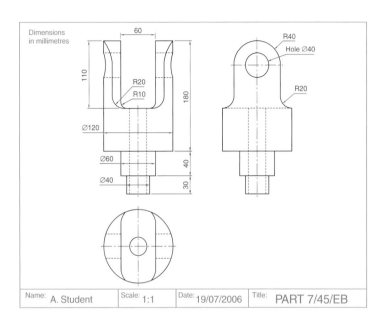

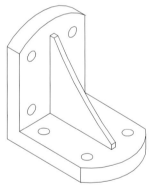

Fig. 7.6 The completed working
drawing of the solid

First angle and third angle

There are two types of orthographic projection – **first angle** and **third angle**. Fig. 7.7 is a pictorial drawing of the solid used to demonstrate the two angles. Fig. 7.8 shows a three-view **first angle projection** and Fig. 7.9 the same views in **third angle**.

Fig. 7.7 The solid used to
demonstrate first and third angles
of projection

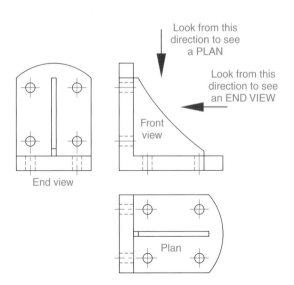

Fig. 7.8 A **first angle** projection

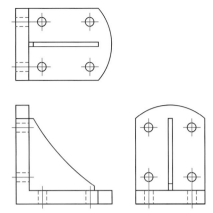

Fig. 7.9 A **third angle** projection

In both angles the viewing is from the same direction. The difference is that the view as seen is placed on the viewing side of the front view in **third angle** and on the opposite side to the viewing in **first angle**.

Sectional views

In order to show internal shapes of a solid being drawn in orthographic projection, the solid is imagined as being cut along a plane and the cut surface then drawn as seen. Common practice is to **hatch** the areas which then show in the cut surface. Note the section plane line, the section label and the hatching in the sectional view in Fig. 7.10.

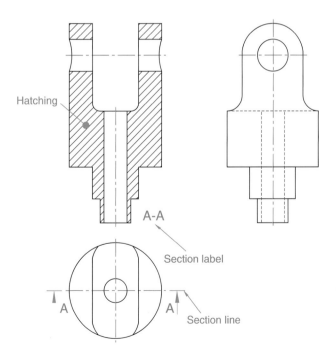

Fig. 7.10 A sectional view

Fig. 7.11 The **Hatch** tool icon
from the **2D Draw** control panel

Adding hatching

To add the hatching as shown in Fig. 7.10:

1. Call the **Hatch** tool – either *left-click* on its tool icon in the **2D Draw control panel** (Fig. 7.11), or *click* the tool in the **Draw** toolbar, or *enter* **h** at the command line. *Note* – do not *enter* **hatch** as this gives a different result. The **Hatch and Gradient** dialog (Fig. 7.12) appears.

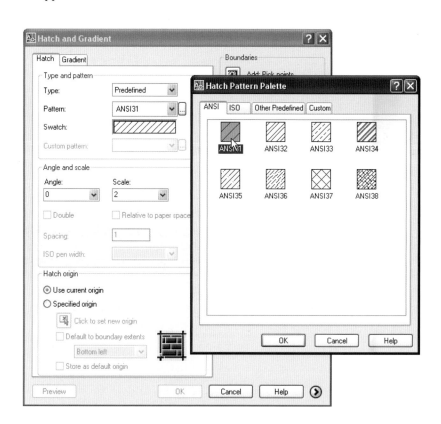

Fig. 7.12 The **Hatch and Gradient** dialog and the **ANSI Hatch Pattern Palette**

2. *Click* in the **Swatch** field. The **Hatch Pattern Palette** appears. *Left-click* the **ANSI** tab and from the resulting pattern icons *double-click* the **ANSI31** icon. The palette disappears and the **ANSI31** pattern appears in the **Swatch** field.
3. In the dialog *left-click* the **Pick an internal point** button (Fig. 7.13). The dialog disappears.
4. In the front view *pick* points as shown in the left-hand drawing of Fig. 7.14. The dialog reappears. *Click* the **Preview** button of the dialog and in the sectional view which reappears, check whether the hatching is satisfactory. In this example it may well be that the **Scale** figure in the dialog needs to be *entered* as **2** in place of the default **1**. Change the figure and **Preview** again. If satisfied *click* the **OK** button of the dialog.

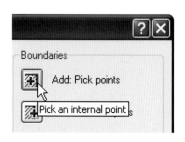

Fig. 7.13 The **Pick an internal point** button of the **Boundary Hatch and Fill** dialog

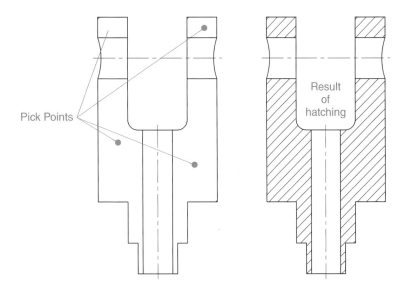

Fig. 7.14 The result of hatching

Isometric drawing

Isometric drawing must not be confused with solid model drawing, examples of which are given in Chapters 13 to 17. Isometric drawing is a 2D method of describing objects in a pictorial form.

Setting the AutoCAD window for isometric drawing

To set the AutoCAD 2008 window for the construction of isometric drawings:

1. At the command line:

   Command: *enter* snap
   Specify snap spacing or [On/Off/Aspect/Rotate/Style/Type] <5>:
      s (Style)
   Enter snap grid style [Standard/Isometric] <S>: i (Isometric)
   Specify vertical spacing <5>: *right-click*
   Command:

   And the grid dots in the window assume an isometric pattern as shown in Fig. 7.15. Note also the cursor hair lines which are set in an **Isometric Left** angle.

2. There are three isometric angles – **Isoplane Top, Isoplane Left** and **Isoplane Right**. These can be set either by pressing the **F5** function key or by pressing the **Ctrl** and **E** keys. Repeated pressing of either of these 'toggles' between the three settings. Fig. 7.16 is an isometric view showing the three isometric planes.

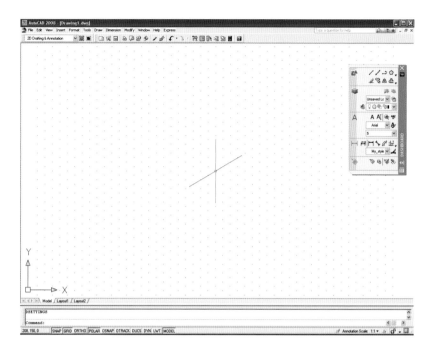

Fig. 7.15 The AutoCAD grid points set for isometric drawing

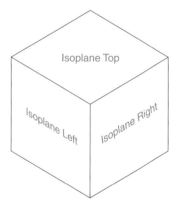

Fig. 7.16 The three isoplanes

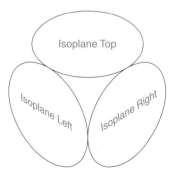

Fig. 7.17 The three isocircles

The isometric circle

Circles in an isometric drawing show as ellipses. To add an isometric circle to an isometric drawing, call the **Ellipse** tool. The command line shows:

> **Command: _ellipse**
> **Specify axis endpoint of ellipse or [Arc/Center/Isocircle]:** *enter* **i** (Isocircle) *right-click*
> **Specify center of isocircle:** *pick* or *enter* coordinates
> **Specify radius of isocircle or [Diameter]:** *enter* a number
> **Command:**

And the isocircle appears. Its isoplane position is determined by which of the isoplanes is in operation at the time the isocircle was formed. Fig 7.17 shows these three isoplanes containing isocircles.

Examples of isometric drawings

First example – isometric drawing (Fig. 7.20)

1. Work to the shapes and sizes given in the orthographic projection in Fig. 7.18. Set Snap on (press the **F9** function key) and Grid on (**F7**).
2. Set Snap to Isometric and set the isoplane to Isoplane Top using **F5**.
3. With **Line**, construct the outline of the top of the model (Fig. 7.19), working to the dimensions given in Fig. 7.18.
4. Call **Ellipse** tool and set to isocircle, and add the isocircle of radius 20 centred in its correct position in the outline of the top (Fig. 7.19).

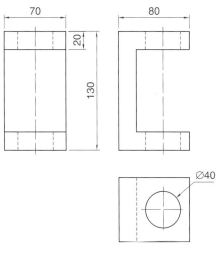

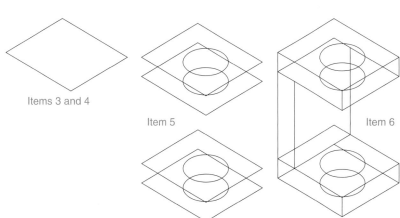

Fig. 7.18 First example –
isometric drawing – the model

Fig. 7.19 First example – isometric
drawing – items **3, 4, 5** and **6**

Items 3 and 4

Item 5

Item 6

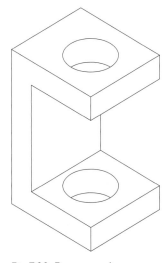

Fig. 7.20 First example –
isometric drawing

5. Set the isoplane to Isoplane Right and, with the **Copy** tool, copy the top with its ellipse vertically downwards three times as shown in Fig. 7.19.
6. Add lines as shown in Fig. 7.19.
7. Finally using **Trim** remove unwanted parts of lines and ellipses to produce Fig. 7.20.

Second example – isometric drawing (Fig. 7.22)

Fig. 7.21 is an orthographic projection of the model from which the isometric drawing is to be constructed. Fig. 7.22 shows the stages in its construction. The numbers refer to the items in the list below.

1. In **Isoplane Right** construct two isocircles of radii 10 and 20.
2. Add lines as in drawing **2** and trim unwanted parts of isocircle.
3. With **Copy**, copy three times as in drawing **3**.
4. With **Trim**, trim unwanted lines and parts of isocircle as in drawing **4**.

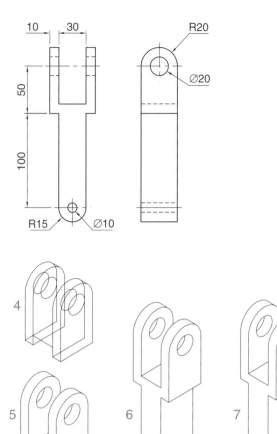

Fig. 7.21 Second example –
isometric drawing – orthographic
projection of model

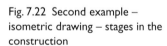

Fig. 7.22 Second example –
isometric drawing – stages in the
construction

5. In **Isoplane Left** add lines as in drawing **5**.
6. In **Isoplane Right** add lines and isocircles as in drawing **6**.
7. With **Trim**, trim unwanted lines and parts of isocircles to complete the
   isometric drawing – drawing **7**.

Revision notes

1. There are, in the main, two types of orthographic projection – first
   angle and third angle.
2. The number of views included in an orthographic projection depend
   upon the complexity of what is being drawn – a good rule to follow is
   to attempt fully describing the object being drawn in as few views as
   possible.

3. Sectional views allow parts of an object which are normally hidden from view to be more fully described in a projection.
4. When a layer is turned **OFF** all constructions on that layer disappear from the screen.
5. If a layer is locked, objects can be added to the layer but no further additions or modifications can be added to the layer. If an attempt is made to modify an object on a locked layer the command line shows:

Command:_erase
Select objects: *pick* **1 found**
1 was on a locked layer

And the object will not be modified.

6. Frozen layers cannot be selected, but note that layer **0** cannot be frozen.
7. Isometric drawing is a 2D pictorial method of producing illustrations showing objects. It is not a 3D method of showing a pictorial view.
8. When drawing ellipses in an isometric drawing, the **Isocircle** prompt of the **Ellipse** tool command line sequence must be used.
9. When constructing an isometric drawing **Snap** must be set to isometric mode before construction can commence.

Exercises

Fig. 7.23 is an isometric drawing of a slider fitment on which exercises **1, 2** and **3** are based.

1. Fig. 7.24 is a first angle orthographic projection of part of the fitment shown in the isometric drawing in Fig. 7.23. Construct a three-view third angle orthographic projection of the part.

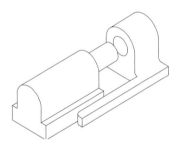

Fig. 7.23 Exercises 1, 2 and 3 – an isometric drawing of the three parts of the slider on which these exercises are based

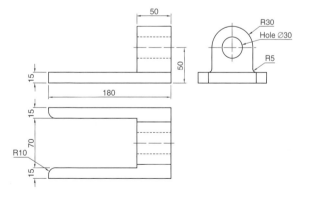

Fig. 7.24 Exercise 1

2. Fig. 7.25 is a first angle orthographic projection of the other part of the fitment. Construct a three-view third angle orthographic projection of the part.

3. Construct an isometric drawing of the part shown in Fig. 7.25.

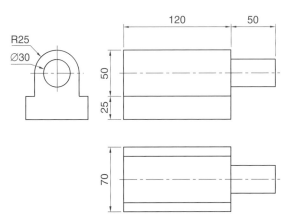

Fig. 7.25 Exercises 2 and 3

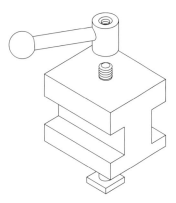

Fig. 7.26 Exercises 4 and 5 – an isometric drawing of the tool holder on which the two exercises are based

Fig. 7.27 Exercises 4 and 5 – orthographic projections of the three parts of the tool holder

4. Construct a three-view orthographic projection in an angle of your own choice of the tool holder assembled as shown in the isometric drawing in Fig. 7.26. Details are given in Fig. 7.27.

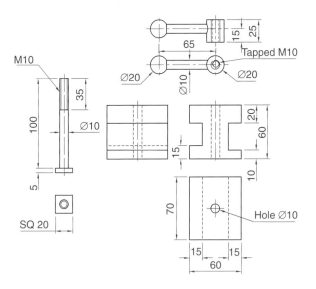

5. Construct an isometric drawing of the body of the tool holder shown in Figs 7.26 and 7.27.
6. Construct the orthographic projection given in Fig. 7.29.
7. Construct an isometric drawing of the angle plate shown in Figs 7.28 and 7.29.

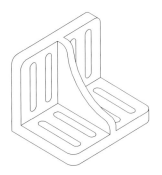

Fig. 7.28 An isometric drawing of the angle plate on which exercises 6 and 7 are based

Fig. 7.29 Exercises 6 and 7 – an orthographic projection of the angle plate

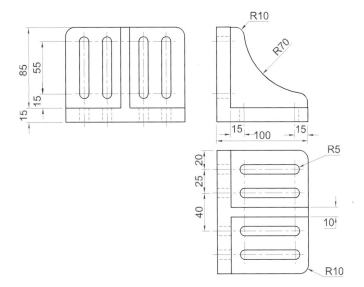

8. Construct a third angle projection of the component shown in the isometric drawing in Fig. 7.30 and the three-view first angle projection in Fig. 7.31.

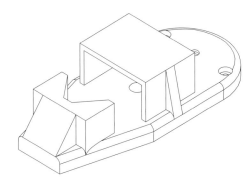

Fig. 7.30 Exercises 8 and 9 – an isometric drawing of the component for the two exercises

9. Construct the isometric drawing shown in Fig. 7.30, working to the dimensions given in Fig. 7.31.

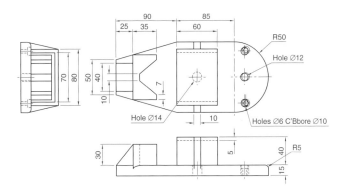

Fig. 7.31 Exercises 8 and 9

CHAPTER 8

Hatching

Aim of this chapter

To describe further examples of the use of hatching in its various forms.

Introduction

In Chapter 7 an example of hatching a sectional view in an orthographic projection was given. Further examples of the use of hatching will be described in this chapter.

There are a large number of hatch patterns available when hatching drawings in AutoCAD 2008. Some examples from the **Other Predefined** set of hatch patterns (Fig. 8.2) in the **Hatch Pattern Palette** sub-dialog are shown in Fig. 8.1.

Other hatch patterns can be selected from the **ISO** or **ANSI** hatch pattern palettes, or the operator can design their own hatch patterns and save them to the **Custom** hatch palette.

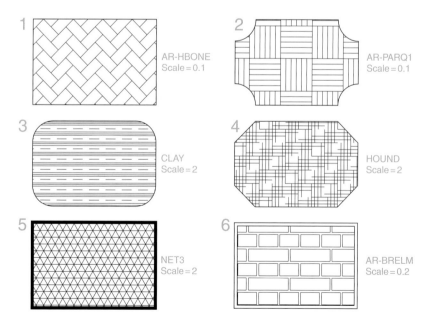

Fig. 8.1 Some hatch patterns from **Predefined** hatch patterns

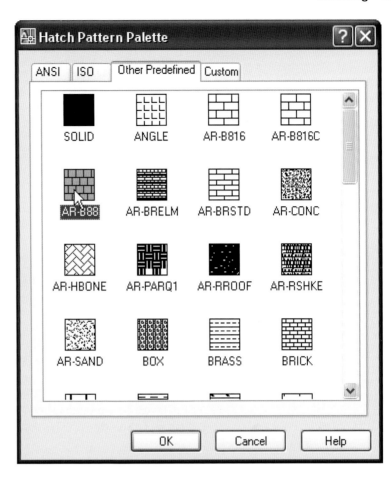

Fig. 8.2 The **Other Predefined** Hatch Pattern Palette

First example – hatching a sectional view (Fig. 8.3)

Fig. 8.3 shows a two-view orthographic projection which includes a sectional end view. Note the following in the drawing:

1. The section plane line, consisting of a centre line with its ends marked **A** and an arrow showing the direction of viewing to obtain the sectional view.
2. The sectional view labelled with the letters of the section plane line.
3. The cut surfaces of the sectional view hatched with the **ANSI31** hatch pattern, which is in general use for the hatching of engineering drawing sections.

Second example – hatching rules (Fig. 8.4)

Fig. 8.4 describes the stages in hatching a sectional end view of a lathe tool holder. Note the following in the section:

1. There are two angles of hatching to differentiate in separate parts of the section.

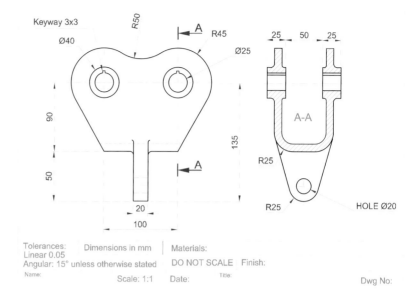

Fig. 8.3 First example – **Hatching**

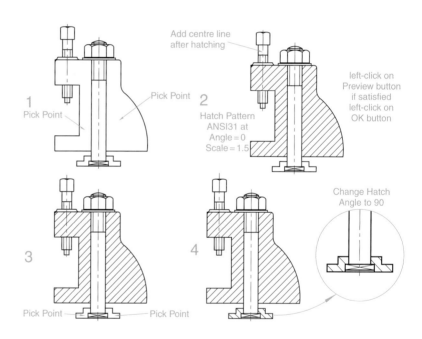

Fig. 8.4 Second example –
hatching rules for sections

2. The section follows the general rule that parts such as screws, bolts, nuts, rivets, other cylindrical objects, webs and ribs and other such features are shown within sections as outside views.

Third example – Associative hatching (Fig. 8.5)

Fig. 8.5 shows two end view of a house. After constructing the left-hand view, it was found that the upper window had been placed in the wrong

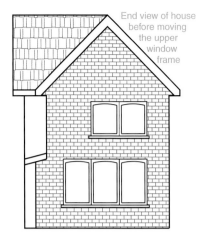 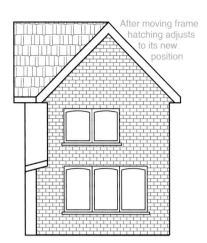

End view of house before moving the upper window frame

After moving frame hatching adjusts to its new position

Fig. 8.5 Third example –
Associative hatching

Fig. 8.6 **Associative** hatching set
On in the **Hatch and Gradient**
dialog

position. Using the **Move** tool, the window was moved to a new position. The brick hatching automatically adjusted to the new position. Such **Associative hatching** is possible only if the check box against **Associative** in the **Options** area of the **Hatch and Gradient** dialog is **ON** – a tick in the check box (Fig. 8.6).

Fourth example – Colour gradient hatching (Fig. 8.9)

Fig. 8.8 shows two examples of hatching from the **Gradient** sub-dialog of the **Hatch and Gradient** dialog.

1. Construct two outlines each consisting of six rectangles (Fig. 8.9).
2. *Click* the **Gradient...** tool icon in the **2D Draw** control panel (Fig. 8.7) or in the **Draw** toolbar. In the **Hatch and Gradient** dialog which appears (Fig. 8.8) *pick* one of the gradient choices, followed with a *click* on the **Pick an internal point** button. *Click* one of the color panels in the dialog and when the dialog disappears, pick a single area of one of the rectangles in the left-hand drawing, followed by a *click* on the dialog's **OK** button when the dialog reappears.
3. Repeat in each of the other rectangles of the left-hand drawing, changing the pattern in each of the rectangles.
4. *Click* the button (**...**) to the right of the **Color** field, select a new colour from the **Select Color** dialog which appears and repeat steps **3** and **4** in the six rectangles.

The result is shown in Fig. 8.9.

Note

If the **Two color** radio button is set on (dot in circle) the colours involved in the gradient hatch can be changed by *clicking* the button marked with three dots (**...**) on the right of the colour field. This brings a **Select Color** dialog on screen, which offers three choices of sub-dialogs from which to select colours.

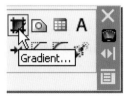

Fig. 8.7 The **Gradient Hatch**
tool icon from the **2D Draw**
control panel

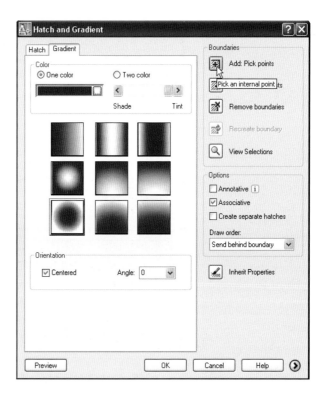

Fig. 8.8 The **Hatch and Gradient** dialog

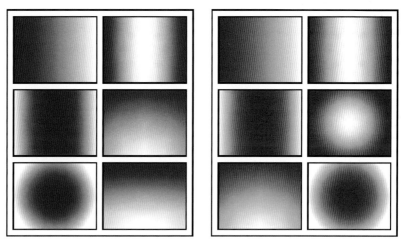

Fig. 8.9 Fourth example – **Colour Gradient** hatching

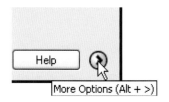

Fig. 8.10 The **More Options** arrow of the **Hatch and Gradient** dialog

Fifth example – Advanced hatching (Fig. 8.12)

If the arrow at the bottom right-hand corner of the **Hatch and Gradient** dialog is *clicked* (Fig. 8.10) the dialog expands to show the **Island Display** selections (Fig. 8.11).

1. Construct a drawing which includes three outlines as shown in the left-hand drawing of Fig. 8.12 and copy it twice to produce three identical drawings.

Fig. 8.11 The **Island display style** selections in the expanded **Hatch and Gradient** dialog

Fig. 8.12 Fifth example – **Advanced** hatching

Fig. 8.13 Sixth example – Text in hatching

2. Select the hatch pattern **HONEY** at an angle of **0** and scale **1**.
3. *Click* in the **Normal** radio button of the **Island display style** area.
4. *Pick* a point in the left-hand drawing. The drawing hatches as shown.
5. Repeat in the centre drawing with the radio button of the **Outer** style set on (dot in button).
6. Repeat in the right-hand drawing with **Ignore** set on.

Sixth example – Text in hatching (Fig. 8.13)

1. Construct a pline rectangle using the sizes given in Fig. 8.13.
2. In the **Text Style Manager** dialog, set the text font to **Arial** and its **Height = 25**.
3. Using the **Dtext** tool *enter* the text as shown central to the rectangle.
4. Hatch the area using the **HONEY** hatch pattern set to an angle of **0** and scale of **1**.

The result is shown in Fig. 8.13.

Note

Text will be entered with a surrounding boundary area free from hatching, providing the **Advanced Normal** radio button is set on.

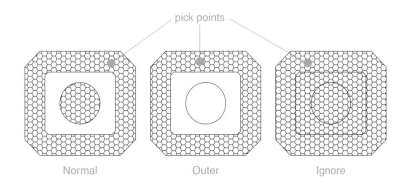

Seventh example – Advanced hatching (Fig. 8.20)

1. From the **Layers** control panel open the **Layer** list with a *click* on the arrow to the right of the layers field.
2. Note the extra added layer (**HATCH**) in Fig. 8.14.
3. With the layer **0** current, construct the outline as given in Fig. 8.15.
4. Make layer **Text** current and construct the lines as shown in Fig. 8.16.

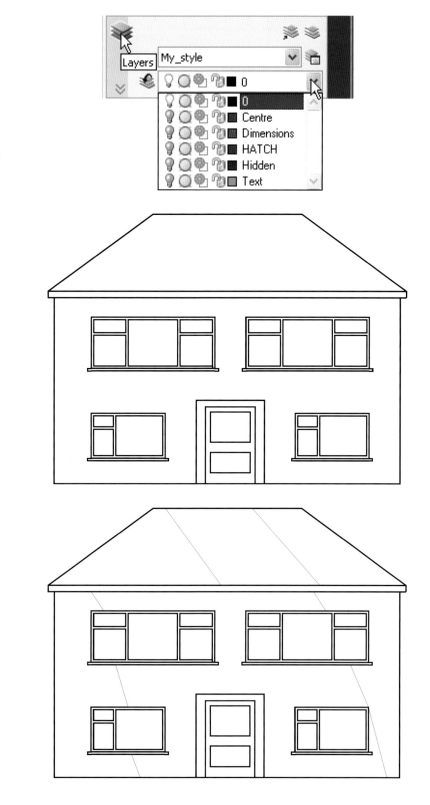

Fig. 8.14 Seventh example – the layers setup for the advanced hatch example

Fig. 8.15 Seventh example – construction on layer **0**

Fig. 8.16 Seventh example – construction on layer **Text**

5. Make the layer **HATCH** current and add hatching to the areas shown in Fig. 8.17 using the hatch patterns **ANGLE** at scale **2** for the roof and **BRICK** at a scale of **0.75** for the wall.
6. Finally turn the layer **Text** off. The result is given in Fig. 8.18.

Fig. 8.17 Seventh example – construction on layer **HATCH**

Fig. 8.18 Seventh example – the finished drawing

Revision notes

1. A large variety of hatch patterns are available when working with AutoCAD 2008.
2. In sectional views in engineering drawings it is usual to show items such as bolts, screws, other cylindrical objects, webs and ribs as outside views.

3. When Associative hatching is set on and an object is moved within a hatched area, the hatching accommodates to fit around the moved object.
4. Colour gradient hatching is available in AutoCAD 2008.
5. When hatching takes place around text, a space around the text will be free from hatching.

Exercises

1. Fig. 8.19 shows a pictorial drawing of the component shown in the three-view orthographic projection in Fig. 8.20. Construct the three views, with the front view as a sectional view based on the section plane **A-A**.
2. Construct the three-view orthographic projection in Fig. 8.21 to the given dimensions with the front view as the sectional view **A-A**.

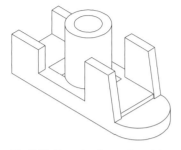

Fig. 8.19 Exercise 1 – a pictorial view

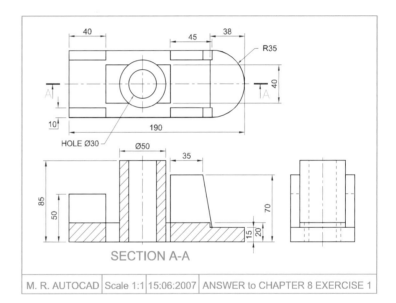

SECTION A-A

| M. R. AUTOCAD | Scale 1:1 | 15:06:2007 | ANSWER to CHAPTER 8 EXERCISE 1 |

Fig. 8.20 Exercise 1

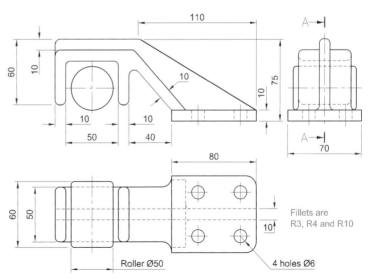

Fillets are R3, R4 and R10

Roller Ø50

4 holes Ø6

Fig. 8.21 Exercise 2

3. Construct the drawing in **Stage 5** following the descriptions of stages given in Fig. 8. 22.

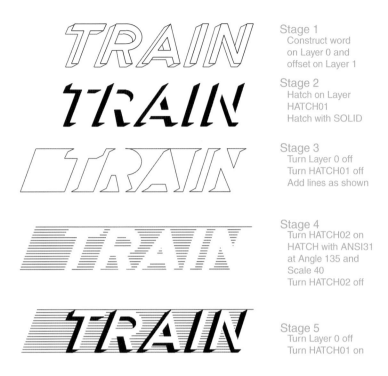

Stage 1
Construct word
on Layer 0 and
offset on Layer 1

Stage 2
Hatch on Layer
HATCH01
Hatch with SOLID

Stage 3
Turn Layer 0 off
Turn HATCH01 off
Add lines as shown

Stage 4
Turn HATCH02 on
HATCH with ANSI31
at Angle 135 and
Scale 40
Turn HATCH02 off

Stage 5
Turn Layer 0 off
Turn HATCH01 on

Fig. 8.22 Exercise 3

4. Fig. 8.23 is a front view of a car with parts hatched. Construct a similar drawing of any make of car, using hatching to emphasise the shape.

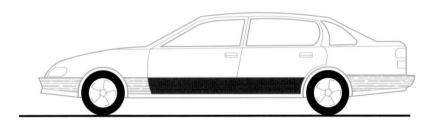

Fig. 8.23 Exercise 4

5. Working to the notes given with the drawing in Fig. 8.24, construct the end view of a house as shown. Use your own discretion about sizes for the parts of the drawing.
6. Working to dimensions of your own choice, construct the three-view projection of a two-storey house as shown in Fig. 8.25.
7. Construct Fig. 8.26 as follows:
   (a) On layer **Text**, construct a circle of radius **90**.
   (b) Make layer **0** current.

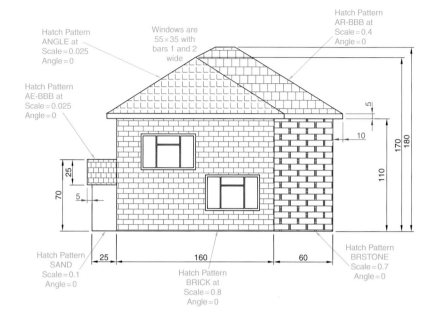

Hatch Pattern
ANGLE at
Scale = 0.025
Angle = 0

Windows are
55×35 with
bars 1 and 2
wide

Hatch Pattern
AR-BBB at
Scale = 0.4
Angle = 0

Hatch Pattern
AE-BBB at
Scale = 0.025
Angle = 0

5

10

170

180

110

25

70

5

Hatch Pattern
SAND
Scale = 0.1
Angle = 0

25

160

60

Hatch Pattern
BRICK at
Scale = 0.8
Angle = 0

Hatch Pattern
BRSTONE
Scale = 0.7
Angle = 0

Fig. 8.24 Exercise 5

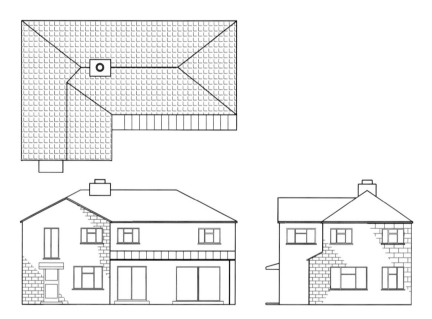

Fig. 8.25 Exercise 6

(c) Construct the small drawing to the details as shown and save as a block with a block name **shape** (see Chapter 9).

(d) Call the **Divide** tool by *entering* **div** at the command line:

Command: *enter* **div** *right-click*
Select object to divide: *pick* the circle
Enter number of segments or [Block]: *enter* **b** *right-click*

Enter name of block to insert: *enter* **shape** *right-click*
Align block with object? [Yes/No] <Y>: *right-click*
Enter the number of segments: *enter* **20** *right-click*
Command:

(e) Turn the layer **Text** off.

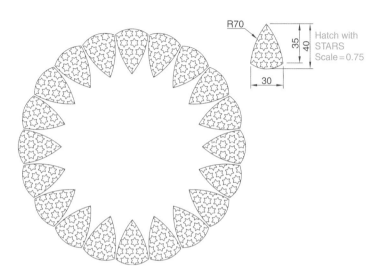

R70

35

40

Hatch with
STARS
Scale=0.75

30

Fig. 8.26 Exercise 7

CHAPTER 9

Blocks and Inserts

Aims of this chapter

1. To describe the construction of **blocks** and **wblocks** (written blocks).
2. To introduce the insertion of blocks and wblocks into other drawings.
3. To introduce the use of the **DesignCenter** palette.
4. To explain the use of the **Explode** and **Purge** tools.

Introduction

Blocks are drawings which can be inserted into other drawings. Blocks are contained in the data of the drawing in which they have been constructed. Wblocks (written blocks) are saved as drawings in their own right, but can be inserted into other drawings if required.

Blocks

First example – Blocks (Fig. 9.3)

1. Construct the building symbols as shown in Fig. 9.1 to a scale of 1:50.

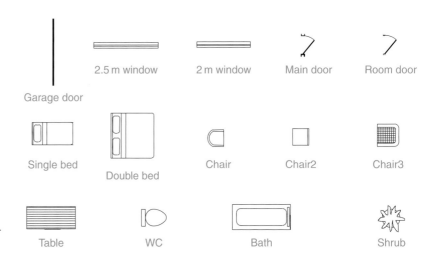

Fig. 9.1 First example – **Blocks** – symbols to be saved as blocks

2. *Left-click* the **Make...** tool in the **Block Attributes** control panel (Fig. 9.2). The **Block Definition** dialog (Fig. 9.3) appears. To make a block of the **Double bed** symbol drawing:

   (a) *Enter* **double bed** in the **Name** field.

   (b) *Click* the **Select objects** button. The dialog disappears. *Window* the drawing of the double bed. The dialog reappears. Note the icon of the double bed in the top right-hand corner of the dialog.

   (c) *Click* the **Pick Point** button. The dialog disappears. *Click* a point on the double bed drawing to determine its **insertion point**. The dialog reappears.

   (d) If thought necessary *enter* a description in the **Description** field of the dialog.

   (e) *Click* the **OK** button. The drawing is now saved as a **block** in the drawing.

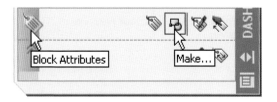

Fig. 9.2 *Click* **Make...** tool icon in the **Block Attributes** control panel

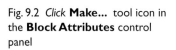
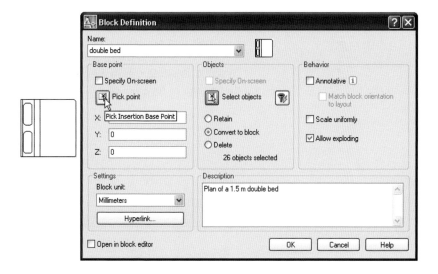

Fig. 9.3 The **Block Definiton** dialog with entries for the **double bed**

3. Repeat steps **1** and **2** to make blocks of all the other symbols in the drawing.

4. Open the **Block Definition** dialog again and *click* the arrow on the right of the **Name** field. Blocks saved in the drawing are listed (Fig. 9.4).

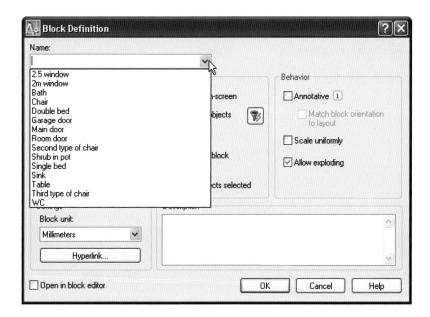

Fig. 9.4 The popup list in the **Name** field of the **Block Definition** dialog showing all blocks saved in the drawing

Inserting blocks into a drawing

There are two methods by which symbols saved as blocks can be inserted into another drawing.

Example – first method of inserting blocks

Ensuring that all the symbols saved as blocks using the **Make Block** tool are saved in the data of the drawing in which the symbols were constructed, erase the drawings of the symbols and in their place construct the outline of the plan of a bungalow to a scale of 1:50 (Fig. 9.5). Then:

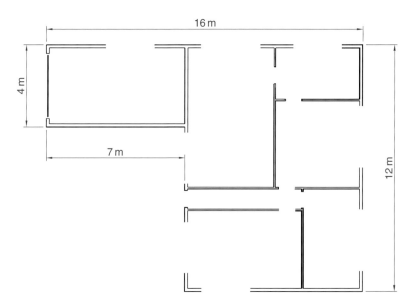

Fig. 9.5 First example – inserting blocks. Outline plan

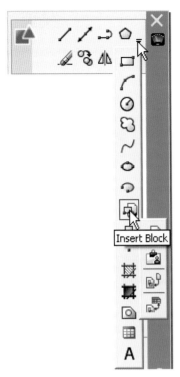

Fig. 9.6 The **Insert Block** tool icon in the **2D Draw** control panel

1. *Left-click* the **Insert Block** tool icon in the **2D Draw** control panel (Fig. 9.6) or the **Insert Block** tool in the **Draw** toolbar. The **Insert** dialog appears on screen (Fig. 9.7). From the **Name** popup list select the name of the block which is to be inserted, in this example the **2.5 window**.
2. *Make sure the checkbox against **Explode** is off (no tick in box). Click* the dialog's **OK** button, the dialog disappears. The symbol drawing appears with its insertion point at the intersection of the cursor hairs ready to be *dragged* into its position in the plan drawing.
3. Once all the block drawings are placed, their positions can be adjusted. Blocks are single objects and can thus be dragged into new positions as required under mouse control. Their angle of position can be amended at the command line, which shows:

Command:
INSERT
Specify insertion point or [Basepoint/Scale/X/Y/Z/Rotate/PScale/ PX/PY/PZ/PRotate]: *enter* **r** (Rotate) *right-click*
Specify insertion angle: *enter* **180** *right-click*
Specify insertion point: *pick*
Command:

Selection from these prompts allows scaling, stretching along any axis, previewing, etc. as the block is inserted.

4. Insert all necessary blocks and add other details as required to the plan outline drawing. The result is given in Fig. 9.8.

Example – second method of inserting blocks

1. Save the drawing which includes all the blocks to a suitable file name (e.g. building_symbols.dwg). Remember this drawing includes data of the blocks in its file.

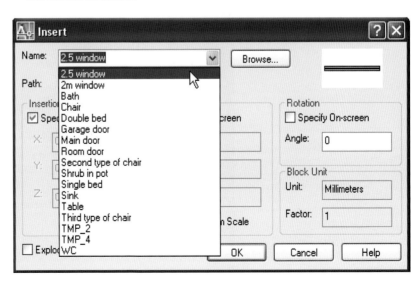

Fig. 9.7 The **Insert** dialog with its **Name** popup list displaying the names of all blocks in the drawing

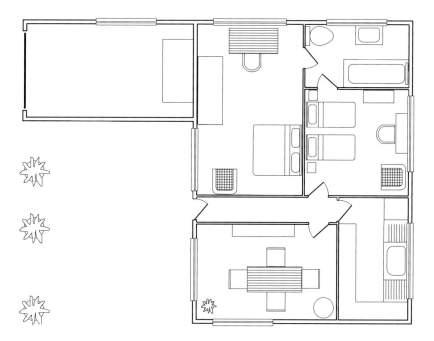

Fig. 9.8 Example – first method of inserting blocks

Fig. 9.9 Selecting **DesignCenter** from the **Standard Annotation** toolbar

2. *Left-click* **DesignCenter** in the **Standard Annotation** toolbar (Fig. 9.9) or press the **Ctrl+2** keys. The **DesignCenter** palette appears on screen (Fig. 9.10).
3. With the outline plan (Fig. 9.5) on screen the symbols can all be *dragged* into position from the **DesignCenter**.

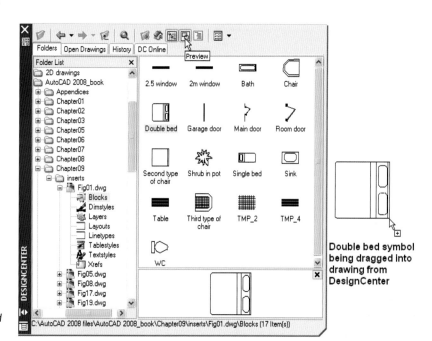

Fig. 9.10 The **DesignCenter** with the double bed block *dragged* on screen

Notes about DesignCenter palette

1. As with other palettes, the **DesignCenter** palette can be re-sized by *dragging* the palette to a new size from its edges or corners.
2. *Clicks* on one of the three icons at the top-right corner of the palette (Fig. 9.11) have the following results:
   (a) **Tree View Toggle** – changes from showing two areas – a **Folder List** and icons of the blocks within a file – to a single area showing the block icons (Fig. 9.12).
   (b) **Preview** – a *click* on the icon opens a small area at the base of the palette, showing an enlarged view of the selected block icon.
   (c) **Description** – a *click* on the icon opens another small area with a description of the block.

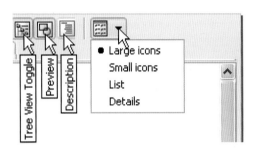

Fig. 9.11 The icons at the top-right corner of the **DesignCenter** palette

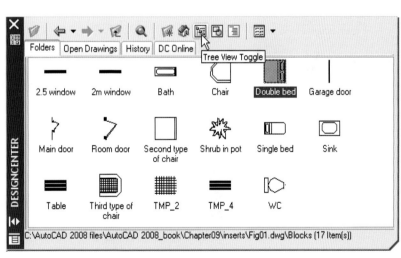

Fig. 9.12 The results of a *click* on **Tree View Toggle**

Fig. 9.13 The **Explode** check box in the **Insert dialog**

The Explode tool

A block is a single object no matter from how many objects it was originally constructed. This enables a block to be *dragged* about the drawing area as a single object.

A check box in the bottom left-hand corner of the **Insert** dialog is labelled **Explode** (Fig. 9.13). If the check box is ticked, **Explode** will be set on and when a block is inserted it will be exploded into the objects from which it was constructed.

Fig. 9.14 The **Explode** tool icon in the **DASHBOARD** palette

Another way of exploding a block would be to use the **Explode** tool from the **DASHBOARD** palette (Fig. 9.14). A *click* on the icon or *entering* **ex** at the command line brings prompts into the command line:

Command:_explode
Select objects: *pick* a block on screen **1 found**.
Select objects: *right-click*
Command:

And the *picked* object is exploded into its original objects.

The Purge tool

The **Purge** tool can be called by *entering* **pu** at the command line or from **Drawing Utilities** in the **File** drop-down menu (Fig. 9.15). When the tool is called the **Purge** dialog appears on screen (Fig. 9.16).

Fig. 9.15 Calling **Purge** from the **Drawing Utilities** sub-menu of the **File** drop-down menu

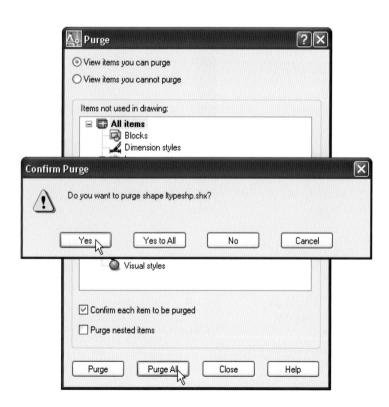

Fig. 9.16 The **Purge** dialog

The **Purge** tool can be used to remove the data of blocks within a drawing thus saving file space when a drawing which includes blocks is saved to disk.

To use the tool, in its dialog *click* the **Purge All** button and a sub-dialog appears naming a block to be purged. A *click* on the **Yes** button clears the data of the block from the drawing. Continue until all blocks that are to be purged are removed.

Take the drawing in Fig. 9.8 (page 154) as an example. If all the blocks are purged from the drawing, the file will be reduced from **145** to **67** Kb when the drawing is saved to disk.

Using the DesignCenter (Fig. 9.19)

1. Construct the set of electric/electronic circuit symbols shown in Fig. 9.17 and make a series of blocks from each of the symbols.
2. Save the drawing to a file **Fig17.dwg**.
3. Open the **acadiso.dwt** template. Open the **DesignCenter** with a *click* on its icon in the **Standard Annotation** toolbar.
4. From the **Folder list** select the file **Fig17.dwg** and *click* on **Blocks** under its file name. Then *drag* symbol icons from the **DesignCenter** into the drawing area as shown in Fig. 9.18. Ensure they are placed in

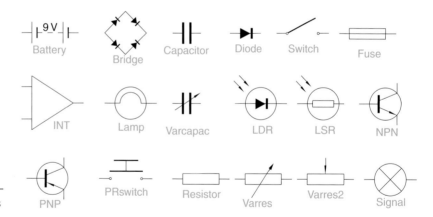

Fig. 9.17 Using the DesignCenter – a set of electric/electronic symbols

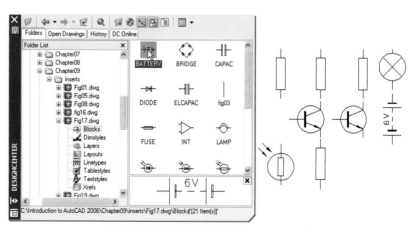

Fig. 9.18 Using the DesignCenter

appropriate positions in relation to each other to form a circuit. If necessary either **Move** and/or **Rotate** the symbols into correct positions.

5. Close the **DesignCenter** palette with a *click* on the **x** in the top left-hand corner.

6. Complete the circuit drawing as shown in Fig. 9.19.

Note

Fig. 9.19 does not represent an authentic electronics circuit.

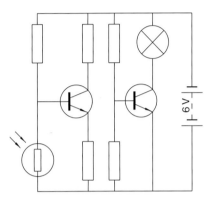

Fig. 9.19 Using the DesignCenter – the completed circuit

Wblocks

Wblocks or written blocks are saved as drawing files in their own right and are not part of the drawing in which they have been saved.

Example – wblock (Fig. 9.20)

1. Construct a light emitting diode (**LED**) symbol and *enter* **w** at the command line. The **Write Block** dialog appears (Fig. 9.20).

2. *Click* the button marked with three dots (**...**) to the right of the **File name and path** field and from the **Browse for Drawing File** dialog which comes to screen select an appropriate directory. The directory name appears in the **File name and path** field. Add **LED.dwg** at the end of the name.

3. Make sure the **Insert units** is set to **Millimetres** in its popup list.

4. *Click* the **Select objects** button, *window* the symbol drawing and when the dialog reappears, *click* the **Pick point** button, followed by selecting the left-hand end of the symbol.

5. Finally *click* the **OK** button of the dialog and the symbol is saved in its selected directory as a drawing file **LED.dwg** in its own right.

Note on the DesignCenter

Drawings can be inserted into the AutoCAD window from the **Design-Center** by *dragging* the icon representing the drawing into the window (Fig. 9.21).

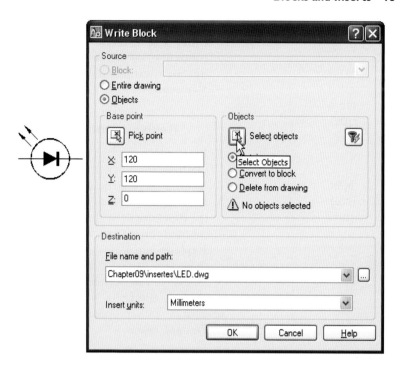

Fig. 9.20 Example – **Wblock**

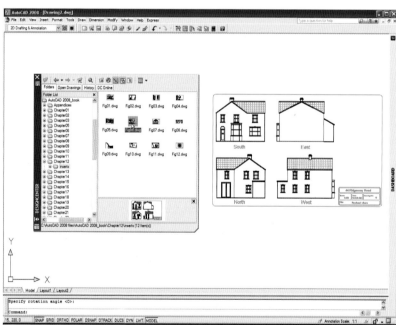

Fig. 9.21 An example of a drawing *dragged* from the **DesignCenter**

When such a drawing is *dragged* into the AutoCAD window, the command line shows a sequence such as:

Command:_INSERT Enter block name or [?] <Fig26>: "Chapter07\inserts\Fig25.dwg"

Specify insertion point or [prompts]: *pick*
Enter X scale factor <1>: *right-click*
Enter Y scale factor <use X scale factor>: *right-click*
Specify rotation angle <0>: *right-click*
Command:

Revision notes

1. Blocks become part of the drawing file in which they were constructed.
2. Wblocks become drawing files in their own right.
3. Drawings or parts of drawings can be inserted in other drawings with the **Block** tool.
4. Inserted blocks or drawings are single objects unless either the **Explode** check box of the **Insert** dialog is checked or the block or drawing is exploded with the **Explode** tool.
5. Drawings can be inserted into the AutoCAD drawing area using the **DesignCenter**.
6. Blocks within drawings can be inserted into drawings from the **DesignCenter**.

Exercises

1. Construct the building symbols in Fig. 9.22 in a drawing saved as **symbols.dwg**. Then using the **DesignCenter** construct a building drawing of the first floor of the house you are living in, making use of the symbols. Do not bother too much about dimensions because this exercise is designed to practise using the idea of making blocks and using the **DesignCenter**.

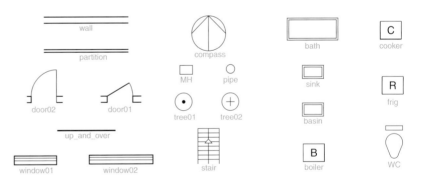

Fig. 9.22 Exercise 1

2. Construct drawings of the electric/electronics symbols in Fig. 9.17 (page 157) and save them as blocks in a drawing file **electronics.dwg**.
3. Construct the electronics circuit given in Fig. 9.23 from the file **electronics.dwg** using the **DesignCenter**.

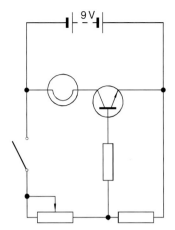

Fig. 9.23 Exercise 3

4. Construct the electronics circuit given in Fig. 9.24 from the file **electronics.dwg** using the **DesignCenter**.

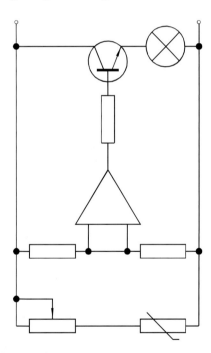

Fig. 9.24 Exercise 4

CHAPTER 10

Other types of file format

Aims of this chapter

1. To introduce Object Linking and Embedding (**OLE**) and its uses.
2. To introduce the use of Encapsulated Postscript (**EPS**) files.
3. To introduce the use of Data Exchange Format (**DXF**) files.
4. To introduce raster files.
5. To introduce **Xrefs**.

Object linking and embedding

First example – copying and pasting (Fig. 10.3)

1. Open any drawing in the AutoCAD 2008 window (Fig. 10.1).
2. *Left-click* **Copy Link** in the **Edit** drop-down menu (Fig. 10.1).

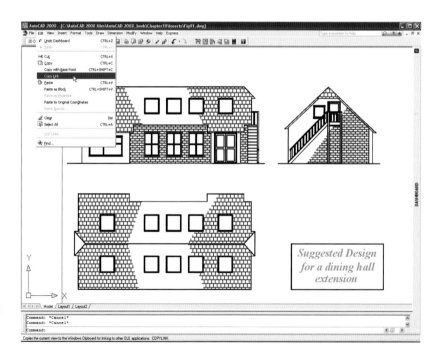

Fig. 10.1 A drawing in the AutoCAD 2008 window showing **Copy Link** selected from the **Edit** drop-down menu

3. *Click* the AutoCAD 2008 **Minimize** button and open the **Clipboard** viewer. The copied drawing appears in the clipboard (Fig. 10.2).

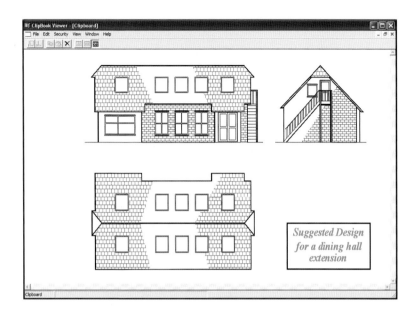

Fig. 10.2 The drawing from AutoCAD copied to the **Clipboard**

4. Open **Microsoft Word** and *click* on **Paste** in the **Edit** drop-down menu (Fig. 10.3). The drawing from the **Clipboard** appears in the **Microsoft Word** document (Fig. 10.3).
5. Add text as required.

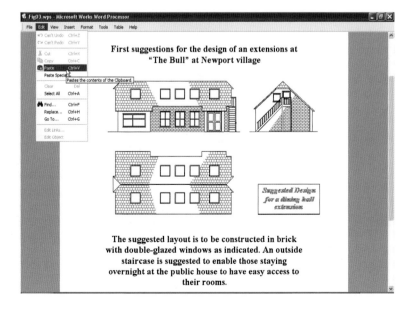

Fig. 10.3 Example – **copying and pasting**

Notes

1. It is not common practice to have a **Clipboard** window showing on screen, since it usually works in the background. It is shown opened here to display its use in acting as an agent for transposing drawings, etc. from one application to another.
2. Similar results can be obtained using the **Copy** and **Copy with Base Point** tools from the **Edit** drop-down menu of AutoCAD 2008.
3. The drawing could also be pasted back into the AutoCAD window – not that there would be much point in doing so, but anything in the **Clipboard** window can be pasted into other applications.

Second example – EPS file (Fig. 10.5)

1. With the same drawing on screen *click* on **Export...** in the **File** drop-down menu. The **Export Data** dialog appears (Fig. 10.4). *Pick* **Encapsulated PS (*.eps)** from the **Files of type** popup list, then *enter* a suitable file name (**building.eps**) in the **File name** field and *click* the **Save** button.

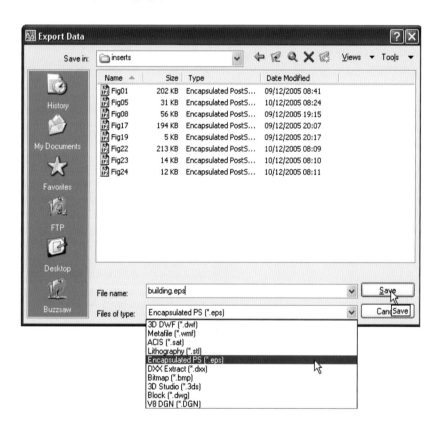

Fig. 10.4 The **Export Data** dialog of AutoCAD 2008

2. Open a desktop publishing application. That shown in Fig. 10.5 is **PageMaker**.
3. From the **File** drop-down menu *click* **Place...** A dialog appears listing files which can be placed in a PageMaker document. Among the files

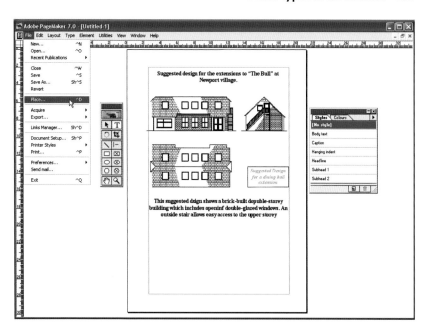

Fig. 10.5 An EPS file placed in position in a PageMaker document

named will be **building.eps**. *Double-click* that file name and an icon appears, the placing of which determines the position of the *.**eps** file drawing in the PageMaker document (Fig. 10.5).

4. Add text as required.
5. Save the PageMaker document to a suitable file name.
6. Go back to the AutoCAD drawing and delete the title.
7. Make a new *.**eps** file with the same file name (**building.eps**).
8. Go back into **PageMaker** and *click* **Links Manager...** in the **File** drop-down menu. The **Links Manager** dialog appears (Fig. 10.6). Against the name of the **building.eps** file name is a dash and a note at the bottom of the dialog explaining that changes have taken place in the drawing from which the *.**eps** had been derived. *Click* the **Update** button and when the document reappears the drawing in PageMaker no longer includes the erased title.

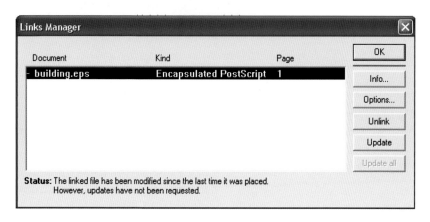

Fig. 10.6 The **Links Manager** dialog of PageMaker

Notes

1. This is **Object linking and embedding**. Changes in the AutoCAD drawing saved as an *.**eps** file are linked to the drawing embedded in another application document, so changes made in the AutoCAD drawing are reflected in the PageMaker document.
2. There is actually no need to use the **Links Manager** because if the file from PageMaker is saved with the old *.**eps** file in place, when it is reopened the file will have changed to the redrawn AutoCAD drawing, without the erased title.

DXF (Data Exchange Format) files

The *.**DXF** format was originated by Autodesk (publishers of AutoCAD), but is now in general use in most **CAD** software. A drawing saved to a *.**dxf** format file can be opened in most other CAD software applications. This file format is of great value when drawings are being exchanged between operators using different CAD applications.

Example – DXF file (Fig. 10.8)

1. Open a drawing in AutoCAD. This example is shown in Fig. 10.7.
2. *Click* on **Save As...** in the **File** drop-down menu and in the **Save Drawing As** dialog which appears, *click* **AutoCAD 2004 DXF [*.dxf]**.

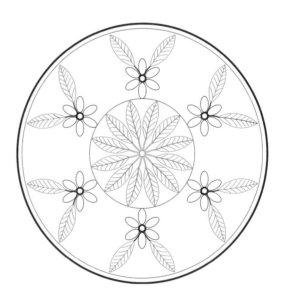

Fig. 10.7 Example – **DXF file**.
Drawing to be saved as a dxf file

3. *Enter* a suitable file name. In this example this is **Fig. 07**. The extension **.dxf** is automatically included when the **Save** button of the dialog is *clicked* (Fig. 10.8).

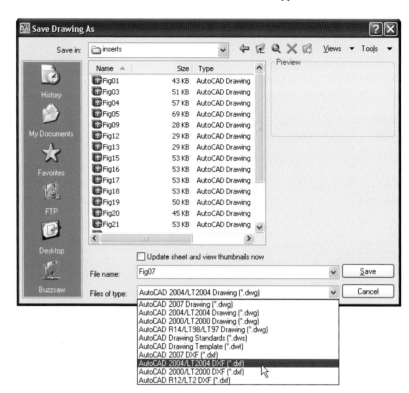

Fig. 10.8 The **Save Drawing** As dialog set up to save drawings in DXF format

4. The **DXF** file can now be opened in the majority of CAD applications and then saved to the drawing file format of the CAD in use.

Note

To open a **DXF** file in AutoCAD 2008, select **Open...** from the **File** drop-down menu and select **DXF [*.dxf]** from the popup list of the **Files of type** field.

Raster images

A variety of raster files can be placed into AutoCAD 2008 drawings from the **Select Image File** dialog brought to screen with a *click* on **Raster Image Reference...** in the **Insert** drop-down menu (Fig. 10.9). In this example the selected raster file is a bitmap (extension *.bmp) of a rendered 3D model drawing constructed to the views in an assembly drawing of a lathe tool post (see Chapter 10 about rendering 3D models).

Example – placing a raster file in a drawing (Fig. 10.13)

1. *Click* **Raster Image Reference...** from the **Insert** drop-down menu. The **Select Image File** dialog appears (Fig. 10.10). *Click* the file name of the image to be inserted, in this example **rendering01.bmp**. A preview appears in the **Preview** area of the dialog.

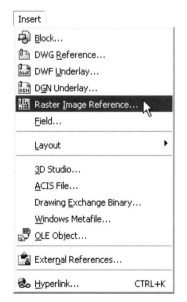

Fig. 10.9 Selecting **Raster Image Reference...** from the **Insert** drop-down menu

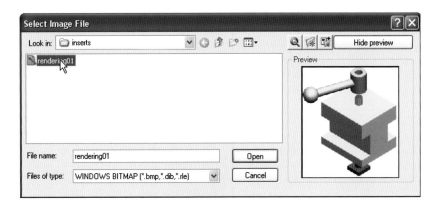

Fig. 10.10 The **Select Image File** dialog

2. *Click* the **Open** button of the dialog. The **Image** dialog appears (Fig. 10.11).

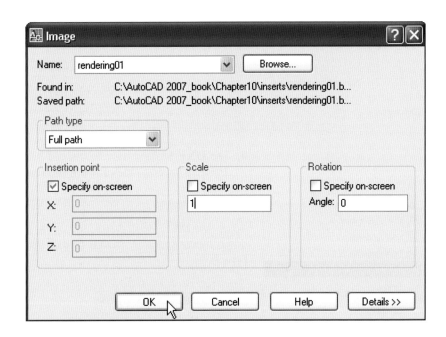

Fig. 10.11 The **Image** dialog

3. In the **Scale** field *enter* a suitable scale figure. The size of the image that will appear in the AutoCAD window can be seen with a *click* on the **Details** button which brings down an extension of the dialog which shows details about the resolution and size of the image.
4. *Click* the **OK** button, the command line shows:

Command:_imageattach
Specify insertion point <0,0>: an outline of the image attached to the intersection of the cursor cross hairs appears *pick* a suitable point on screen
Command:

And the raster image appears at the *picked* point (Fig. 10.12).

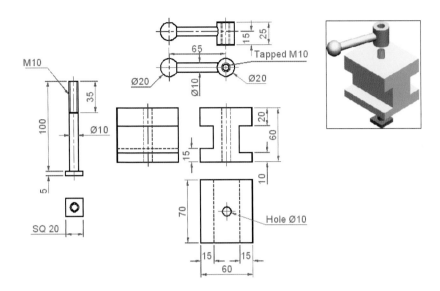

Fig. 10.12 Example – placing a raster file in a drawing

Notes

As can be seen from the **Insert** drop-down menu (Fig. 10.9) a variety of different types of raster and other images can be inserted into an Auto-CAD drawing. Some examples are:

Blocks – see Chapter 9.
External References (Xrefs) – see later in this chapter.
Field name – a *click* on the name brings up the **Field** dialog. Practise inserting various categories of field names from the dialog.
Layout – a wizard appears allowing new layouts to be created and saved for new templates.
3D Studio – allows the insertion of images constructed in the Autodesk software **3D Studio** from files with the format *.**3ds**.
OLE Objects – allows raster images to be placed as OLE images from a variety of other applications.

External References (Xrefs)

If a drawing is inserted into another drawing as an external reference, any changes made in the original Xref drawing are automatically reflected in the drawing into which the Xref has been inserted.

Example – External References (Fig. 10.19)

1. Construct the three-view orthographic drawing in Fig. 10.15. Dimensions of this drawing will be found on page 276. Save the drawing to a suitable file name.

2. As a separate drawing construct Fig. 10.16. Save it as a wblock with the name of **Fig16.dwg** and with a base insertion point at one end of its centre line.

3. In the **Insert** drop-down menu *click* **External References...** The **EXTERNAL REFERENCES** palette appears (Fig. 10.13).

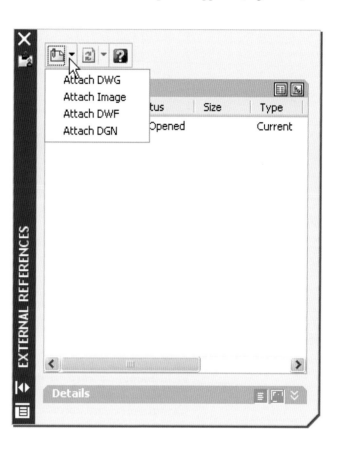

Fig. 10.13 The **EXTERNAL REFERENCES** palette

4. *Click* its **Attach** button and select **Attach DWG** from the popup list which appears when a *left-click* is held on the button. Select the drawing of a spindle (**Fig16.dwg**) from the **Select Reference File** dialog which appears followed by a *click* on the dialog's **Open** button. This brings up the **External Reference** dialog (Fig. 10.14) showing **Fig16** in its **Name** field. *Click* the dialog's **OK** button.

5. The spindle drawing appears on screen ready to be *dragged* into position. Place it in position as indicated in Fig. 10.17.

6. Save the drawing with its Xref to its original file name.

7. Open the drawing **Fig16.dwg** and make changes as shown in Fig. 10.18.

8. Now reopen the original drawing. The **external reference** within the drawing has changed in accordance with the alterations to the spindle drawing (Fig. 10.19).

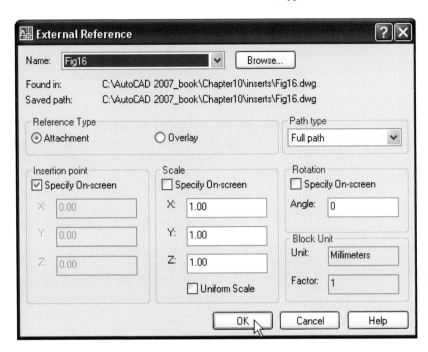

Fig. 10.14 The **External Reference** dialog

Fig. 10.15 Example – **External references** – original drawing

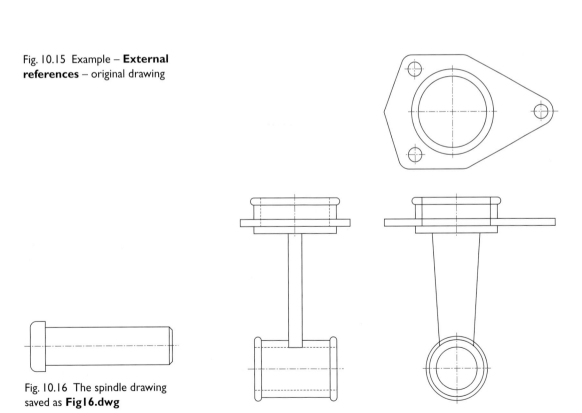

Fig. 10.16 The spindle drawing saved as **Fig16.dwg**

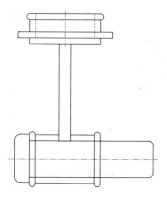

Fig. 10.17 The spindle in place in the original drawing

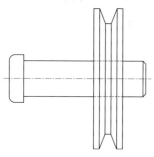

Fig. 10.18 The revised **spindle.dwg** drawing

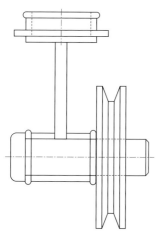

Fig. 10.19 Example – **Xrefs**

Fig. 10.20 Example – a drawing in MicroStation V8

Note

In this example, to ensure accuracy of drawing, the **external reference** will need to be exploded and parts of the spindle changed to hidden detail lines.

Dgnimport and Dgnexport

Drawings constructed in MicroStation V8 format (*.**dgn**) can be imported into AutoCAD 2008 format using the command **dgnimport** at the command line. AutoCAD drawings in AutoCAD 2004 format can be exported into MicroStation *.**dgn** format using the command **dgnexport**.

Example of importing a *.dgn drawing into AutoCAD

1. Fig. 10.20 is an example of an orthographic drawing constructed in MicroStation V8.
2. In AutoCAD 2008 at the command line *enter* **dgnimport**. The dialog in Fig. 10.21 appears on screen from which the required drawing file name can be selected. When the **Open** button of the dialog is *clicked* a warning window appears informing the operator of steps to take in order to load the drawing. When completed the drawing loads (Fig. 10.22).

In a similar manner AutoCAD drawing files can be exported to MicroStation using the command **dgnexport** *entered* at the command line. The files must be exported in AutoCAD 2004 format.

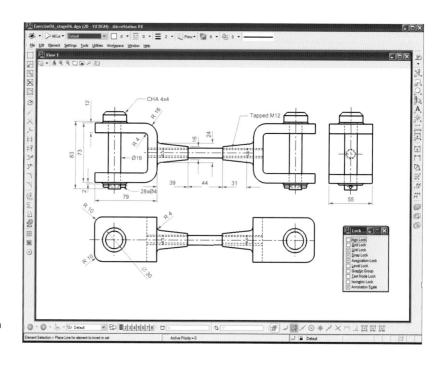

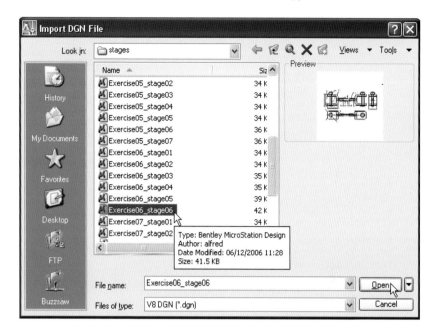

Fig. 10.21 The **Import DGN File** dialog

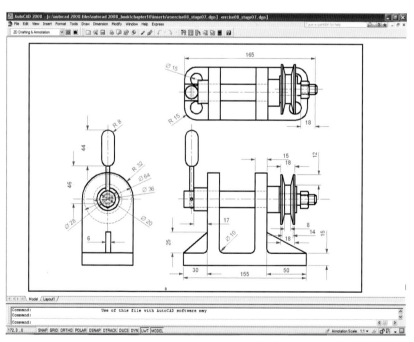

Fig. 10.22 The *.**dgn** file imported into AutoCAD 2008

Multiple Document Environment (MDE)

1. Open several drawings in AutoCAD, in this example four separate drawings have been opened.
2. In the **Window** drop-down menu, *click* **Tile Horizontally**. The four drawings rearrange as shown in Fig. 10.23.

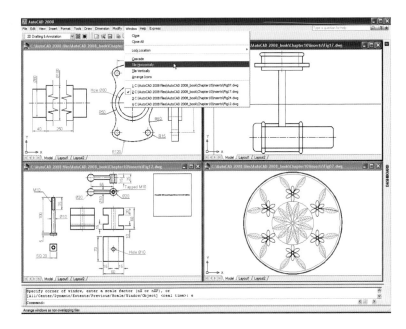

Fig. 10.23 Four drawings in the **Multiple Document Environment**

Note

The names of the drawings appear in the **Window** drop-down menu, showing their directories, file names and file name extensions.

Revision notes

1. The **Edit** tools **Copy with Base Point, Copy** and **Copy Link** enable objects from AutoCAD 2008 to be copied for **Pasting** onto other applications.
2. Objects can be copied from other applications to be pasted into the AutoCAD 2008 window.
3. Drawings saved in AutoCAD as **DXF (*.dxf)** files can be opened in other CAD applications.
4. Similarly drawings saved in other CAD applications as ***.dxf** files can be opened in AutoCAD 2008.
5. **Raster** files of the format types ***.bmp**, ***.jpg**, ***.pcx**, ***.tga**, ***.tif** among other raster type file objects can be inserted into AutoCAD 2008 drawings.
6. Drawings saved to the Encapsulated Postscript (***.eps**) file format can be inserted into documents of other applications.
7. Changes made in a drawing saved as an ***.eps** file will be reflected in the drawing inserted as an ***.eps** file in another application.
8. When a drawing is inserted into another drawing as an **external reference**, changes made to the inserted drawing will automatically be updated in the drawing into which it has been inserted.
9. A number of drawings can be opened in the AutoCAD 2008 window.
10. Drawings constructed in MicroStation V8 can be imported into Auto-CAD 2008 using the command **dgnimport**.

11. Drawings constructed in AutoCAD 2008 can be saved as MicroStation *.**dgn** drawings to be opened in MicroStation V8.

Exercises

1. Fig. 10.24 shows a pattern formed by inserting an **external reference** and then copying or arraying the **external reference**.

Fig. 10.24 Exercise 1 – original pattern

The hatched parts of the **external reference** drawing were then changed using a different hatch pattern. The result of the change in the Xref is shown in Fig. 10.25.

Fig. 10.25 Exercise 1

Construct a similar **Xref** drawing, insert as an **Xref**, array or copy to form the pattern, then change the hatching, save the **Xref** drawing and note the results.

2. Fig 10.26 is a rendering of a roller between two end holders.Fig. 10.27 gives details of the end holders and the roller in orthographic projections.

Fig. 10.26 Exercise 2 – a rendering of the holders and roller

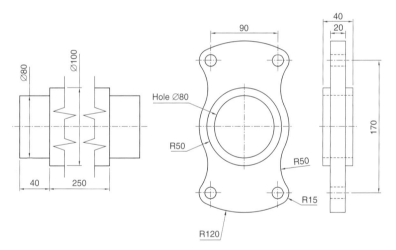

Fig. 10.27 Exercise 2 – details of the parts of the roller and holders

Construct a full size front view of the roller and save to a file name **roller .dwg**. Then as a separate drawing construct a front view of the two end holders in their correct positions to receive the roller and save to the file name **assembly.dwg**.

Insert the roller drawing into the assembly drawing as an **Xref**. Open the **roller.dwg** and change its outline as shown in Fig. 10.28. Save the drawing. Open the **assembly.dwg** and note the change in the inserted **Xref**.

3. *Click* **Raster Image...** in the **Insert** drop-down menu and insert a **JPEG** image (**.jpg* file) of a photograph into the AutoCAD 2008 window. An example is given in Fig. 10.29.

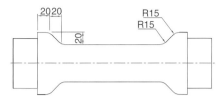

Fig. 10.28 The amended **Xref** drawing

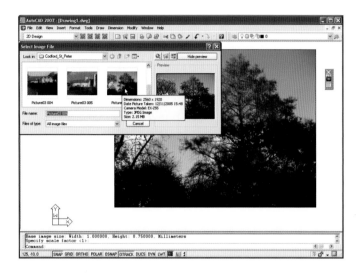

Fig. 10.29 Exercise 3 – example

4. Using **Copy** from the **Insert** drop-down menu, copy a drawing from AutoCAD 2008 into a Microsoft Word document. An example is given in Fig. 10.30. Add some appropriate text.
5. The plan in Figs 10.1,10.2 and 10.3 is incorrect in that some details have been missed from the drawing. Can you identify the error?

Fig. 10.30 Exercise 4 – an example

CHAPTER 11

Sheet sets

Aims of this chapter

1. To introduce sheet sets.
2. To describe working in the **Sheet Layout and Publishing** workspace.
3. To give an example of a sheet set based on the design of a two-storey house.

Sheet sets

When anything is to be manufactured or constructed, whether it be a building, an engineering design, an electronics device or any other form of manufactured artefact, a variety of documents, many in the form of technical drawings, will be needed to convey to those responsible for constructing the design information necessary to be able to proceed according to the wishes of the designer. Such sets of drawings may be passed between the people or companies responsible for the construction, enabling all those involved to make adjustments or suggest changes to the design. In some cases there may well be a considerable number of drawings required in such sets of drawings. In AutoCAD 2008 all the drawings from which a design is to be manufactured can be gathered together in a **sheet set**. This chapter shows how a much reduced sheet set of drawings for the construction of a house at 62 Pheasant Drive can be formed. Some other drawings, particularly detail drawings, would be required in this example, but to save page space, the sheet set described here consists of only four drawings and a subset of another four.

A sheet set for 62 Pheasant Drive

1. Construct a template **62 Pheasant Drive.dwt** based upon the **acadiso.dwt** template, but including a border and a title block. Save the template in a **Layout1** format. An example of the title block from one of the drawings constructed in this template is shown in Fig. 11.1.
2. Construct each of the drawings which will form the sheet set in this drawing template. The whole set of drawings is shown in Fig. 11.2. Save the drawings in a directory – in this example this has been given the name **62 Pheasant Drive**.

Fig. 11.1 The title block from Drawing number **2** of the sheet set

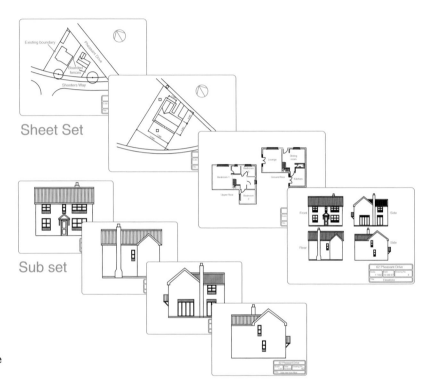

Fig. 11.2 The eight drawings in the **62 Pheasant Drive** sheet set

Fig. 11.3 Selecting **New Sheet Set...** from the **File** drop-down menu

3. *Click* **New Sheet Set** in the **File** drop-down menu (Fig. 11.3). The first of a series of **Create Sheet Set** dialogs appears – the **Begin** dialog (Fig. 11.4). *Click* the radio button next to **Existing drawings**, followed by a *click* on the **Next** button and the next dialog **Sheet Set Details** appears (Fig. 11.5).

4. *Enter* details as shown in the dialog in Fig. 11.5. Then *click* the **Next** button to bring the **Choose Layouts** dialog to screen (Fig. 11.6).

5. *Click* its **Browse...** button and from the **Browse for Folder** list which comes to screen, *pick* the directory **62 Pheasant Drive**. *Click* the **OK** button and the drawings held in the directory appear in the **Choose Layouts** dialog (Fig. 11.6). If satisfied the list is correct, *click* the **Next** button. A **Confirm** dialog appears (Fig. 11.7). If satisfied *click* the **Finish** button and the **Sheet Set Manager** palette appears showing the drawings which will be in the **62 Pheasant Drive** sheet set (Fig. 11.8).

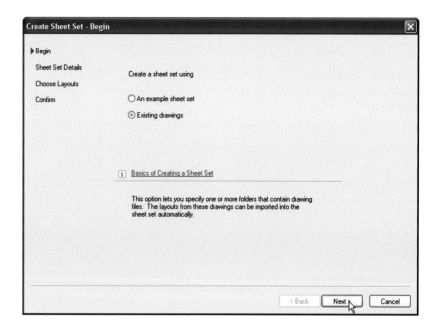

Fig. 11.4 The first of the **Create Sheet Set** dialogs – **Begin**

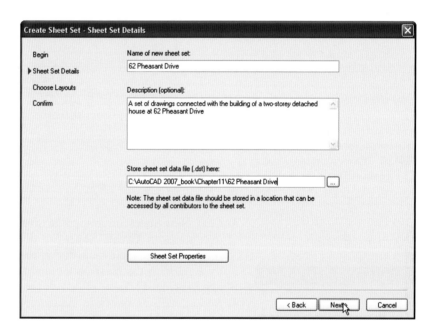

Fig. 11.5 The **Sheet Set Details** dialog

Notes

1. The eight drawings in the sheet set are shown in Fig. 11.8. If any of the drawings in the sheet set are subsequently amended or changed, when the drawing is opened again from the **62 Pheasant Drive** Sheet Set Manager palette, the drawing will include any changes or amendments.

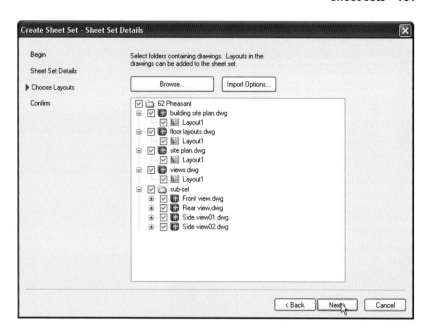

Fig. 11.6 The **Choose Layouts** dialog

Fig. 11.7 The **Confirm** dialog

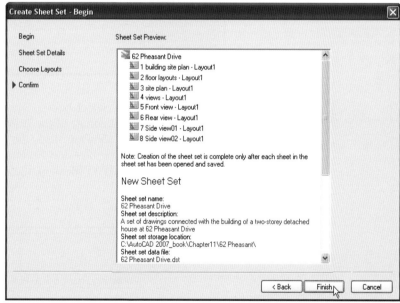

Fig. 11.8 The **Sheet Set Manager** palette for **62 Pheasant Driv**

2. Drawings can only be placed into sheet sets if they have been saved in a **Layout** screen. Note that all the drawings shown in the **62 Pheasant Drive** Sheet Set Manager have **Layout1** after the drawing names because each has been saved after being placed in a **Layout1** screen.
3. Sheet sets in the form of **DWF** (Design Web Format) files can be sent via email to others who are using the drawings or placed on an intranet. The method of producing a **DWF** for the **62 Pheasant Drive** Sheet Set follows.

Fig. 11.9 The **Publish to DWF** icon in the **Sheet Set Manager**

62 Pheasant Drive DWF

1. In the **62 Pheasant Drive** Sheet Set Manager *click* the **Publish to DWF** icon (Fig. 11.9). The **Select DWF File** dialog appears (Fig. 11.10). *Enter* **62 Pheasant Drive** in the **File name** field followed

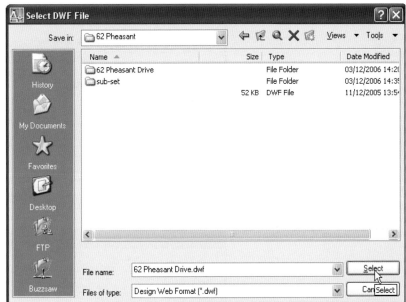

Fig. 11.10 The **Select DWF File** dialog

by a *click* on the **Select** button. The **Publish in Progress** icon at the bottom right-hand corner of the AutoCAD 2008 window starts fluctuating in shape showing that the DWF file is being processed (Fig. 11.11). When the icon becomes stationary *right-click* the icon and *click* **View DWFfile...** in the *right-click* menu which appears (Fig. 11.12).

Fig. 11.11 The **Publish Job in Progress** icon

Fig. 11.12 The *right-click* menu of the icon

2. The **Autodesk DWF Viewer** window appears showing the **62 Pheasant Drive.dwf** file (Fig. 11.13). *Click* in any of the icons of the thumbnails of the drawings in the viewer and the drawing appears in the right-hand area of the viewer.

3. If required the DWF Viewer file can be sent between people by email as an attachment, opened in a company's intranet or, indeed, be included within an Internet webpage.

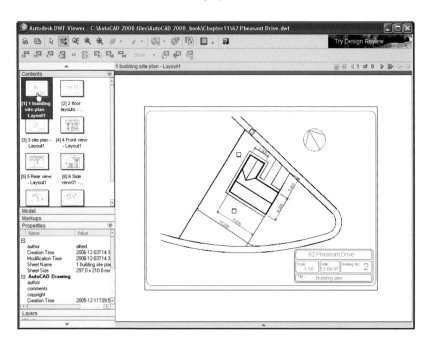

Fig. 11.13 The **Autodesk DWF Viewer** showing details of the **62 Pheasant Drive.dwf** file

Revision notes

1. To start off a new sheet set, *click* **New Sheet Set...** in the **File** drop-down menu.
2. Sheet sets can only contain drawings saved in **Layout** form.
3. Sheet sets can be published as **Design Web Format (*.dwf)** files which can be sent between offices by email, published on an intranet or published on a webpage.
4. Sub sets can be included in sheet sets.
5. Changes or amendments made to any drawings in a sheet set are reflected in the sheet set drawings when the sheet set is opened.

Exercises

1. Fig. 11.14 is an exploded orthographic projection of the parts of a piston and its connecting rod. There are four parts in the assembly. Small drawings of the required sheet set are shown in Fig. 11.16.

Construct the drawing in Fig. 11.14 and also the four drawings of its parts. Save each of the drawings in a **Layout1** format and construct the sheet set which contains the five drawings.

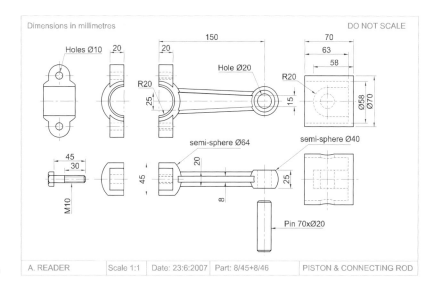

Fig. 11.14 Exercise 1 – the
exploded orthographic projection

Construct the **DWF** file of the sheet set. Experiment sending it to a friend via email as an attachment to a document, asking him/her to return the whole email to you without changes. When the email is returned, open its DWF file and *click* each drawing icon in turn to check the contents of the drawings.

Note

Fig. 11.15 shows a DWF for the sheet set from exercise 1 with the addition of a sixth drawing which is a 3D exploded model drawing of the

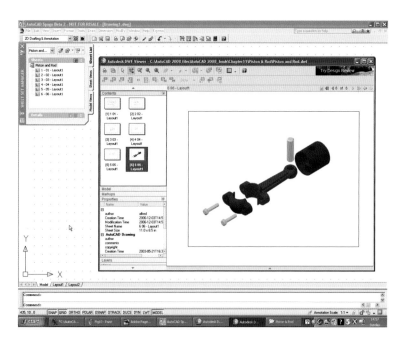

Fig. 11.15 The **DWF** for exercise 1

five parts of the piston and connecting rod which has been Gourand shaded – see Chapter 16. This illustration has been included here to show that such shaded 3D models can be included in a sheet set.

2. Construct a similar sheet set as in the answer to Exercise 1 from the exploded orthographic drawing of a **Machine adjusting spindle** given in Fig. 11.17.

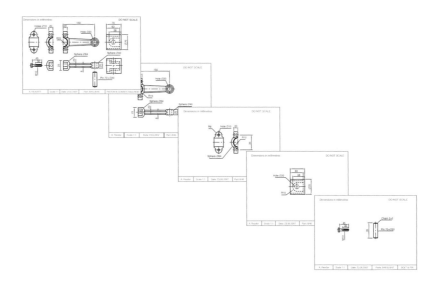

Fig. 11.16 Exercise 1 – the five drawings in the sheet set

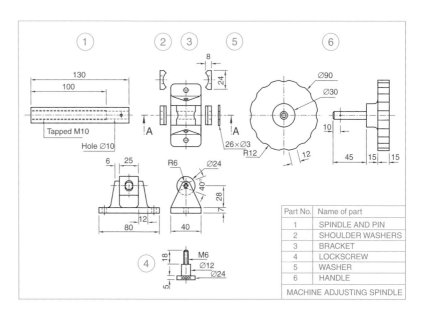

Fig. 11.17 Exercise 2

CHAPTER 12

Building drawing

Aim of this chapter

To show that AutoCAD 2008 is a suitable CAD software package for the construction of building drawings.

Building drawings

There are a number of different types of drawings related to the construction of any form of building. As fairly typical examples of a set of building drawings, in this chapter, seven drawings are shown related to the construction of an extension to an existing two-storey house (44 Ridgeway Road). These show:

1. A site plan of the original two-storey house, drawn to a scale of **1:200** (Fig. 12.1).
2. A site layout plan of the original house, drawn to a scale of **1:100** (Fig. 12.2).

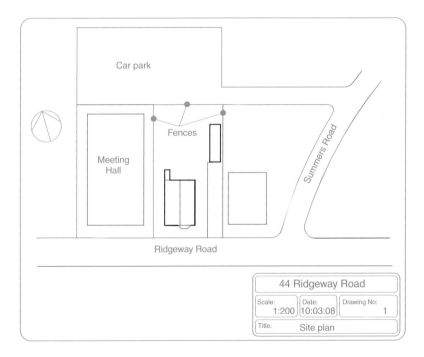

Fig. 12.1 A site plan

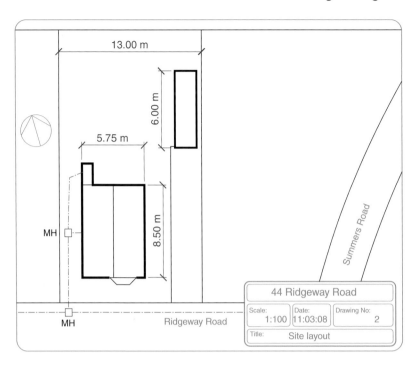

Fig. 12.2 A site layout plan

3. Floor layouts of the original house, drawn to a scale of **1:50** (Fig. 12.3).

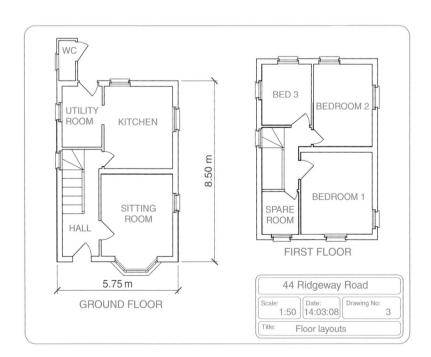

Fig. 12.3 A floor layouts drawing of the original house

4. Views of all four sides of the original house drawn to a scale of **1:50** (Fig. 12.4).

Fig. 12.4 Views of the original house

5. Floor layouts including the proposed extension, drawn to a scale of **1:50** (Fig. 12.5).

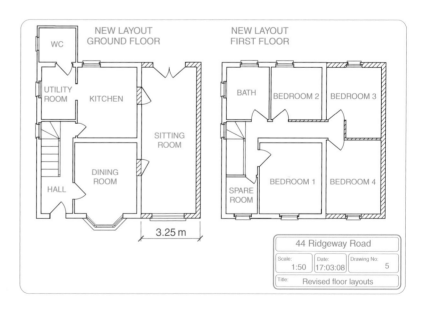

Fig. 12.5 Floor layouts drawing of the proposed extension

6. Views of all four sides of the house including the proposed extension, drawn to a scale of **1:50** (Fig. 12.6).

Fig. 12.6 Views including the
proposed extension

7. A sectional view through the proposed extension, drawn to a scale of
1:50 (Fig. 12.7).

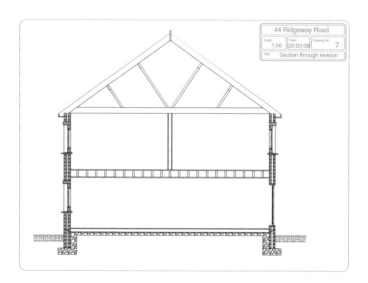

Fig. 12.7 A section through the
proposed extension

Notes

1. Other types of drawings will be constructed which show the details of
   parts such as doors, windows, floor structures, etc. These are often
   shown in sectional views.
2. Although the seven drawings related to the proposed extension of the
   house at 44 Ridgeway Road are shown here as having been constructed on either A3 or A4 layouts, it is common practice to include
   several types of building drawings on larger sheets such as A1 sheets
   of a size 820 mm × 594 mm.

Floor layouts

When constructing floor layout drawings it is advisable to build up a library of block drawings of symbols representing features such as doors, windows, etc. These can then be inserted into layouts from the DesignCenter. A suggested small library of such block symbols is shown in Fig. 12.8.

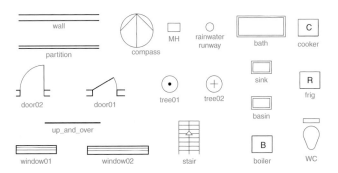

Fig. 12.8 A small libray of building symbols

Revision notes

There are a number of different types of building drawings – site plans, site layout plans, floor layouts, views, sectional views, detail drawings, etc. AutoCAD 2008 is a suitable CAD program to use when constructing building drawings.

Exercises

1. Fig. 12.9 is a site plan drawn to a scale of 1:200 showing a bungalow to be built in the garden of an existing bungalow.

Construct the library of symbols shown in Fig. 12.8 and by inserting the symbols from the DesignCenter construct a scale 1:50 drawing of the floor layout plan of the proposed bungalow.

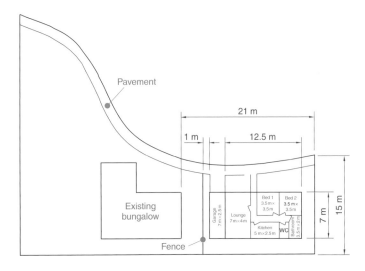

Fig. 12.9 Exercise 1

2. Fig. 12.10 is a site plan of a two-storey house to be built on abuilding plot. Design and construct to a scale 1:50, a suggested pair of floor layouts for the two floors of the proposed house.

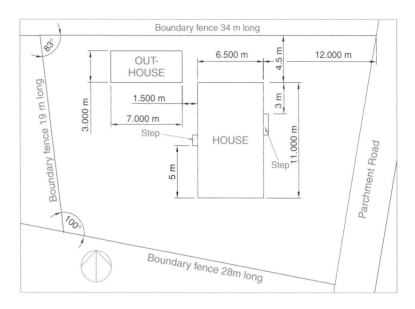

Fig. 12.10 Exercise 2

3. Fig. 12.11 showsascale 1:100 site plan for the proposed bungalow at 4 Caretaker Road. Construct the floor layout for the proposed house shown in the drawing in Fig. 12.12.

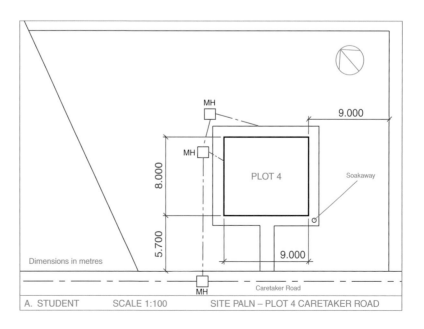

Fig. 12.11 Exercise 3 – site plan

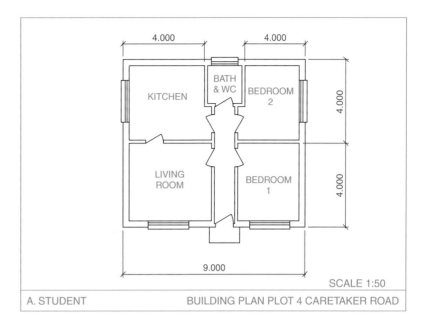

Fig. 12.12 Exercise 3

PART II

3D Design

CHAPTER 13

Introducing 3D modelling

Aims of this chapter

1. To introduce the tools used for the construction of 3D solid models.
2. To give examples of the construction of 3D solid models using tools from the **3D Make** control panel.
3. To give examples of 2D outlines suitable as a basis for the construction of 3D solid models.
4. To give examples of constructions involving the Boolean operators – **Union, Subtract** and **Intersect**.

Introduction

As shown in Chapter 1 the AutoCAD coordinate system includes a third coordinate direction **Z**, which, when dealing with 2D drawings in previous chapters, has not been used. 3D model drawings make use of this third **Z** coordinate.

The 3D Modeling workspace

It is possible to construct 3D model drawings in the **AutoCAD Classic** or **2D Drafting & Annotation** workspaces, but in this part of the book we will be working in the **3D Modeling** workspace in the template **acadiso3D.dwt**. To set this workspace *left-click* **New...** in the **File** drop-down menu (Fig. 13.1) and from the **Select template** dialog *click* **acadiso3D** in the **Name** list (Fig. 13.2). The **acadiso3D** template appears (Fig. 13.3). In this window the seven main 3D control panels of the **DASHBOARD** are shown. It is not necessary to have the **DASHBOARD** on screen. It is up to the operator to decide which of the available methods of calling tools for 3D modelling they wish to use – control panels, toolbars, *entering* tool names or abbreviation or from drop-down menus.

The **acadiso3D** window in Fig. 13.3 shows the grid in a **Parallel** layout, brought about by a *click* on the **Parallel Projection** icon in the **3D Navigate** control panel. This is the window in which the examples in this chapter have been constructed.

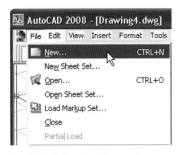

Fig. 13.1 Selecting **New...** from the **File** drop-down menu

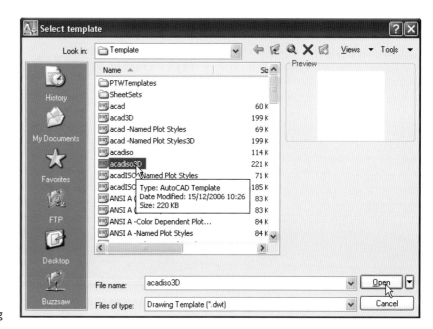

Fig. 13.2 Selecting **acadiso3D** from the **Select template** dialog

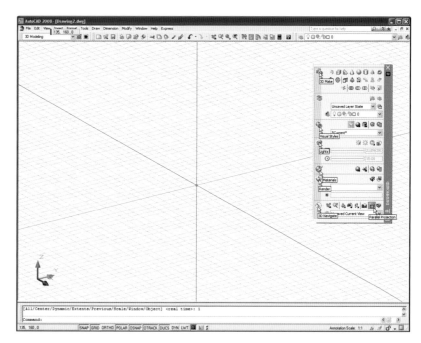

Fig. 13.3 The **acadiso3D** template screen showing seven of the 3D control panels

Methods of calling tools for 3D modelling

When calling the tools for the construction of 3D model drawings, the five same methods apply as that used when constructing 2D drawings:

1. A *click* on a tool icon in the **3D Make** control panel.
2. A *click* on a tool icon in the **Modeling** toolbar.

3. A *click* on the name of a tool from a drop-down menu brings the tool into action.
4. *Entering* the tool name at the command line in the command window, followed by pressing the *Return* button of the mouse or the **Return** key of the keyboard, brings the tool into action.
5. Some of the 3D tools have an abbreviation which can be *entered* at the command line instead of its full name.

Fig. 13.4 shows the tools and tooltips in the **3D Make** control panel.

Notes

1. As when constructing 2D drawings, no matter which method is used – most operators will use a combination of these five methods – the result of calling a tool results in prompts sequences appearing at the command prompt as in the following example:

Command: *enter* **box** *right-click*
Specify first corner or [CEnter]: *enter* **90,120** *right-click*
Specify other corner or [Cube/Length]:

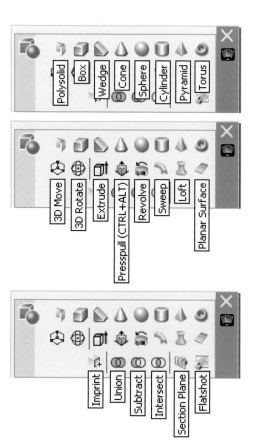

Fig. 13.4 The tool icons and tooltips in the **3D Make** control panel

Or, if the tool is called from its tool icon or from a drop-down menu:

Command:_box
Specify first corner or [CEnter]: *enter* **90,120** *right-click*
Specify other corner or [Cube/Length]:

2. In the following pages, if the tool's sequences are to be repeated, they may be replaced by an abbreviated form such as:

Command:_box
[prompts]: 90,120
[prompts]:

The Polysolid tool (Fig. 13.6)

1. Make a new layer **Construct** of colour **black**. Make this layer current.
2. *Click* **Top** in the **3D Navigate** control panel's popup list (Fig. 13.5).
3. Construct an octagon of edge length **60** using the **Polygon** tool.
4. Set layer **0** current and from the **3D Navigate** drop-down menu select **Southeast Isometric**.
5. Call the **Polysolid** tool with a *click* on its tool icon in the **3D Make** control panel (Fig. 13.4). The command line shows:

Command:_Polysolid Height = 0, Width = 0, Justification = Center
Specify start point or [Object/Height/Width/Justify]<Object>:
  enter **h** (Height)
Specify height <4>: 60
Height = 60, Width = 0, Justification = Center
Specify start point or [Object/Height/Width/Justify] <Object>:
  enter **w** (Width)

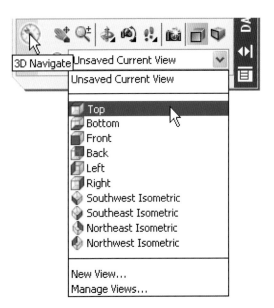

Fig. 13.5 Selecting **Top** from the **3D Navigate** control panel's popup list

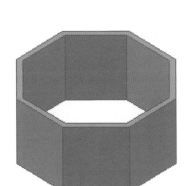

Fig. 13.6 Example – Polysolid

Specify width <0>: 5
Height = 60, Width = 5, Justification = Center
Specify start point or [Object/Height/Width/Justify]<Object>:
Specify next point or [Arc/Undo]: *pick* one corner of octagon
Specify next point or [Arc/Undo]: *pick* second corner
Specify next point or [Arc/Close/Undo]: *pick* third
Specify next point or [Arc/Close/Undo]: *pick* fourth
Specify next point or [Arc/Close/Undo]: *pick* fifth
Specify next point or [Arc/Close/Undo]: *pick* sixth
Specify next point or [Arc/Close/Undo]: *pick* seventh
Specify next point or [Arc/Close/Undo]: *pick* last
Specify next point or [Arc/Close/Undo]: *enter* **c** (Close)
Command:

And the **Polysolid** forms (Fig. 13.6).

2D outlines suitable for 3D models

When constructing 2D outlines suitable as a basis for constructing some forms of 3D model, use tools from the **2D Draw** control panel. If constructed using tools such as **Line, Circle** and **Ellipse**, before being of any use for 3D modelling, outlines must be changed into regions with the **Region** tool (**2D Draw** control panel – Fig. 13.8). Closed polylines can be used without the need to use the **Region** tool.

First example – Line outline and Region (Fig. 13.7)

1. Construct the left-hand drawing of Fig. 13.7 using the **Line** tool.

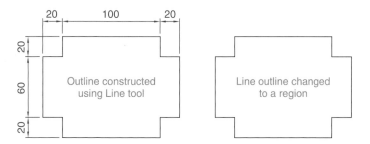

Fig. 13.7 First example – Line outline and Region

2. *Left-click* on **Region** tool in the **2D Draw** control panel (Fig. 13.8), or *enter* **reg** at the command line. The command line shows:

Command:_region
Select objects: *window* the drawing **12 found**
Select objects: *right-click*
1 Region created
Command:

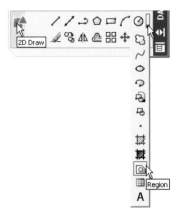

A

Fig. 13.8 Selecting **Region** from a flyout in the **2D Draw** control panel

And the **Line** outline is changed to a region – right-hand drawing of Fig. 13.7.

Second example – Union, Subtract and regions (Fig. 13.9)

1. In the **Top** view, construct drawing **1** of Fig. 13.9 and with the **Copy** tool (**2D Draw** control panel), copy the drawing three times to produce drawings **2, 3** and **4**.

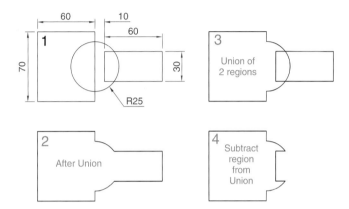

Fig. 13.9 Second example – Union, Subtract and regions

2. With the **Region** tool change all the outlines into regions.
3. Drawing **2** – call the **Union** tool from the **3D Make** control panel (Fig. 13.10). The command line shows:

Command: _union
Select objects: *pick* the left-hand region **1 found**
Select objects: *pick* the circular region **1 found, 2 total**
Select objects: *pick* the right-hand region **1 found, 3 total**
Command:

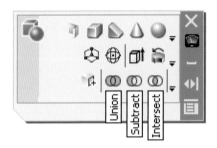

Fig. 13.10 The **Union, Subtract** and **Intersect** tool icons in the **3D Make** control panel

4. Drawing **3** – with the **Union** tool form a union of the left-hand region and the circular region.
5. Drawing **4** – call the **Subtract** tool (Fig. 13.10). The command line shows:

Command:_subtract Select solids and regions to subtract from...
Select objects: *pick* the region just formed **1 found**

Select objects: *right-click*
Select solids and regions to subtract: *pick* the right-hand region **1 found**
Select objects: *right-click*
Command:

Third example – Intersection and regions (Fig. 13.11)

1. Construct drawing **1** of Fig. 13.11.
2. With the **Region** tool, change the three outlines into regions.
3. With the **Copy** tool, copy the three regions.
4. Drawing **2** – call the **Intersect** tool from the **3D Make** control panel. The command line shows:

Command:_intersect
Select objects: *pick* one of the circles **1 found**
Select objects: *pick* the other circle **1 found, 2 total**
Select objects: *right-click*
Command:

And the two circular regions are intersect with each other to form a region.

5. Drawing **3** – repeat using the **Intersect** tool on the intersection of the two circles and the rectangular region.

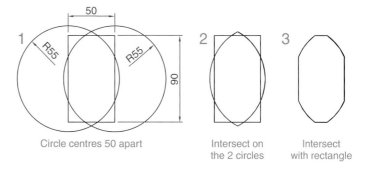

Fig. 13.11 Third example – Intersection and regions

Circle centres 50 apart

2 Intersect on the 2 circles

3 Intersect with rectangle

The Extrude tool

The **Extrude** tool can be called either with a *click* on its tool icon in the **3D Make** control panel (Fig. 13.4, page 197), or from the **Modeling** tool-bar, or from the **Draw** drop-down menu, or by *entering* **extrude** or its abbreviation **ext** at the command line.

Note

In this chapter 3D models are shown in illustrations as they appear in the **acadiso3D.dwt** template screen. In later chapters, 3D models are sometimes shown in outline only. This is to allow the reader to see the parts of 3D models in future chapters more clearly in the illustrations.

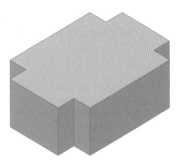

Fig. 13.12 First example –
Extrude

Examples of the use of the Extrude tool

The three examples of forming regions given in Figs. 13.7, 13.9 and 13.11 are used here to show results of using the **Extrude** tool.

First example – Extrude (Fig. 13.12)

From the first example of forming a region:

1. Call the **Extrude** tool. The command line shows:

   Command: _extrude
   Current wire frame density: ISOLINES=4
   Select objects to extrude: *pick* region **1 found**
   Select objects to extrude: *right-click*
   Specify height of extrusion or [Direction/Path/Taper angle] <45>:
       enter **50** *right-click*
   Command:

2. Select **Southwest Isometric** from the popup list in the **3D Navigate** control panel (Fig. 13.5, page 198). The extrusion appears in an isometric view.
3. Call **Zoom** and zoom to **1**.

   Notes

1. In the above example we made use of one of the isometric views possible from the **3D Navigate** control panel (Fig. 13.5). These views will be used frequently in examples to show 3D solid model drawings in a variety of positions in 3D space.
2. Note the **Current wire frame density: ISOLINES=4** in the prompts sequence when **Extrude** is called. The setting of **4** is suitable when extruding plines or regions consisting of straight lines, but when arcs are being extruded it may be better to set **ISOLINES** to a higher figure as follows:

   Command: *enter* isolines *right-click*
   Enter new value for ISOLINES <4>: *enter* **16** *right-click*
   Command:

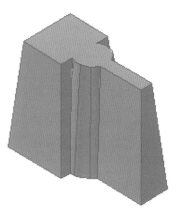

Fig. 13.13 Second example –
Extrude

Second example – Extrude (Fig. 13.13)

From the second example of forming a region:

1. Set **ISOLINES** to **16**.
2. Call the **Extrude** tool. The command line shows:

   Command: _extrude
   Current wire frame density: ISOLINES=16
   Select objects to extrude: *pick* the region **1 found**
   Select objects to extrude: *right-click*
   Specify height of extrusion or [Direction/Path/Taper angle]: *enter* **t**
       right-click

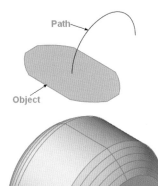

Fig. 13.14 Third example –
Extrude

Specify angle of taper for extrusion: *enter* **5** *right-click*
Specify height of extrusion or [Direction/Path/Taperangle]: *enter*
    100 *right-click*
Command:

3. *Click* **Southwest Isometric** in the **3D Navigate** control panel's popup list.
4. **Zoom** to **1**.

Third example – Extrude (Fig. 13.14)

From the third example of forming a region:

1. Place the screen in the **Front** view.
2. Construct a semicircular arc from the centre of the region.
3. Place the screen in the **Top** view.
4. With the **Move** tool, move the arc to the centre of the region.
5. Place the screen in the **Southwest Isometric** view.
6. Set **ISOLINES** to **24**.
7. Call the **Extrude** tool. The command line shows:

Command: _extrude
Current wire frame density: ISOLINES = 24
Select objects to extrude: *pick* the region **1 found**
Select objects to extrude: *right-click*
Specify height of extrusion or [Direction/Path/Taper angle] <100>:
    enter **p** *right-click*
Select extrusion path or [Taper angle]: *pick* the path
Command:

The Revolve tool

The **Revolve** tool can be called either with a *click* on its tool icon in the
Modeling toolbar, or by a *click* on its tool icon in the **3D Make** control
panel, or by a *click* on its name in the **Modeling** sub-menu of the **Draw**
drop-down menu, or by *entering* **revolve**, or its abbreviation **rev**, at the
command line.

Examples of the use of the Revolve tool

Solids of revolution can be constructed from closed plines or from regions.

First example – Revolve (13.16)

1. Construct the closed polyline in Fig. 13.15.
2. Set **ISOLINES** to **24**.
3. Call the **Revolve** tool from the **3D Make** control panel (Fig. 13.4). The
   command line shows:

Command:
Command: _revolve
Current wire frame density: ISOLINES=24

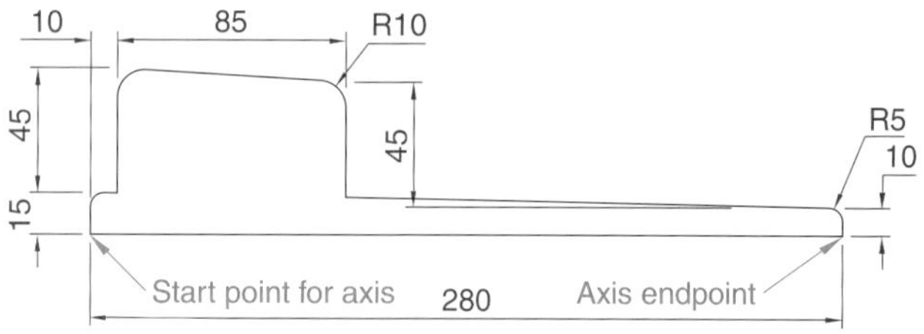

Fig. 13.15 First example –
Revolve. The closed pline

Fig. 13.16 First example –
Revolve

Select objects to revolve: *pick* the polyline **1 found**
Select objects to revolve: *right-click*
Specify axis start point or define axis by [Object/X/Y/Z] <Object>:
      pick
Specify axis endpoint: *pick*
Specify angle of revolution or [STart angle] <360>: *right-click*
Command:

4. Place in the **Southwest Isometric** view. **Zoom** to **1**.

Second example – Revolve (Fig. 13.18)

1. Place the screen in the **Front** view. **Zoom** to **1**.
2. Construct the pline outline (Fig. 13.17).
3. Set **ISOLINES** to **24**.
4. Call the **Revolve** tool and construct a solid of revolution.
5. Place the screen in the **Southwest Isometric** view. **Zoom** to **1**.

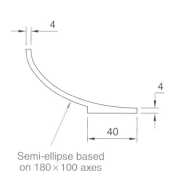

Fig. 13.17 Second example –
Revolve. The pline outline

Third example – Revolve (Fig. 13.19)

1. Construct the pline (left-hand drawing of Fig. 13.19). The drawing must be either a closed pline or a region.
2. Call **Revolve** and form a solid of revolution through 180°.
3. Place the model in the **Northeast Isometric** view. **Zoom** to **1**.

Other tools from the 3D Make control panel

First example – Box (Fig. 13.20)

1. Place the window in the **Front** view.
2. *Click* the **Box** tool icon in the **3D Make** control panel. The command line shows:

Fig. 13.18 Second example –
Revolve

Command: _box
Specify first corner or [Center]: *enter* **90, 90** *right-click*
Specify other corner or [Cube/Length]: *enter* **110,−30** *right-click*
Specify height or [2Point]: *enter* **75** *right-click*
Command: *right-click*
BOX Specify first corner or [Center]: 110,90
Specify other corner or [Cube/Length]: 170,70
Specify height or [2Point]: 75
Command:

BOX Specify first corner or [Center]: 110,−10
Specify other corner or [Cube/Length]: 200,−30
Specify height or [2Point]: 75
Command:

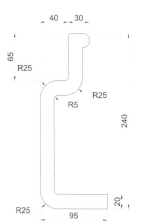
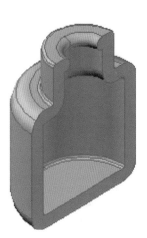

Fig. 13.19 Third example –
Revolve. The outline to be
revolved and the solid of
revolution

3. Place in the **Southeast Isometric View** and **Zoom** to **1**.
4. Call the **Union** tool from the **3D Make** control panel. The command line shows:

Command:_union
Select objects: *pick* one of the boxes **1 found**
Select objects: *pick* the second box **1 found, 2 total**
Select objects: *pick* the third box **1 found, 3 total**
Select objects: *right-click*
Command:

And the three boxes are joined in a single union.

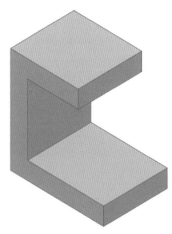

Fig. 13.20 First example – **3D Objects**

Second example – Sphere and Cylinder (Fig. 13.21)

1. Set **ISOLINES** to **16**.
2. *Click* the **Sphere** tool icon from the **3D Make** control panel. The command line shows:

Command: _sphere
Specify center point or [3P/2P/Ttr]: 180,170
Specify radius or [Diameter]: 50
Command:

3. *Click* the **Cylinder** tool icon in the **3D Make** control panel. The command line shows:

Command: _cylinder
Specify center point of base or [3P/2P/Ttr/Elliptical]: 180,170
Specify base radius or [Diameter]: 25
Specify height or [2Point/Axis endpoint]: 110
Command:

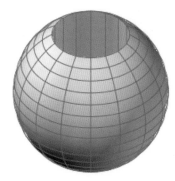

Fig. 13.21 Second example – **3D Objects**

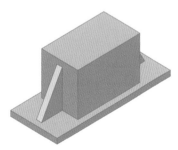

4. Place the screen in the **Front** view and **Zoom** to **1**.
5. With the **Move** tool (from the **2D Draw** control panel), move the cylinder vertically down so that the bottom of the cylinder is at the bottom of the sphere.
6. *Click* the **Subtract** tool icon in the **3D Make** control panel. The command line shows:

   Command: _subtract Select solids and regions to subtract from...
   Select objects: *pick* the sphere **1 found**
   Select objects: *right-click*
   Select solids and regions to subtract
   Select objects: *pick* the cylinder **1 found**
   Select objects: *right-click*
   Command:

7. Place the screen in the **3D Views/SW Isometric** view and **Zoom** to **1**.
8. Call **Hide**.

Fig. 13.22 Third example – **3D Objects**

Third example – Cylinder, Cone and Sphere (Fig. 13.22)

1. Call the **Cylinder** tool and with a centre **170,150** construct a cylinder of radius **60** and height **15**.
2. *Click* the **Cone** in the **3D Make** control panel. The command line shows:

   Command: _cone
   Specify center point of base or [3P/2P/Ttr/Elliptical]: 170,150
   Specify base radius or [Diameter]: 40
   Specify height or [2Point/Axis endpoint/Top radius]: 150
   Command:

3. Call the **Sphere** tool and construct a sphere of centre **170,150** and radius **45**.
4. Place the screen in the **Front** view and with the **Move** tool, move the cone and sphere so that the cone is resting on the cylinder and the centre of the sphere is at the apex of the cone.
5. Place in the **Southwest Isometric** view, **Zoom** to **1** and with **Union** form a single 3D model from the three objects.

Fourth example – Box and Wedge (Fig. 13.23)

1. *Click* the **Box** tool icon in the **3D Make** control panel and construct two boxes: the first from corners **70,210** and **290,120** of height **10**, the second of corners **120,200,10** and **240,130,10** and of height **80**.
2. Place the screen in the **Front** view and **Zoom** to **1**.
3. *Click* the **Wedge** tool icon in the **3D Make** control panel. The command line shows:

   Command: _wedge
   Specify first corner or [Center]: 120,170,10
   Specify other corner or [Cube/Length]: 80,160,10
   Specify height or [2Point]: 70

Fig. 13.23 Fourth example – **3D Objects**

Fig. 13.24 Fifth example – **3D Objects**

Command: *right-click*
WEDGE
Specify first corner of wedge or [Center]: 240,170,10
Specify corner or [Cube/Length]: 280,160,10
Specify height or [2Point]: 70
Command:

4. Place the screen in the **Southwest Isometric** view and **Zoom** to **1**.
5. Call the **Union** tool from the **3D Make control panel** and in response to the prompts in the tool's sequences *pick* each of the four objects in turn to form a union of the four objects.

Fifth example – Cylinder and Torus (Fig. 13.24)

1. Using the **Cylinder** tool from the **3D Make control panel**, construct a cylinder of centre **180,160**, of radius **40** and height **120**.
2. *Click* the **Torus** tool icon in the **3D Make** control panel. The command line shows:

Command: _torus
Specify center point or [3P/2P/Ttr]: 180,160,10
Specify radius or [Diameter]: 40
Specify tube radius or [2Point/Diameter]: 10
Command: *right-click*
TORUS
Specify center point or [3P/2P/Ttr]: 180,160,110
Specify radius or [Diameter] <40>: *right-click*
Specify tube radius or [2Point/Diameter] <10>: *right-click*
Command:

3. Call the **Cylinder** tool and construct another cylinder of centre **180,160**, of radius **35** and height **120**.
4. Place in the **Southwest Isometric** view and **Zoom** to **1**.
5. *Click* the **Union** tool icon in the **3D Make control panel** and form a union of the larger cylinder and the two torii.
6. *Click* the **Subtract** tool icon in the **3D Make** control panel and subtract the smaller cylinder from the union.

The Chamfer and Fillet tools

The **Chamfer** and **Fillet** tools from the **2D Draw** control panel (Fig. 13.25), which are used to create chamfers and fillets in 2D drawings in AutoCAD 2008, can just as well be used when constructing 3D models.

Example – Chamfer and Fillet (Fig. 13.28)

1. Using the **Box** and **Cylinder** tools, construct the 3D model in Fig. 13.26.
2. Place in the **Southwest Isometric** view. **Union** the two boxes and, with the **Subtract** tool, subtract the cylinders from the union (Fig. 13.27).

2D Draw
Chamfer
Fillet

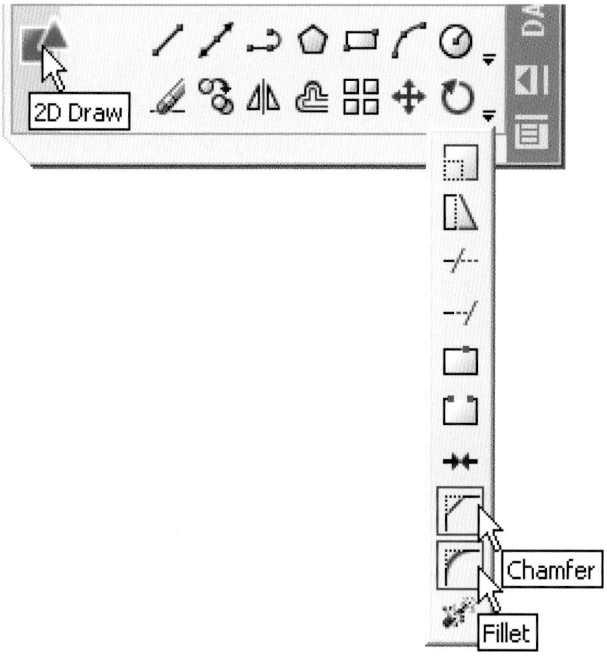

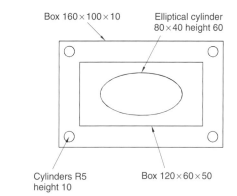

Fig. 13.25 The **Chamfer** and **Fillet** tools in the **2D Draw** control panel

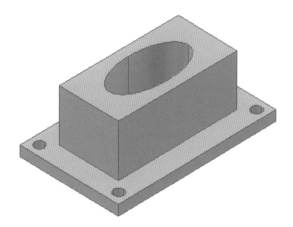

Box 160 × 100 × 10
Elliptical cylinder 80 × 40 height 60
Cylinders R5 height 10
Box 120 × 60 × 50

Fig. 13.26 Example – **Chamfer and Fillet** – the model before using the tools

Fig. 13.27 Example – isometric view – **Chamfer and Fillet** – the model before using the tools

Note

To construct the elliptical cylinder:

Command: _cylinder
Specify center point of base or [3P/2P/Ttr/Elliptical]: *enter* **e** *right-click*
Specify endpoint of first axis or [Center]: 130,160
Specify other endpoint of first axis: 210,160
Specify endpoint of second axis: 170,180
Specify height or [2Point/Axis endpoint]: 50
Command:

3. *Click* the **Fillet** tool icon in the **2D Draw** control panel (Fig. 13.25). The command line shows:

Command:_fillet
Current settings: Mode = TRIM. Radius = 1
Specify first object or [Undo/Polyline/Radius/Trim/Multiple]: *enter* **r** (Radius) *right-click*
Specify fillet radius <1>: 10
Select first object: *pick* one corner
Select an edge or [Chain/Radius]: *pick* a second corner
Select an edge or [Chain/Radius]: *pick* a third corner
Select an edge or [Chain/Radius]: *pick* the fourth corner
Select an edge or [Chain/Radius]: *right-click*
4 edge(s) selected for fillet.
Command:

4. *Click* the **Chamfer** tool icon in the **2D Draw** control panel (Fig. 13.25). The command line shows:

Command:_chamfer
(TRIM mode) Current chamfer Dist1 = 1, Dist2 = 1
Select first line or [Undo/Polyline/Distance/Angle/Trim/mEthod/ Multiple] *enter* **d** (Distance) *right-click*
Specify first chamfer distance <1>: 10
Specify second chamfer distance <10>: *right-click*
Select first line: *pick* one corner – One side of the box highlights
Base surface selection... Enter surface selection [Next/OK (current)] <OK>: *right-click*
Specify base surface chamfer distance <10>: *right-click*
Specify other surface chamfer distance <10>: *right-click*
Select an edge or [Loop]: *pick* the edge again **Select an edge:** *pick* the second edge
Select an edge [or Loop]: *right-click*
Command:

And two edges are chamfered. Repeat to chamfer the other two edges (Fig. 13.28).

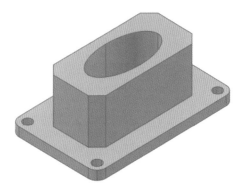

Fig. 13.28 Example – **Chamfer and Fillet**

Note on the tools Union, Subtract and Intersect

The tools **Union, Subtract** and **Intersect** found in the **Solids Editing** toolbar are known as the **Boolean** operators after the mathematician Boolean. They can be used to form unions, subtractions or intersection between extrusions, solids of revolution or any of the 3D Objects.

Note on using 2D Draw tools on 3D models

As was seen above when using the **Move, Chamfer** and **Fillet** tools from the **2D Draw** control panel, so also can other tools like **Copy, Mirror, Rotate** and **Scale** from the control panel be used in connection with the construction of 3D models.

Constructing 3D surfaces using the Extrude tool

In this example of the construction of a 3D surface model the use of the **DYN** (Dynamic input) method of construction will be shown.

1. Place the AutoCAD drawing area in the **SW Isometric** view.
2. *Click* the **DYN** button in the status bar to make dynamic input active.

Example (Fig. 13.31)

1. Using the **line** tool construct the outline in Fig. 13.29.
2. Call the **Extrude** tool and *window* the line outline.
3. Extrude to a height of **100**.
4. In the **Visual Styles** control panel *click* the **Visual Styles** button and in the dialog which appears *click* the **3D Hidden** icon (Fig. 13.30). All lines behind the surfaces are hidden (Fig. 13.31).

The stages of producing the extrusion are shown in Fig. 13.29. The resulting 3D model is a surface model.

The Sweep tool

The modelling tool **Sweep** is new to AutoCAD 2008. To call the tool *click* on its tool icon in the **3D Make** control panel (Fig. 13.4, page 197).

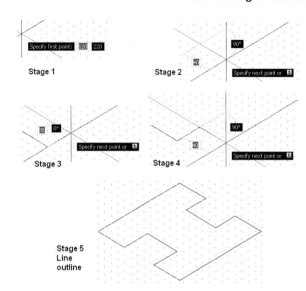

Fig. 13.29 Example – constructing
the line outline

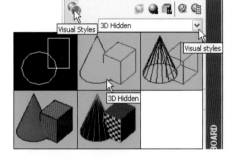

Fig. 13.30 Calling **3D Hidden**
from the **Visual Styles** dialog

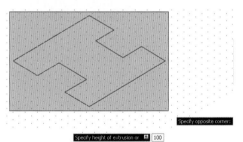

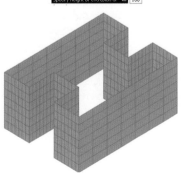

Fig. 13.31 Example – constructing
3D surfaces using the **Extrude**
tool

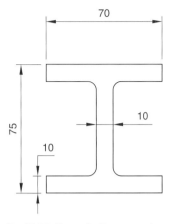

Fig. 13.32 Example **Sweep** – the outline to be swept

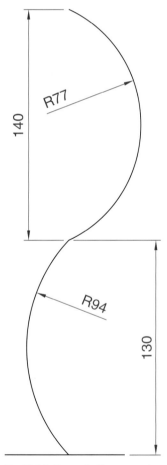

Fig. 13.33 Example **Sweep** – the pline path

Example – Sweep (Fig. 13.34)

1. Construct the pline outline in Fig. 13.32 in the **Top** view.
2. Change to the **3D Views/Front** view, **Zoom** to **1** and construct a pline as shown in Fig. 13.33 as a path central to the ellipse.
3. Place the window in the **3D Views/SW Isometric** view and *click* the **Sweep** tool icon. The command line shows:

Command: _sweep
Current wire frame density: ISOLINES=4
Select objects to sweep: *pick* the ellipse **1 found**
Select objects to sweep: *right-click*
Select sweep path or [Alignment/Base point/Scale/Twist]: *pick* the pline
Command:

4. From the **Visual Styles** control panel set the model to **3D Hidden**.

The result is shown in Fig. 13.34.

The Loft tool

The modelling tool **Loft** is new to AutoCAD 2008. To call the tool *click* on its tool icon in the **3D Make** control panel (Fig. 13.4, page 197).

Example – Loft (Fig. 13.37)

1. Construct the seven circles shown in Fig. 13.35 at vertical distances of **30** units apart.
2. Place the drawing area in the **Southwest Isometric** view.
3. Call the **Loft** tool with a *click* on its tool icon in the **3D Make** control panel (Fig. 13.4, page 197).
4. The command line shows:

Command: _loft
Select cross-sections in lofting order: <Snap off> *pick* the bottom circle **1 found**
Select cross-sections in lofting order: *pick* the next circle **1 found, 2 total**
Select cross-sections in lofting order: *pick* the next circle **1 found, 3 total**
Select cross-sections in lofting order: *pick* the next circle **1 found, 4 total**
Select cross-sections in lofting order: *pick* the next circle **1 found, 5 total**
Select cross-sections in lofting order: *pick* the next circle **1 found, 6 total**
Select cross-sections in lofting order: *pick* the next circle **1 found, 7 total**
Select cross-sections in lofting order: *right-click*

And the **Loft Settings** dialog appears (Fig. 13.36).

Fig. 13.34 Example – **Sweep**

5. *Click* the **Smooth Fit** button, followed by a *click* on the **OK** button. The loft appears.
6. From the **Visual Styles** control panel set the model to **3D Hidden**.

The result is shown in Fig. 13.37.

Revision notes

1. In the AutoCAD 3D coordinate system, positive Z is towards the operator away from the monitor screen.
2. A 3D face is a mesh behind which other details can be hidden.
3. **3D Hidden** from the **Visual Styles** control panel can be used to hide details behind the 3D meshes of 3D solid models.
4. The **Extrude** tool can be used for extruding closed plines or regions to stated heights, to stated slopes or along paths.
5. The **Revolve** tool can be used for constructing solids of revolution through any angle up to 360°.
6. 3D models can be constructed from the 3D Objects **Box, Sphere, Cylinder, Cone, Torus** and **Wedge**. Extrusions and/or solids of revolutions may form part of models constructed using the 3D Objects.
7. Tools such as **Chamfer** and **Fillet** from the **Modify** toolbar can be used when constructing 3D models.

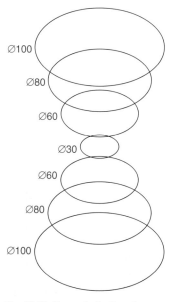

Fig. 13.35 Example **Loft** – the cross sections

Fig. 13.36 The **Loft Settings** dialog

Fig. 13.37 Example **Loft**

8. The tools **Union, Subtract** and **Intersect** are known as the **Boolean** operators.
9. When outlines which are not closed polylines or regions are acted upon by the **Extrude** tool the resulting models will be 3D Surface models.

Exercises

The exercises which follow require using tools from the **3D Make** control panel in association with tools from other control panels.

1. Fig. 13.38 shows the pline outline from which the polysolid outline in Fig. 13.39 has been constructed to a height of **100** and Width of **3**. When the polysolid has been constructed, construct extrusions which can then be subtracted from the polysolid. Sizes of the extrusions are left to your judgement.

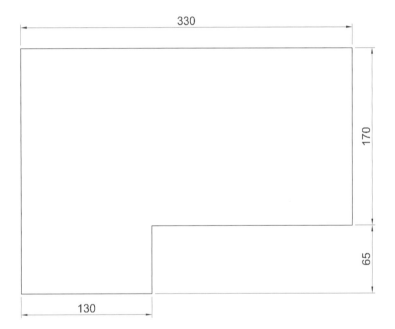

Fig. 13.38 Exercise 1 – outline for polyline

2. Fig. 13.40 shows a 3D model constructed from four polysolids which have been formed into a union using the **Union** tool from the **3D Make** control panel. The original polysolid was formed from a hexagon of edge length **30**. The original polysolid was of height **40** and Width **5**. Construct the union.

3. Fig. 13.41 shows the 3D model from Exercise 2 acted upon by the **Presspull** tool from the **3D Make** control panel (Fig. 13.42).

   With the 3D model from Exercise 2 on screen and using the **Presspull** tool, construct the 3D model shown in Fig. 13.41. The distance of the pull can be estimated.

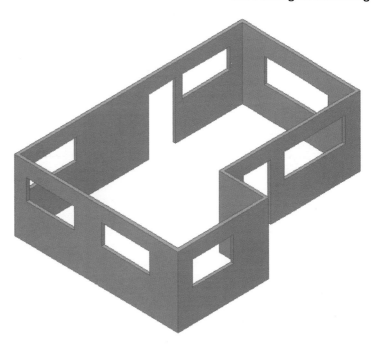

Fig. 13.39 Exercise 1

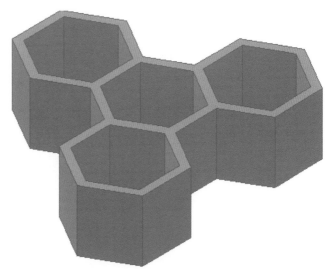

Fig. 13.40 Exercise 2

4. Construct the 3D model of a wine glass as shown in Fig. 13.44, working to the dimensions given in the outline drawing in Fig. 13.43.

You will need to construct the outline and change it into a region
before being able to change the outline into a solid of revolution using
the **Revolve** tool. This is because the semi-elliptical part of the outline
has been constructed using the **Ellipse** tool, resulting in part of the outline being a spline, which cannot be acted upon by **Polyline Edit** to
form a closed pline.

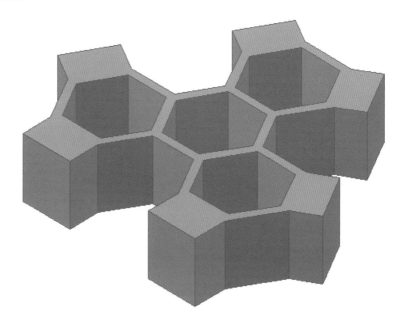

Fig. 13.41 Exercise 3

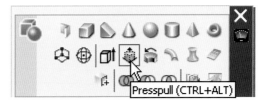

Fig. 13.42 Exercise 3 – the **Presspull** tool from the **3D Make** control panel

Fig. 13.43 Exercise 4 – outline drawing

Fig. 13.44 Exercise 4

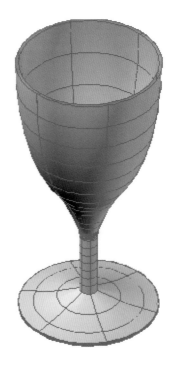

5. Fig. 13.45 shows the outline from which a solid of revolution can be constructed. Using the **Revolve** tool construct the solid of revolution.

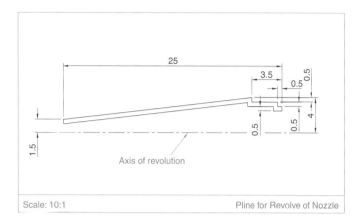

Fig. 13.45 Exercise 5

6. Construct the 3D solid model of a bracket, working to the information given in Fig. 13.46.

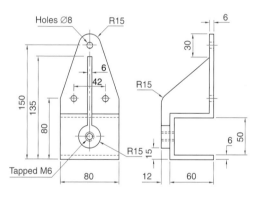

Fig. 13.46 Exercise 6

7. Working to the dimensions given in Fig. 13.47, construct an extrusion of the plate to a height of **5** units.

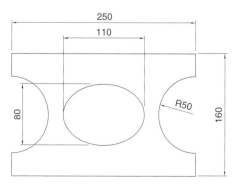

Fig. 13.47 Exercise 7

8. Working to the details given in the orthographic projection in Fig. 13.48, construct a 3D model of the assembly.

After constructing the pline outline(s) required for the solid(s) of revolution, use the **Revolve** tool to form the 3D solid.

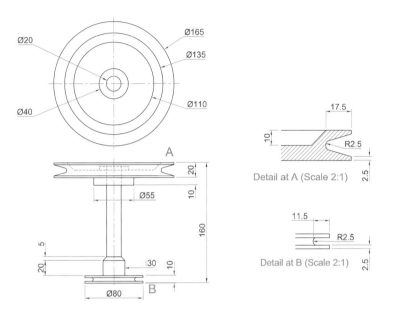

Fig. 13.48 Exercise 8

9. Working to the polylines shown in Fig. 13.49, construct the **Sweep** shown in Fig. 13.50.

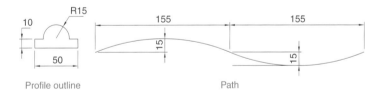

Fig. 13.49 Exercise 9 – profile and path dimensions

Profile outline   Path

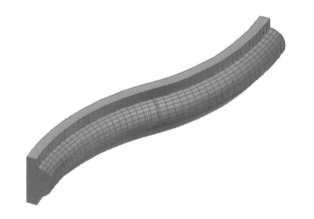

Fig. 13.50 Exercise 9

10. Construct the cross sections as shown in Fig. 13.51, working to suitable dimensions. From the cross sections construct the lofts shown in Fig. 13.52. The lofts are topped with a sphere constructed using the **Sphere** tool.

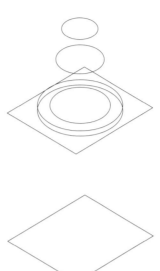

Fig. 13.51 The cross sections for Exercise 10

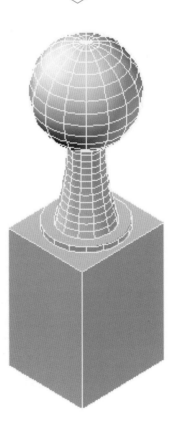

Fig. 13.52 Exercise 10

CHAPTER 14

3D models in viewports

Aim of this chapter

To give examples of 3D solid models constructed in multiple viewport settings.

Setting up viewport systems

One of the better methods of constructing 3D models is in different viewport settings. This allows what is being constructed to be seen from a variety of viewing positions. To set up a new viewport system:

1. *Click* **View** in the menu bar and from the drop-down menu which appears *click* **Viewports** and in the sub-menu which then appears *click* **New Viewports...** (Fig. 14.1). The **Viewports** dialog appears (Fig. 14.2).

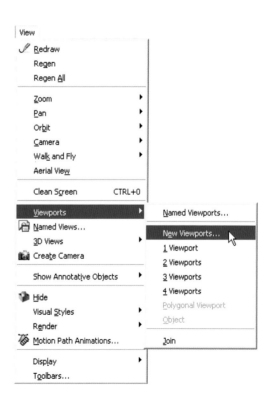

Fig. 14.1 Selecting **New Viewports...** from the **View** drop-down menu

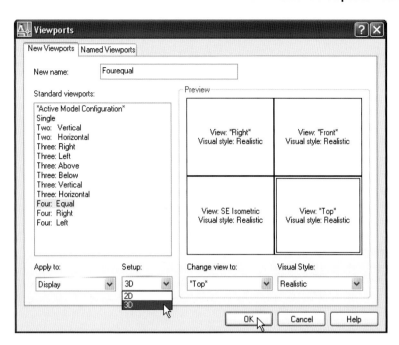

Fig. 14.2 The **Viewports** dialog

2. *Click* the **New Viewports** tab and a number of named viewports systems appears in the **Standard Viewports** list in the dialog.
3. *Click* the name **Four: Equal**, followed by a *click* on **3D** in the **Setup** popup list. A preview of the **Four: Equal** viewports screen appears showing the views appearing in each of the four viewports.
4. *Click* the **OK** button of the dialog and the AutoCAD 2008 drawing area appears showing the four viewport layout (Fig. 14.3).

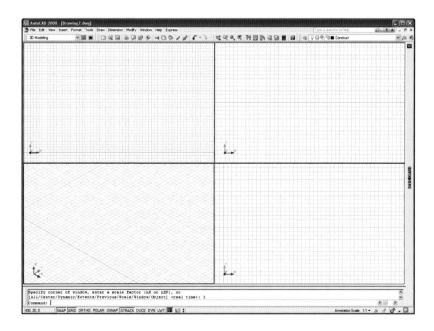

Fig. 14.3 The **Four: Equal** viewports layout

First example – Four: Equal viewports (Fig. 14.7)

Fig. 14.4 shows a first angle orthographic projection of a support. To construct a **Scale 1:1** 3D model of the support in a **Four: Equal** viewport setting:

1. *Click* **View** in the menu bar, followed by a *click* on **Viewports** in the drop-down menu, followed by another *click* on **New Viewports...** in the **Viewports** sub-menu. Make sure the **3D** option is selected from the **Setup** popup list and *click* the **OK** button of the dialog. The AutoCAD 2008 drawing area appears in a **Four: Equal** viewport setting.

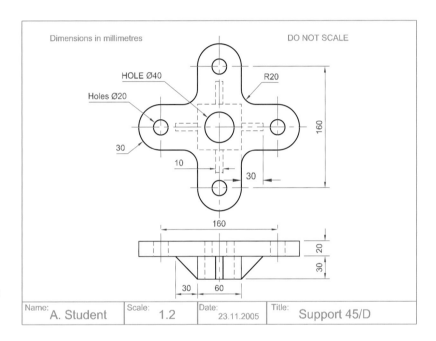

Fig. 14.4 Orthographic projection of the support for the first example

2. *Click* in each viewport in turn, making the selected viewport active, and **Zoom** to **1**.
3. Set **ISOLINES** to **4**.
4. Using the **Polyline** tool, construct the outline of the plan view of the plate of the support, including the holes (Fig. 14.5). Note the views in the other viewports.
5. Call the **Extrude** tool from the **Solids** toolbar and extrude the plan outline and the circles to a height of **20**.
6. With the **Subtract** tool from the **Solids Editing** toolbar, subtract the holes from the plate (Fig. 14.6).
7. Call the **Box** tool and in the centre of the plate construct a box of Width=**60**, Length=**60** and Height=**30**.
8. Call the **Cylinder** tool and in the centre of the box construct a cylinder of Radius=**20** and Height=**30**.
9. Call **Subtract** and subtract the cylinder from the box.

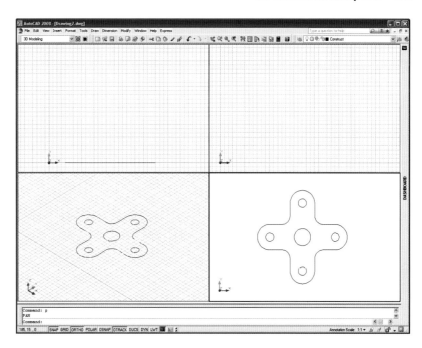

Fig. 14.5 The plan view drawn

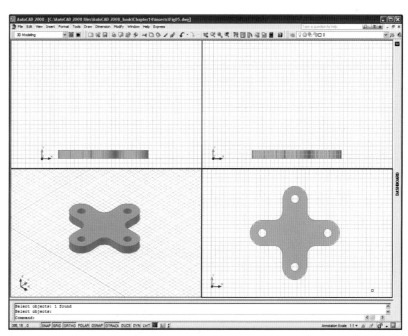

Fig. 14.6 The four views
after using the **Extrude** and
Subtract tools

10. *Click* in the **Right** viewport and with the **Move** tool, move the box
and its hole into the correct position with regard to the plate.
11. With **Union**, form a union of the plate and box.
12. *Click* in the **Front** viewport and construct a triangle for one of the
webs attached between the plate and the box. With **Extrude**, extrude

the triangle to a height of **10**. With the **Mirror** tool, mirror the web to the other side of the box.

13. *Click* in the **Right** viewport and with the **Move** tool, move the two webs into their correct positions between the box and the plate. Then, with **Union**, form a union between the webs and the 3D model.

14. While in the **Right** viewport, construct the other two webs and in the **Front** viewport, move, mirror and union the webs as in steps **12** and **13**.

Fig. 14.7 shows the resulting four-viewport scene.

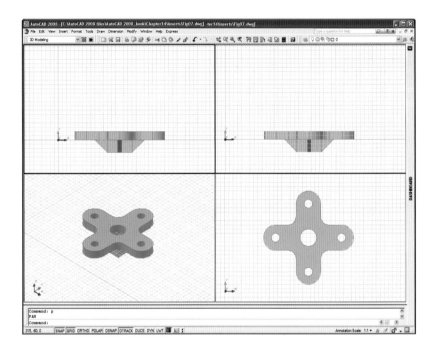

Fig. 14.7 First example – **Four: Equal viewports**

Second example – Four: Left viewports (Fig. 14.9)

1. Open the **Four: Left** viewport layout from the **Viewports** dialog.
2. Make a new layer of colour **Magenta** and make that layer current.
3. In the **Top** viewport construct an outline of the web of the Support Bracket shown in Fig. 14.8. With the **Extrude** tool, extrude the parts of the web to a height of **20**.
4. With the **Subtract** tool, subtract the holes from the web.
5. In the **Top** viewport, construct two cylinders central to the extrusion, one of radius **50** and height **30**, the second of radius **40** and height **30**. With the **Subtract** tool, subtract the smaller cylinder from the larger.
6. *Click* in the **Front** viewport and move the cylinders vertically by **5** units. With **Union** form a union between the cylinders and the web.

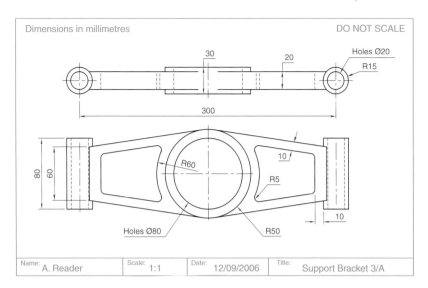

Fig. 14.8 Working drawing for the second example

7. Make the **Front** viewport active and at one end of the union, construct two cylinders, the first of radius **10** and height **80**, the second of radius **15** and height **80**. Subtract the smaller from the larger.

8. With the **Mirror** tool, mirror the cylinders to the other end of the union.

9. Make the **Top** viewport current and with the **Move** tool, move the cylinders to their correct positions at the ends of the union. Form a union between all parts on screen.

10. Make the **SE Isometric** viewport current. From the **Visual Styles** control panel popup list select **Conceptual**.

Fig. 14.9 shows the result.

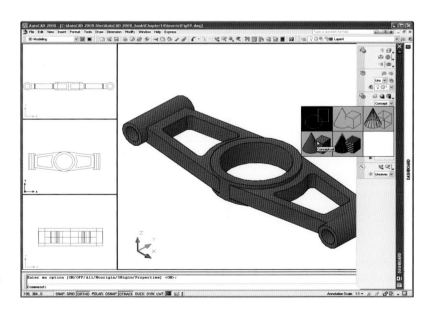

Fig. 14.9 Second example – **Four: Left viewports**

Third example – Three: Right viewports (Fig. 14.11)

1. Open the **Three: Right** viewport layout from the **Viewports** dialog. Make sure **3D** setup is chosen.
2. Make a new layer of colour **Green** and make that layer current.
3. In the **Front** viewport (top left-hand), construct a pline outline to the dimensions in Fig. 14.10.

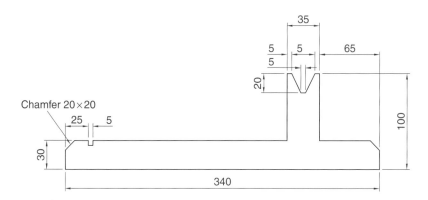

Fig. 14.10 Third example – outline for solid of revolution

4. Call the **Revolve** tool from the **3D Make** control panel and revolve the outline through 360°.
5. Make the **SE Isometric** viewport current. In the **Visual Styles** control panel select **Conceptual** from its popup list.

The result is shown in Fig. 14.11.

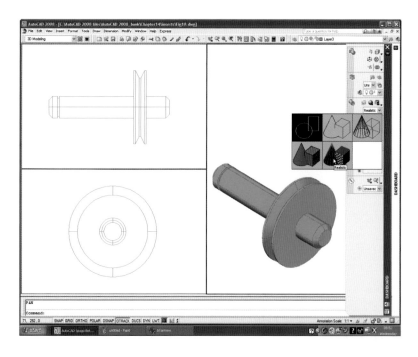

Fig. 14.11 Third example – **Three: Right viewports**

Notes

1. When working in viewport layouts such as in the above three examples, it is important to make good use of the **Zoom** tool, mainly because the viewports are smaller than the single viewport when working in AutoCAD 2008.
2. As in all other forms of constructing drawings in AutoCAD 2008 frequent toggling of **SNAP, ORTHO** and **GRID** will allow speedier and more accurate working.

Revision notes

1. Outlines suitable for use when constructing 3D models can be constructed using the 2D tools such as **Line, Arc, Circle** and **Polyline**. Such outlines must be changed either to closed polylines or to regions before being incorporated in 3D models.
2. The use of multiple viewports can be of value when constructing 3D models in that various views of the model appear enabling the operator to check the accuracy of the 3D appearance throughout the construction period.

Exercises

1. Using the **Cylinder, Box, Sphere, Wedge** and **Fillet** tools, together with the **Union** and **Subtract** tools and working to any sizes thought suitable, construct the 'head' as shown in the **Three: Right** viewport in Fig. 14.12.

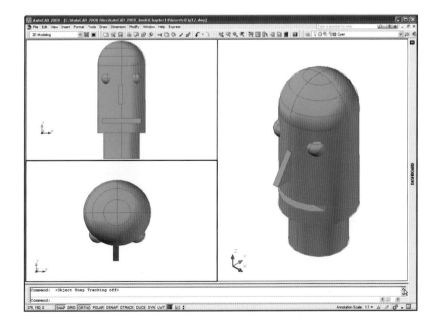

Fig. 14.12 Exercise 1

2. Using the tools **Sphere, Box, Union** and **Subtract** and working to the dimensions given in Fig. 14.14, construct the 3D solid model as shown in the isometric drawing in Fig. 14.13.

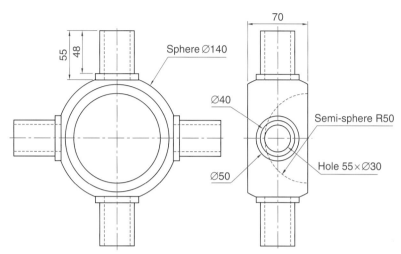

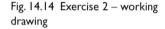

Fig. 14.13 Exercise 2

Fig. 14.14 Exercise 2 – working drawing

3. Each link of the chain shown in Fig. 14.15 has been constructed using the **Extrude** tool, extruding a small circle along an elliptical path. Copies of the link were then made, half of which were rotated in a **Right** view and then moved into their positions relative to the other links. Working to suitable sizes, construct a link and from the link construct the chain as shown.

Fig. 14.15 Exercise 3

4. A two-view orthographic projection of a rotatable lever from a machine is given in Fig. 14.16, together with an isometric drawing

of the 3D model constructed to the details given in the drawing in
Fig. 14.17. Construct the 3D model drawing in a **Four: Equal** viewport setting.

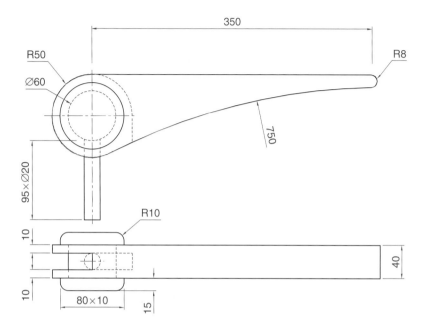

Fig. 14.16 Exercise 4 –
orthographic projection

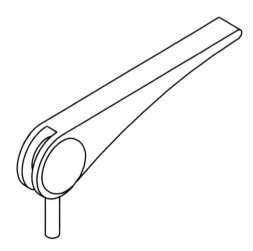

Fig.14.17 Exercise 4

5. Working in a **Three: Left** viewport setting, construct a 3D model of
the faceplate to the dimensions given in Fig. 14.18. With the **Mirror**
tool, mirror the model to obtain an opposite facing model. In the
Isometric viewport call the **Hide** tool (Fig. 14.19).

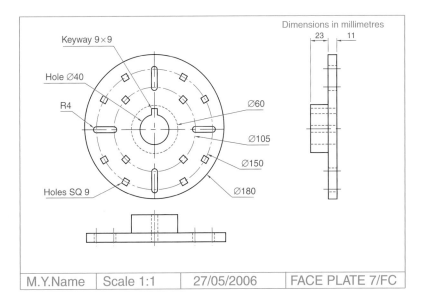

Fig. 14.18 Exercise 5 – dimensions

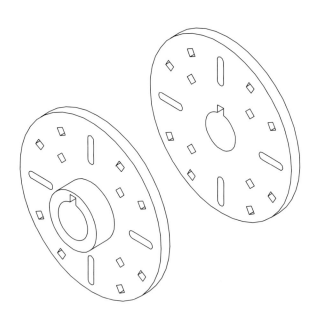

Fig. 14.19 Exercise 5

CHAPTER 15

The modification of 3D models

Aims of this chapter

1. To demonstrate how 3D models can be saved as blocks for insertion into other drawings via the DesignCenter.
2. To show how a library of 3D models in the form of blocks can be constructed to enable the models to be inserted into other drawings.
3. To give examples of the use of the tools from the **Operations** submenu from the **Modify** drop-down menu:

   3D Array – Rectangular and Polar 3D arrays
   Mirror 3D
   Rotate 3D.

4. To give examples of the use of the **Section Plane** tool from the **3D Make** control panel.
5. To give examples of the use of the **Helix** tool.
6. To give a further example of construction involving the **DYN** method.
7. To show how to obtain different views of 3D models in 3D space using:

   Views from the 3D **Navigate** drop-down menu
   Viewpoint Presets.

Creating 3D model libraries

In the same way as 2D drawings of parts such as electronics symbols, engineering parts, building symbols and the like can be saved in a file as blocks and then opened into another drawing by *dragging* the appropriate block drawing from the DesignCenter, so can 3D models.

First example – inserting 3D blocks (Fig. 15.4)

1. Construct individual 3D models of the parts for a lathe milling wheel holder to details as given in Fig. 15.1 on layers of different colours.
2. Save each of the 3D models of the parts to file names as given in Fig. 15.1 as blocks using the **Make Block** tool from the **2D Draw** control panel. When all seven blocks have been saved, the drawings on screen can be deleted. Save the drawing with its blocks to a suitable file name. In this example this is **Fig01.dwg**.
3. Set up a **Four: Equal** viewports setting.

Flat 12x5

Nut 15xØ25
tapped M8x1.5

Washers 20xR9
with hole Ø8

M8

20

R8

29

Arms (2) 60x16x15

Screw
75xØ8

10

23

15

2.5

20

10

Holes Ø8

32

T-Bar 90x15x10

R8

Pins (2)
20xØ6

Fig. 15.1 The components of a
lathe milling wheel holder

Fig. 15.2 Calling the
DesignCenter to screen

4. Open the **DesignCenter** with a *click* on its icon in the **Standard** toolbar (Fig. 15.2), or by pressing the **Ctrl** and **2** keys of the keyboard.
5. In the **DesignCenter** *click* the directory **Chapter 15**, followed by another *click* on **Fig01.dwg** and yet another *click* on **Blocks**. The saved blocks appear as icons in the right-hand area of the **DesignCenter**.
6. *Drag* and *drop* the blocks one by one into one of the viewports on screen. Fig. 15.3 shows the **Nut** block ready to be *dragged* into position in the **Right** viewport. As the blocks are *dropped* on screen, they will need moving into their correct positions in relation to other parts of the assembly by using the **Move** tool from the **2D Draw** control panel in suitable viewports.
7. Using the **Move** tool, move the individual 3D models into their final places on screen and render the **Southeast Isometric** viewport. Shade using **Visual Styles/Conceptual** shading (Fig. 15.4).

Notes

1. It does not matter which of the four viewports any one of the blocks is *dragged* and *dropped* into – the part automatically assumes the view of the viewport.
2. If a block destined for layer **0** is *dragged* and *dropped* into the layer **Centre** (which in our **acadiso.dwt** is of colour **red** and linetype **CEN-TER2**), the block will take on the colour (red) and linetype of that layer (**CENTER2**).
3. In this example, the blocks are 3D models and there is no need to use the **Explode** tool option.

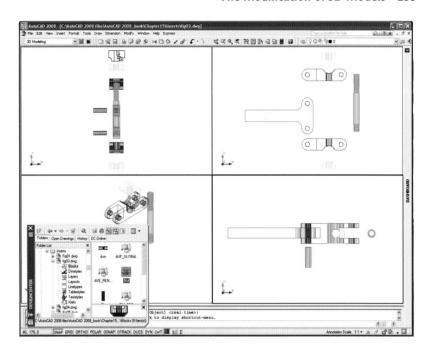

Fig. 15.3 First example –
inserting 3D blocks

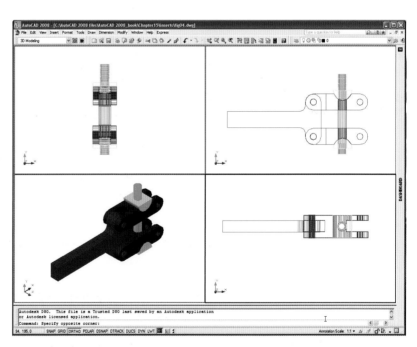

Fig. 15.4 First example –
inserting 3D blocks

Second example – a library of fastenings (Fig. 15.6)

1. Construct a number of engineering fastenings. The number constructed
does not matter. In this example only five have been constructed – a
10 mm round head rivet, a 20 mm countersunk head rivet, a cheese

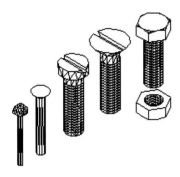

Fig. 15.5 Second example – the
five fastenings

head bolt, a countersunk head bolt and a hexagonal head bolt together
with its nut (Fig. 15.5). With the **Make Block** tool save each separately
as a block, erase the original drawings and save the file to a suitable
file name – in this example this is **Fig05.dwg**.

2. Open the DesignCenter, *click* on the **Chapter15** directory, followed by
   a *click* on **Fig05.dwg**. Then *click* again on **Blocks** in the content list of
   Fig05.dwg. The five 3D models of fastenings appear as icons in the
   right-hand side of the DesignCenter (Fig. 15.6).
3. Such engineering fastenings can be *dragged* and *dropped* into position
   in any engineering drawing where the fastenings are to be included.

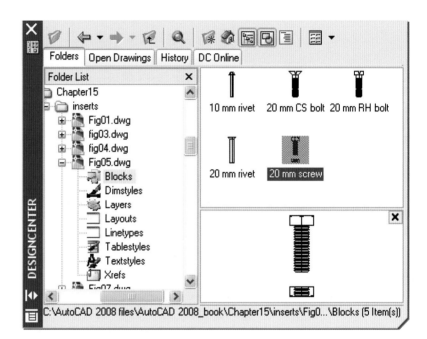

Fig. 15.5 Second example – the
five fastenings

Fig. 15.6 Second example – a
library of fastenings

Constructing a 3D model (Fig. 15.9)

A three-view projection of a pressure head is shown in Fig. 15.7. To construct a 3D model of the head:

1. From the **3D Navigate** control panel select the **Front** view.
2. Construct the outline to be formed into a solid of revolution (Fig. 15.8)
   on a layer colour magenta and with the **Revolve** tool, produce the 3D
   model of the outline.
3. Place the screen in the **3D Navigate/Top** view and with the **Cylinder**
   tool, construct cylinders as follows:
   (a) In the centre of the solid already constructed – radius **50** and
       height **50**.
   (b) With the same centre – radius **40** and height **40**. Subtract this
       cylinder from that of radius **50**.

Fig. 15.7 Orthographic drawing for the example of constructing a 3D model

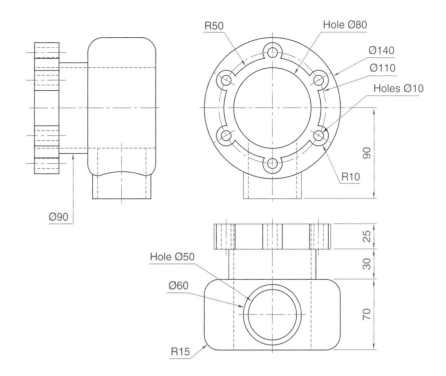

Fig. 15.8 Example of constructing a 3D model – outline for solid of revolution

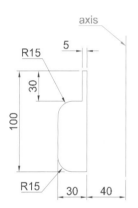

(c) At the correct centre – radius **10** and height **25**.

(d) At the same centre – radius **5** and height **25**. Subtract this cylinder from that of radius **10**.

4. With the **Array** tool, form a six times polar array of the last two cylinders based on the centre of the 3D model.

5. Place the drawing in the **Front** view.

6. With the **Move** tool, move the array and the other two cylinders to their correct positions relative to the solid of revolution so far formed.

7. With the **Union** tool form a union of the array and other two solids.

8. Place the screen in the **3D Navigate/Right** view.

9. Construct a cylinder of radius **30** and height **25** and another of radius **25** and height **60** central to the lower part of the 3D solid so far formed.

10. Place the screen in the **3D Navigate/Top** view and with the **Move** tool move the two cylinders into their correct positions relative to the 3D solid.

11. With **Union**, form a union between the radius **30** cylinder and the 3D model and with **Subtract**, subtract the radius **25** cylinder from the **3D** model.

12. *Click* **Visual Styles/Conceptual** (Fig. 15.9).

Note

Fig. 15.9 Example of constructing a 3D model

This 3D model could equally as well have been constructed in a three or four viewports setting.

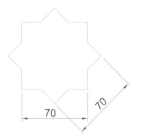

Fig. 15.10 Example – 3D Array –
the star pline

Fig. 15.11 Selecting **3D Array**
from the **Modify** drop-down
menu

The 3D Array tool

First example – a Rectangular Array (Fig. 15.12)

1. Construct the star-shaped pline on a layer colour green (Fig. 15.10) and extrude it to a height of **20**.
2. *Click* on **Modify** in the menu bar and in the drop-down menu which appears *click* on **3D Operation**, followed by another *click* on **3D Array** in the sub-menu which appears (Fig. 15.11). The command line shows:

Command:_3darray
Select objects: *pick* the extrusion **1 found**
Select objects: *right-click*
Enter the type of array [Rectangular/Polar] <R>: *right-click*
Enter the number of rows (—) <1>: *enter* **3** *right-click*
Enter the number of columns (III): *enter* **3** *right-click*
Enter the number of levels (...): *enter* **4** *right-click*
Specify the distance between rows (—): 100
Specify the distance between columns (III): 100
Specify the distance between levels (...): 300
Command:

3. Place the screen in the **3D Navigate/Southwest Isometric** view.
4. Shade using **Visual Styles/Conceptual** (Fig. 15.12).

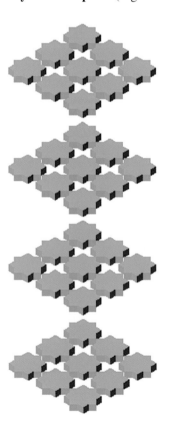

Fig. 15.12 First example – a
Rectangular Array

Second example – a Polar Array (Fig. 15.13)

1. Use the same star-shaped 3D model.
2. Call the **3D Array** tool again. The command line shows:

   Command:_3darray
   Select objects: *pick* the extrusion **1 found**
   Select objects: *right-click*
   Enter the type of array [Rectangular/Polar] <R>: *enter* p (Polar) *right-click*
   Enter number of items in the array: 12
   Specify the angle to fill (+=ccw, −=cw) <360>: *right-click*
   Rotate arrayed objects? [Yes/No] <Y>: *right-click*
   Specify center point of array: 235,125
   Specify second point on axis of rotation: 300,200
   Command:

3. Place the screen in the **3D Navigate/Southwest Isometric** view.
4. *Click* **Visual Styles/Conceptual** (Fig. 15.13).

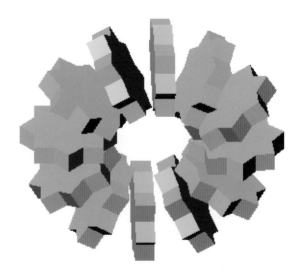

Fig. 15.13 Second example – a **Polar Array**

Third example – a Polar Array (Fig. 15.15)

1. Working on a layer of colour red, construct a solid of revolution in the form of an arrow to the dimensions as shown in Fig. 15.14.
2. Call **3D Array** from the **Modify** drop-down menu. The command line shows:

   Command: _3darray
   Select objects: *pick* the arrow **1 found**
   Select objects: *right-click*
   Enter the type of array [Rectangular/Polar] <R>: *enter* **p** *right-click*
   Enter the number of items in the array: *enter* **12** *right-click*

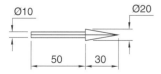

Fig. 15.14 Third example – a **Polar Array** – the 3D model to be arrayed

Specify the angle to fill (+=ccw, −=cw) <360>: *right-click*
Rotate arrayed objects? [Yes/No] <Y>: *right-click*
Specify center point of array: *enter* **40,170,20** *right-click*
Specify second point on axis of rotation: *enter* **60,200,100** *right-click*
Command:

3. Place the array in the **3D Navigate/Southwest Isometric** view and shade to **Visual Styles/Realistic**. The result is shown in Fig. 15.15.

Fig. 15.15 Third example – a
Polar Array

The Mirror 3D tool

First example – Mirror 3D (Fig. 15.17)

1. Working on a layer colour magenta, construct the outline in Fig. 15.16.
2. Extrude the outline to a height of **20**.
3. Extrude the region to a height of **5** and render. A **Visual Styles/ Conceptual** style shading is shown in Fig. 15.17 (left-hand drawing).
4. *Click* on **Mirror 3D** in the **3D Operations** sub-menu of the **Modify** drop-down menu. The command line shows:

Command:_mirror3d
Select objects: *pick* the extrusion **1 found**
Select objects: *right-click*
Specify first point of mirror plane (3 points): *pick*
Specify second point on mirror plane: *pick*
Specify third point on mirror plane or [Object/Last/Zaxis/View/ XY/YZ/ZX/3points]: *enter* **.xy** *right-click* **of (need Z):** *enter* **1** *right-click*
Delete source objects? [Yes/No] <N>: *right-click*
Command:

The result is shown in the right-hand illustration of Fig. 15.17.

Second example – Mirror 3D (Fig. 15.19)

1. Construct a solid of revolution in the shape of a bowl in the **3D Navigate/Front** view (Fig. 15.18).
2. *Click* **Mirror 3D** in the **3D Operations** sub-menu of the **Modify** drop-down menu. The command line shows:

Command:_mirror3d
Select objects: *pick* the bowl **1 found**
Select objects: *right-click*

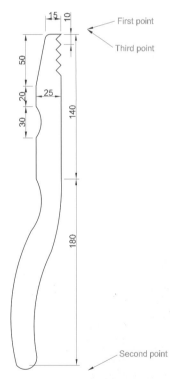

Fig. 15.16 First example – **Mirror 3D** – outline of object to be mirrored

Fig. 15.17 First example – **Mirror 3D** – before and after mirror

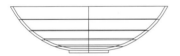

Fig. 15.18 Second example **Mirror 3D** – the 3D model

Specify first point of mirror plane (3 points): *pick*
Specify second point on mirror plane: *pick*
Specify third point on mirror plane: *enter* **.xy** *right-click*
(need Z): *enter* **1** *right-click*
Delete source objects:? [Yes/No] <N>: *right-click*
Command:

3. Place in the **3D Navigate/Southwest Isometric** view.
4. *Click* **Visual Styles/Conceptual**. The result is shown in Fig. 15.19.

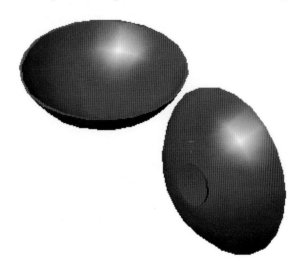

Fig. 15.19 Second example – **Mirror 3D** – the result in a front view

The Rotate 3D tool

Example – Rotate 3D (Fig. 15.20)

1. Use the same 3D model of a bowl as in the last example. Call the **Rotate 3D** tool from the **3D Operations** sub-menu of the **Modify** drop-down menu.
2. The command line shows:

   Command: _3DROTATE
   Current positive angle in UCS: ANGDIR=counterclockwise
       ANGBASE=0
   Select objects: *pick* the bowl **1 found**
   Select objects: *right-click*
   Specify base point: *pick* the centre bottom of the bowl
   Specify rotation angle or [Copy/Reference] <0>: *enter* **60** *right-click*
   Command:

3. Place in the **3D Navigate/Southwest Isometric** view and *click* **Visual Styles/Conceptual**.

The result is shown in Fig. 15.20.

The Slice tool

First example – Slice (Fig. 15.24)

1. Construct a 3D model of the rod link device shown in the two-view projection in Fig. 15.21 on a layer colour green.

Fig. 15.20 Example – **Rotate 3D**

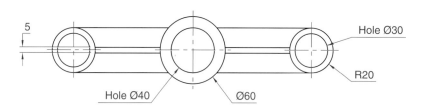

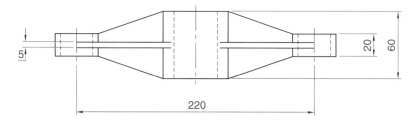

Fig. 15.21 First example – **Slice** – the two-view drawing

2. Place the 3D model in the **3D Navigate/Top** view.
3. Call the **Slice** tool from the **Modify/3D Operations** sub-menu (Fig. 15.22).

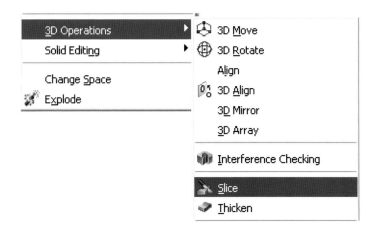

Fig. 15.22 The **Slice** tool icon
from the **Modify** toolbar

The command line shows (Fig. 15.23 shows the *picked* points):

Command:_slice
Select objects: *pick* the 3D model
Select objects to slice: *right-click*
**Specify start point of slicing plane or [planar Object/Surface/
    Zaxis/View/XY/YZ/ZX/3points] <3points>:** *pick*
Specify second point on plane: *pick*
Specify a point on desired side or [keep Both sides] <Both>: *right-
    click*
Command:

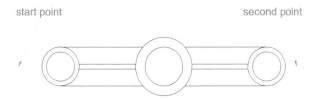

start point   second point

Fig. 15.23 First example – **Slice** –
the *pick* points

4. With the **Move** tool, move the lower half of the sliced model away
   from the upper half.
5. Place the 3D model(s) in a **Southwest Isometric** view.
6. *Click* **Visual Styles/Conceptual**. The result is shown in Fig. 15.24.

Second example – Slice (Fig. 15.25)

1. Construct the closed pline (left-hand drawing of Fig. 15.25) and with
   the **Revolve** tool, form a solid of revolution from the pline.
2. With the **Slice** tool and working to the same sequence as for the first
   Slice example, form two halves of the 3D model and render.

Fig. 15.24 First example – **Slice**

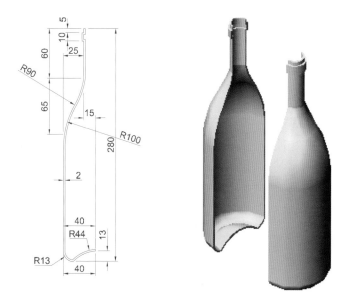

Fig. 15.25 Second example –
Slice

The Section tool

First example – Section Plane (Fig. 15.27)

1. Construct a 3D model to the information given in Fig. 15.26 on layers of different colours. Note there are three objects in the model – a box, a lid and a cap.

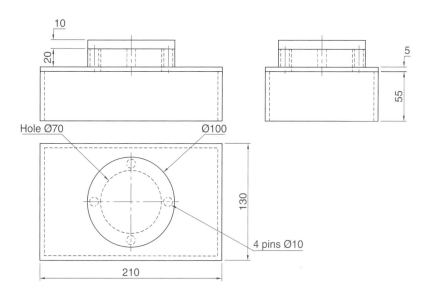

Fig. 15.26 First example –
Section – orthographic
projection

2. Place the model in the **Top** view.
3. *Click* the **Section Plane** tool icon in the **3D Make** control panel. The command line shows:

Command: _sectionplane Select face or any point to locate section line or [Draw section/Orthographic]: *enter* **o** (Orthographic) *right-click*
Align section to: [Front/bAck/Top/Bottom/Left/Right]: *enter* **f** (Front) *right-click*
Command:

4. Place the drawing in the **Front** view.
5. Move the two upper parts vertically away from the bottom part.

The result is shown in Fig. 15.27.

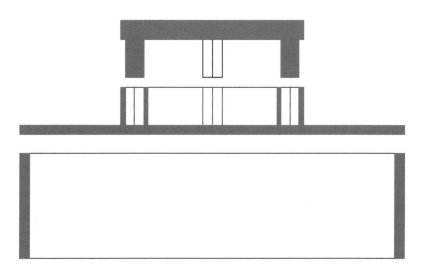

Fig. 15.27 First example –
Section

Second example – Section Plane (Fig. 15.28)

1. Open the drawing of the lathe tool holder constructed in answer to the first example in this chapter (Fig. 15.4). The drawing is in a **Four: Equal** viewports setting. *Click* in the **Top** viewport and from the **View** drop-down menu *click* **1 Viewport** in the **Viewports** sub-menu. The assembly appears in a full size single viewport.
2. Call the **Section Plane** tool and proceed as in the first example above.

The result is shown in Fig. 15.28.

Views of 3D models

Fig. 15.29 is a two-view projection of a model of an arrow.

Some of the possible viewing positions of a 3D model which can be obtained by using the **3D Navigate/Views** have already been seen in this book. Fig. 15.30 shows the viewing positions of the 3D model of the arrow using the viewing positions from the **3D Navigate/Views**.

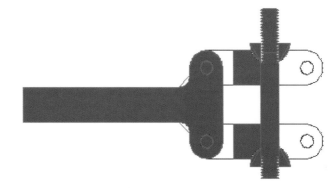

The drawing below shows the
section after moving its parts

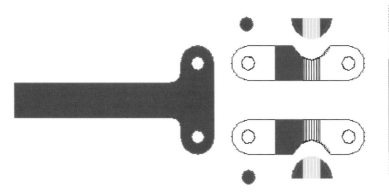

Fig. 15.28 Second example –
Section

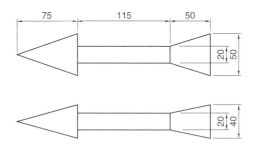

Fig. 15.29 Two views of the arrow

The Viewpoint Presets dialog

There are other methods of obtaining a variety of viewing positions of a
3D model. One method using the **UCS** (User Coordinate System) will be
described in a later chapter. Another method is by using the **Viewpoint
Presets** dialog called with a *click* on **Viewpoint Presets...** in the **3D
Views** sub-menu of the **View** drop-down menu (Fig. 15.31).

When the dialog appears with a 3D model on screen, *entering* figures
for degrees in the **X Axis** and **XY Plane** fields, followed by a *click* on the
dialog's **OK** button, causes the model to take up the viewing position
indicated by these two angles.

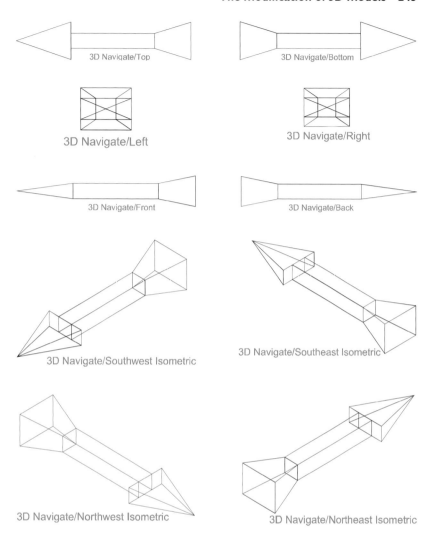

Fig. 15.30 The views from **3D Navigate/Views**

Note

The **Relative to UCS** radio button must be checked on to allow the 3D model to position along the two angles.

Example – Viewpoint Presets

1. With the 3D model of the arrow on screen, *click* **Viewpoint Presets...** in the **3D Views** sub-menu of the **Views** drop-down menu. The dialog appears.
2. *Enter* **330.0** in the **From X Axis** and **−30.0** in the **From XY Plane** fields and *click* the **OK** button of the dialog.
3. The 3D model takes up the viewing position indicated by the two angles (Fig. 15.32).

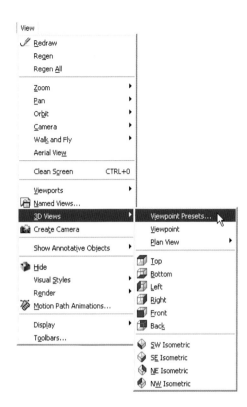

Fig. 15.31 Calling the **Viewpoint Presets...** dialog

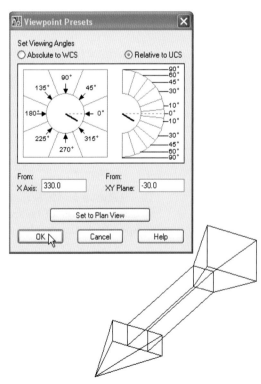

Fig. 15.32 Example – **Viewpoint Presets**

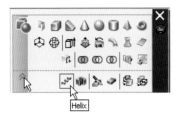

Fig. 15.33 The **Helix** tool icon in the extension of the **3D Make** control panel

The Helix tool

The **Helix** tool can be called with a *click* on its tool icon in the extension of the **3D Make** control panel (Fig. 15.33).

First example – Helix (Fig. 15.36)

1. Construct the triangular outline shown in Fig. 15.34 using the **Polyline** tool. Make sure the pline outline is placed at right angles to the bottom end of the helix as shown in Fig. 15.34. This may mean moving and rotating the outline in a selection of the **3D Views**.

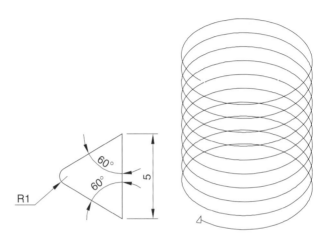

Fig. 15.34 First example **Helix** – the polyline outline and the helix

2. Call the **Helix** tool from the **3D Make** control panel (Fig. 15.33) or from the **Modeling** toolbar. The command line shows:

   Command: _Helix
   Number of turns = 3   Twist = CCW
   Specify center point of base: *enter* **160,160** *right-click*
   Specify base radius or [Diameter] <1>: *pick* **160, 200**
   Specify top radius or [Diameter] <1>: *enter* **40** *right-click*
   Specify helix height or [Axis endpoint/Turns/turn Height/tWist]
       <1>: *enter* **t** (Turns) *right-click*
   Enter number of turns <3>: *enter* **10** *right-click*
   Specify helix height or [Axis endpoint/Turns/turn Height/tWist]
       <1>: *enter* **100** *right-click*
   Command:

3. Call the **Extrude** tool form the **3D Make** control panel and extrude the outline along the path of the helix. The command line shows:

   Command: _extrude
   Current wire frame density: ISOLINES = 4
   Select objects to extrude: *pick* the outline **1 found**
   Select objects to extrude: *right-click*

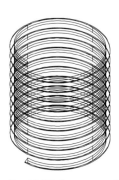

Fig. 15.35 First example **Helix** –
the resulting helix

Fig. 15.36 First example **Helix**

Fig. 15.37 Second example **Helix**

Specify height of extrusion or [Direction/Path/Taperangle]: *enter*
p (path) *right-click*
Select extrusion path or [Taper angle]: *pick* the helix
Command:

The result is shown in Fig. 15.35.

4. Add three cylinders – one to fit inside the helix, the second to form the shank of the screw, the third for the head of the screw. Subtract a box from the head for the screw slot. Then union the four parts of the screw.
5. Shade the screw using the **Visual Styles/Conceptual** form of shading.

The result is shown in Fig. 15.36.

Second example – Helix (Fig. 15.38)

Fig. 15.37 shows a 3D hidden view model of a helix formed from a circle of **5** units radius extruded along a helical path of **six** turns and a radius of **40** and height of **100**.

Using DYN

As with all other tools (commands) in AutoCAD 2008 a helix can be formed working with the **DYN** (Dynamic Input) system. Fig. 15.38 shows the stages (**1** to **5**) in the construction of the helix in the second example. Set **DYN** on with a *click* on its button in the status bar.

1. *Click* the **Helix** tool icon in the **3D Make** control panel. The first of the prompts in **DYN** form appears. *Enter* **160,160** at the command line or *drag* the cursor until **160,160** appears in the **DYN** tip and *right-click*.
2. Move the cursor until the dimension **40** shows and *right-click*.
3. Press the down-arrow key of the keyboard and *click* **Turns** in the menu which appears.
4. *Enter* **6** and *right-click*.
5. Press the down-arrow key of the keyboard and *enter* **100** in the menu as shown.

3D Surfaces

As mentioned on page 199 surfaces can be formed using the **Extrude** tool on lines and polylines. Two examples are given below in Figures 15.40 and 15.42.

First example – 3D Surface (Fig. 15.40)

1. In the **Top** view on a layer colour **magenta**, construct the polyline in Fig. 15.39.
2. In the **Southwest Isometric** view, call the **Extrude** tool from the **3D Make** control panel and extrude the polyline to a height of **80**. The result is shown in Fig. 15.40.

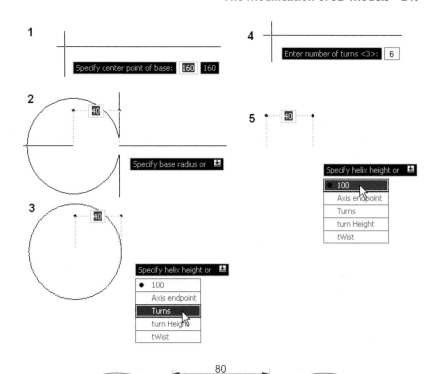

Fig. 15.38 Constructing the helix
for the second example with
the aid of **DYN**

Fig. 15.39 First example – **3D
Surface** – polyline to be
extruded

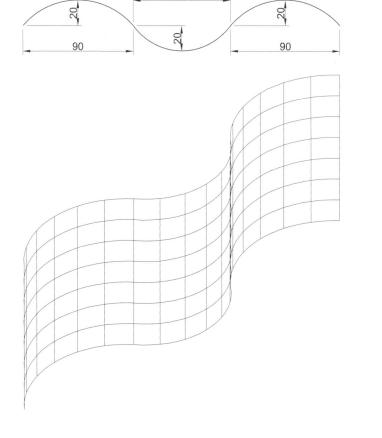

Fig. 15.40 First example – **3D
Surface**

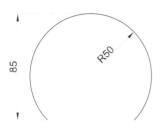

Fig. 15.41 Second example – **3D Surface** – the part circle to be extruded

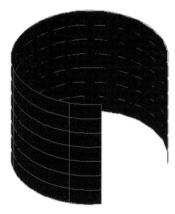

Fig. 15.42 Second example – **3D Surface**

Fig. 15.43 Exercise 1 – a shaded view

Second example – 3D Surface (Fig. 15.42)

1. In the **Top** view on a layer colour **red**, construct the circle in Fig. 15.41. Using the **Break** tool, break the circle as shown.
2. In the **Southwest Isometric** view, call the **Extrude** tool and extrude the part circle to a height of **80**. Shade **Visual Styles/Realistic**.

The result is shown in Fig. 15.42.

Revision notes

1. 3D models can be saved as blocks in a similar manner to the method of saving 2D drawings as blocks.
2. Libraries can be made from 3D model drawings.
3. 3D models saved as blocks can be inserted into other drawings via the DesignCenter.
4. Arrays of 3D model drawings can be constructed in 3D space using the **3D Array** tool.
5. 3D models can be mirrored in 3D space using the **Mirror 3D** tool.
6. 3D models can be rotated in 3D space using the **Rotate 3D** tool.
7. 3D models can be cut into parts with the **Slice** tool.
8. Sectional views can be obtained from 3D models using the **Section Plane** tool.
9. Helices can be constructed using the **Helix** tool. The helices so formed can be used as paths for extruding outlines.
10. Both **3D Views** viewing positions and **Viewpoint Presets** can be used for the placing of 3D models in different viewing positions in 3D space.
11. The **DYN** (Dynamic Input) method of construction can be used equally as well when constructing 3D model drawings as when constructing 2D drawings.
12. 3D Surfaces can be formed from polylines and lines using the **Extrude** tool.

Exercises

1. Fig. 15.43 shows a shaded view of the 3D model for this exercise. Fig. 15.44 is a three-view projection of the model. Working to the details given in Fig. 15.44, construct the 3D model.
2. Construct a 3D model drawing of the separating link shown in the two-view projection (Fig. 15.45). With the **Slice** tool, slice the model into two parts and remove the rear part. Place the front half in a suitable iso-metric view from the **3D Views** sub-menu. Shade the resulting model.
3. Working to the dimensions given in the two orthographic projections (Fig. 15.47), construct an assembled 3D model of the one part inside the other.

With the **Slice** tool, slice the resulting 3D model into two equal parts, place in an isometric view and call the **Hide** tool as indicated in Fig. 15.46.

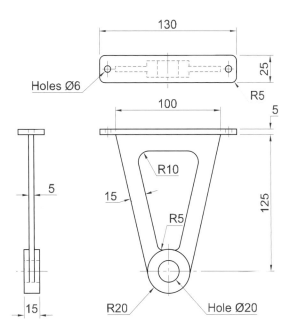

Fig. 15.44 Exercise 1 – three-view projection

Fig. 15.45 Exercise 2

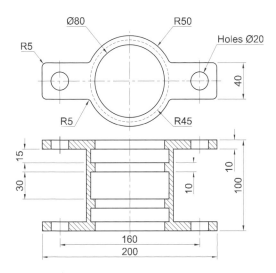

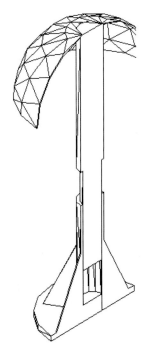

Fig. 15.46 Exercise 3

4. Construct a solid of revolution of the jug shown in the orthographic projection (Fig. 15.48). Construct a handle from an extrusion of a circle along a semicircular path. Union the two parts. Place the 3D model in a suitable isometric view and render.

5. In the **Top** view on a layer colour **blue**, construct the four polylines in Fig. 15.49. Call the **Extrude** tool and extrude the polylines to a height of **80** and place in the **Southwest Isometric** view. Then shade using **Visual Styles/Conceptual** shading (Fig. 15.50).

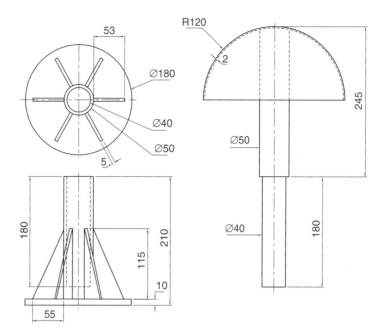

Fig. 15.47 Exercise 3 –
orthographic projections

Fig. 15.48 Exercise 4

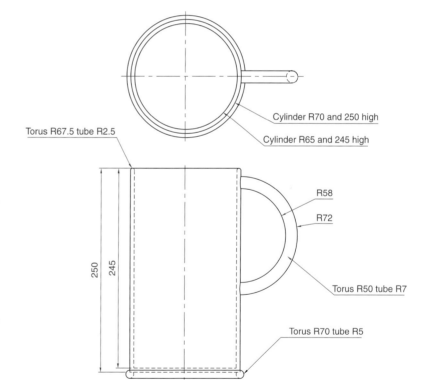

Fig. 15.49 Exercise 5 – outline to
be extruded

Fig. 15.50 Exercise 5

Fig. 15.51 Exercise 6 – outline to be extruded

6. In the **Right** view construct the lines and arc in Fig. 15.51 on a layer colour **green**. Extrude the lines and arc to a height of **180**, place in the **Southwest Isometric** view and in the shade style **Visual Styles/ Realistic** (Fig. 15.52).

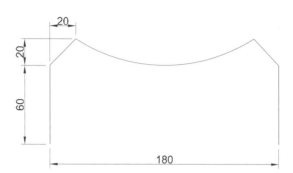

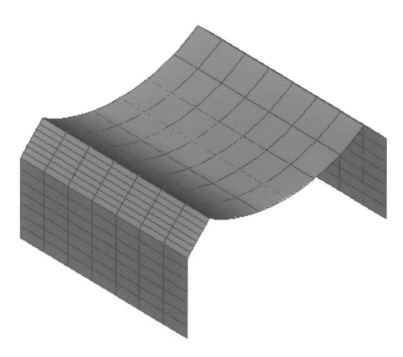

Fig. 15.52 Exercise 6

CHAPTER 16

Rendering

Aims of this chapter

1. To construct a template for 3D modelling to be used as the drawing base for further work in 3D in this book.
2. To introduce the use of the **Render** tools in producing photographic-like images of 3D solid models.
3. To show how to illuminate a 3D solid model to obtain good lighting effects when rendering.
4. To give examples of the rendering of 3D solid models.
5. To introduce the idea of adding materials to 3D solid models in order to obtain a realistic appearance to a rendering.
6. To demonstrate the use of the forms of shading available while using **Visual Styles** shading.
7. To demonstrate methods of printing rendered 3D solid models.

Setting up a new 3D template

So far in the earlier chapters of this book, we have been constructing both 2D and 3D drawings in the **acadiso.dwt** template. Now we will be constructing 3D model drawings in the **acadiso3D.dwt** template. To prepare this template for the remaining drawings in this book:

1. *Click* **New...** in the **File** drop-down menu, followed by a *click* on **acadiso3D** in the file list (Fig. 16.1).
2. When the template appears on screen, ensure the following seven control panels are showing in the **DASHBOARD – 3D Make, Layers, Visual Styles, Lights, Materials, Render** and **3D Navigate**.
3. *Click* the arrow to the right of the **Visual Styles** field in the **Visual Styles** control panel and select **3D Wireframe** from the icons which appear in a popup (Fig. 16.2).
4. Open the **Options** dialog (*right-click* in command window). *Click* the **Display** tab followed by a *click* on the **Colors...** button. Then *click* **3D parallel projection** and set **Uniform background** to **White** (Fig. 16.3).
5. Set **Units** to a **Precision** of **0**, **Snap** to **5** and **Grid** to **10**.
6. The AutoCAD window should appear as in Fig. 16.4.
7. In the **Options** dialog *click* the **Files** label and *click* **Default Template File Name for QNEW** (Fig. 16.5), followed by a *click* on the **Browse...** button which brings up the **Select template** dialog, from

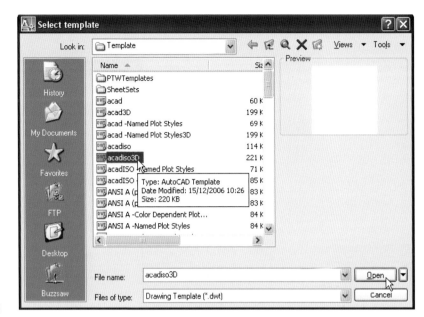

Fig. 16.1 Selecting **acadiso3D**
from the **Select template** dialog

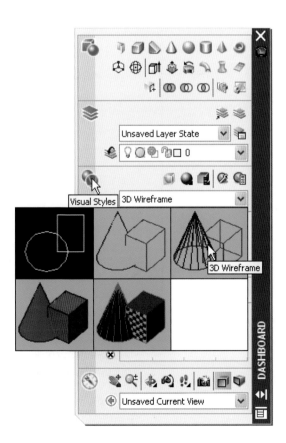

Fig. 16.2 Selecting **3D**
Wireframe from **Visual Styles**

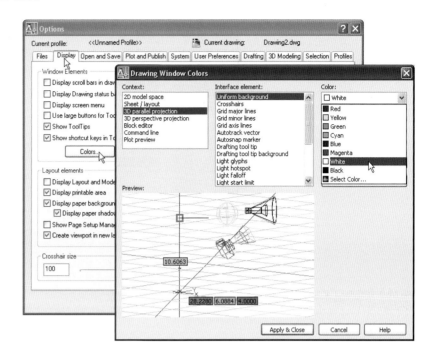

Fig. 16.3 Set **Uniform background** colours to **White**

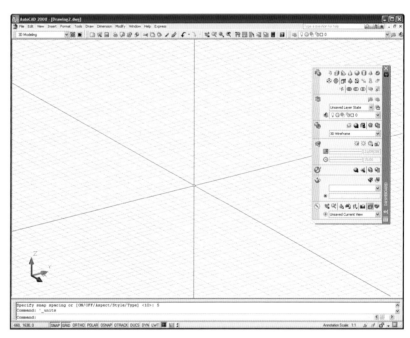

Fig. 16.4 The **acadios3D** screen

which the **acadiso3d.dwt** can be selected. Now when AutoCAD 2008 is opened from the desktop, the **acadiso3D.dwt** template will open.

8. Set up five layers of different colours. In the author's template these have been named after the colours (Fig. 16.6).

9. Save the template to the name **acadiso3D** and then *enter* a suitable name in the **Template Definition** dialog.

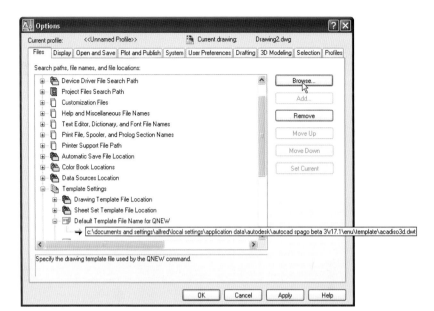

Fig. 16.5 Setting the default window in the **Options** dialog

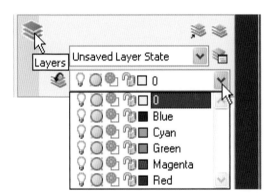

Fig. 16.6 Set up five new layers

10. Note (Fig. 16.4) the screen is in **Parallel** projection. Some operators may prefer the screen to be set to **Perspective** projection.

The Render tools and dialogs

The tool and dialog icons in the **Render** control panel are shown in Fig. 16.7.

The Lights tools

The tools from the **Lights** control panel are shown in Fig. 16.8. There are eight forms of lighting available when using AutoCAD 2008.

1. Ambient lighting is taken as the general overall light that is all around and surrounding any object. Usually left at 30%.

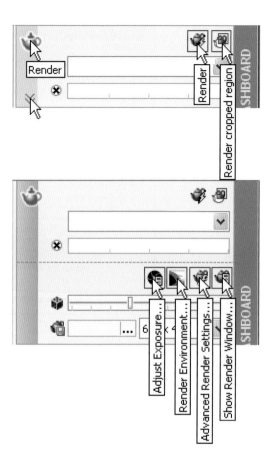

Fig. 16.7 The tool and dialog icons
in the **Render** control panel

2. **Point** lights shed light in all directions from the position in which the light is placed.
3. **Distant** lights send parallel rays of light from their position in the direction chosen by the operator.
4. **Spotlights** illuminate as if from a spotlight. The light is in a direction set by the operator and is in the form of a cone, with a 'hotspot' cone giving a brighter spot on the model being lit.
5. **Photometric lighting**. In this form of lighting lights of a selected wattage can be placed in a lighting scene. The set variable **LIGHTIN-GUNITS** must be set to **1** or **2** for photometric lights to function.
6. **Viewport lighting mode** in **Default lighting** or **User light/sunlight**.
7. **Sun** light which can be edited.
8. **Sky background and illumination**.

In this book we are only concerned with the use of **Point** and **Direct** lights, together with **Default lighting**.

Placing lights to illuminate a 3D model

Any number of the three types of lights – **Point, Distant** and **Spotlight** – can be positioned in 3D space as wished by the operator.

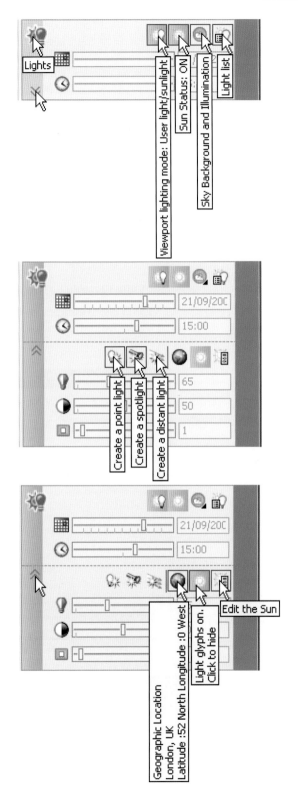

Fig. 16.8 The tool icons in the **Lights** control panel

In general reasonably good lighting effects can be obtained by placing a **Point** light high above the object(s) being illuminated, with a **Distant** light placed pointing towards the object at a distance from the front and above the general height of the object(s) and with a second **Distant** light pointing towards the object(s) from one side and not as high as the first **Distant** light. If desired **Spotlights** can be used either on their own or in conjunction with the other two forms of lighting.

Setting rendering background colour

The default background colour for rendering in AutoCAD 2008 is usually black. In this book, all renderings are shown on a white background in the viewport in which the 3D model drawing was constructed. To set the background to white for renderings:

1. At the command line:

   Command: *enter* **view** *right-click*

   The **View Manager** dialog appears (Fig. 16.9). *Click* **Current** in its **Views** list, followed by a *click* on the **New...** button.

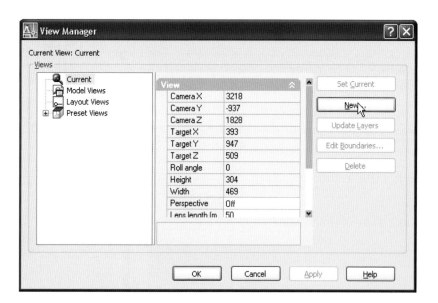

Fig. 16.9 **The View Manager** dialog

2. The **New View** dialog (Fig. 16.10) appears. *Enter* **Bookview** (or similar) in the **View name** field. In the **Background** popup list *click* **Solid**. The **Background** dialog appears (Fig. 16.11)
3. In the **Background** dialog *click* in the **Color** field. The **Select Color** dialog appears (Fig. 16.11).
4. In the **Select Color** dialog *drag* the slider as far upwards as possible to change the colour to white (**255, 255, 255**). Then *click* the dialog's **OK**

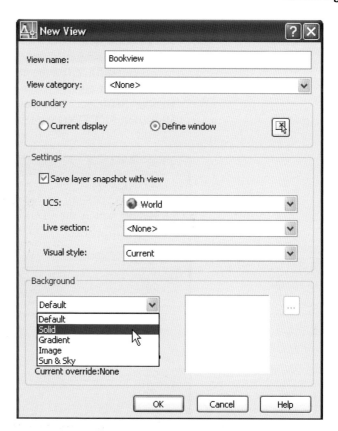

Fig. 16.10 The **New View** dialog

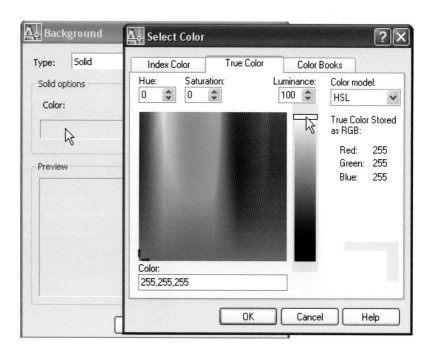

Fig. 16.11 The **Background** and
Select Color dialogs

button. The **Background** dialog reappears showing white in the **Color** and **Preview** fields. *Click* the **Background** dialog's **OK** button.

5. The **View Manager** dialog reappears, showing **Bookview** highlighted in the **Views** list. *Click* the dialog's **OK** button (Fig. 16.12).

6. In the **Render** control panel of the **DASHBOARD** *click* the **Advanced Render Settings...** icon (see Fig. 16.7 on page 5). The **ADVANCED RENDER SETTINGS** palette appears (Fig. 16.13).

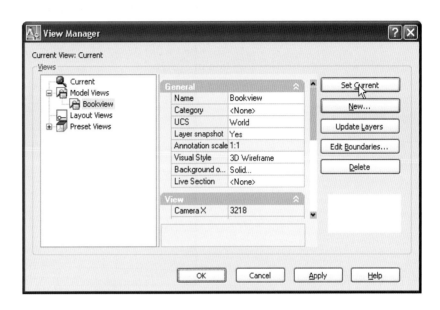

Fig. 16.12 The **View Manager** dialog

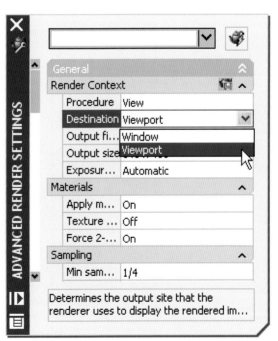

Fig. 16.13 The **ADVANCED RENDER SETTINGS** palette

7. In the palette *click* in the **Procedure** field and select **View**; *click* in the **Destination** field and select **Viewport** as the rendering destination (Fig. 16.13).
8. Close the palette and save the screen with the new settings as the template **3dacadiso.dwt**. This will ensure renderings are made in the viewport in which the 3D model was constructed – on a white background.

First example – rendering a 3D model (Fig. 16.21)

1. Construct a 3D model of the wing nut shown in the two-view projection in Fig. 16.14.

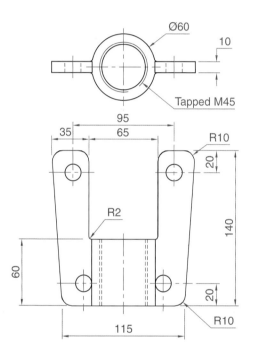

Fig. 16.14 First example – **rendering** – two-view projection

2. Place the 3D model in the **3D Views/Top** view, **Zoom** to **1** and with the **Move** tool, move the model to the upper part of the AutoCAD drawing area.
3. *Click* the **Create a point light** tool icon in the **Lights** control panel (Fig. 16.8). The **Viewport Lighting Mode** warning window appears (Fig. 16.15). *Click* its **Yes** button.
4. A **New Point Light** icon appears and the command line shows:

Command: _pointlight
Specify source location <0,0,0>: *enter* **.xy** *right-click of click at centre of model* (**need Z**): *enter* **500** *right-click*
Enter an option to change [Name/Intensity/Status/shadoW/Attenuation/Color/eXit] <eXit>: *enter* **n** (Name) *right-click*

Enter light name <Pointlight1>: *right-click*
Enter an option to change [Name/Intensity/Status/shadoW/Attenu-
ation/Color/eXit] <eXit>: *right-click*
Command:

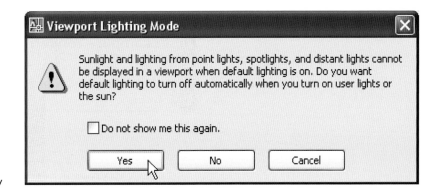

Fig. 16.15 The **Viewpoint**
Lighting Mode warning window

5. *Click* the **Create a distant light** tool icon in the **Lights** control panel.
   The command line shows:

   Command: _distantlight
   Specify light direction FROM <0,0,0> or [Vector]: *enter* **.xy** *right-*
   click **of** *click to* the left and below the 3D model (**need Z**) *enter* **400**
   right-click
   Specify light direction TO <1,1,1>: *enter* **.xy** *right-click* **of** *click* at
   centre of mode (**need Z**) *enter* **70** *right-click*
   Enter an option to change [Name/Intensity/Status/shadoW/Color/
   eXit] <eXit>: *enter* **n** *right-click*
   Enter light name <Distantlight1>: *right-click*
   Enter an option to change [Name/Intensity/Status/shadoW/Color/
   eXit] <eXit>: *right-click*
   Command:

6. Place another **Distant Light (Distantlight2)** in the same position **TO**
   and **FROM** the front and below the model at **Z** of **300**.

   Note

   The **Intensity** of the lights can be set, **Shadow** can **be** set off or on in a
   Sharp or **Soft** setting, and the **Color** of a light can be changed as needed
   in response to the prompts appearing when a light is added to a view.

7. When the model has been rendered if a light requires to be changed in
   intensity, shadow, position or colour, *click* the **Light list** icon in the
   Lights control panel and the **LIGHTS IN MODEL** palette appears.
   Click a light name and the **PROPERTIES** palette for the light appears
   in which modifications can be made (Fig. 16.16). Make any amendments as thought necessary.

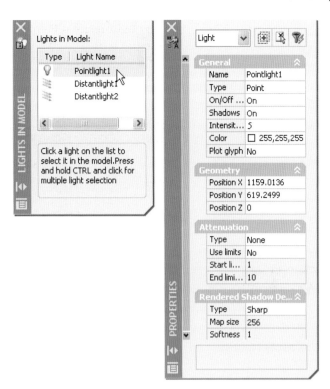

Fig. 16.16 The **LIGHTS IN MODEL** and **PROPERTIES** palettes

Note

In this example the **Intensity factor** has been set at **5** for all three lights. This is possible because the lights are close to the model. In larger size models the **Intensity factor** may have to be set to a much higher figure.

Adding a material to a model

1. *Click* the **Materials...** tool icon in the **Materials** control panel. The **MATERIALS** palette appears (Fig. 16.17).
2. *Click* the **Select Image...** button in the **Diffuse map** area of the palette. The **Select Image File** dialog appears. Select **Metals, Ornamental Metals, Copper** from the **Name** list. Note the change in the **Available Materials in Drawing** swatch at the top of the palette.
3. *Right-click* in the **Available Materials in Drawing** part of the palette and *click* the **Apply Material to Objects** icon (Fig. 16.18).
4. *Click* any part of the 3D model to apply the material to the model.
5. *Right-click* in the **Type** field of the **Material Editor – Global** section of the palette and select **Realistic** in the *right-click* menu (Fig. 16.19).
6. *Click* in the **Global** field and select the name of the material from the popup list which appears. An **Offset** and **Review** part of the palette appears showing the appearance of the material which has been selected (Fig. 16.19). A *click* in either icon to the left or to the right in

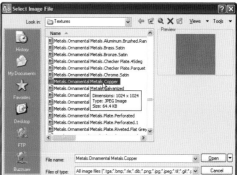

Fig. 16.17 The **MATERIALS** palette

Fig. 16.18 The **Apply Material to Objects** icon

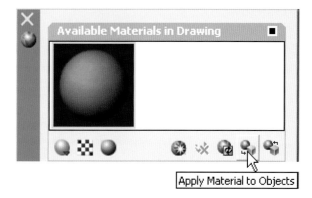

Apply Material to Objects

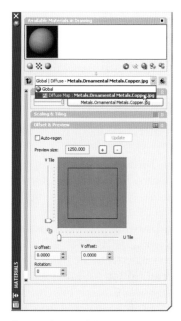

Fig. 16.19 The **Offset and Review** area of the **Materials** palette

this field brings back the **Materials Editor** in which changes can be made using the sliders against the features which can be adjusted.

7. *Click* the **Render cropped region** icon in the **Render** control panel (Fig. 16.7, page 258) and *window* the 3D model. The model renders.
8. If necessary adjust the sliders in the **Materials Editor – Global** part of the palette, rendering after each adjustment to obtain the best possible rendering.
9. *Click* the **Advanced Render Settings...** tool in the **Render** control panel (Fig. 16.7, page 258) and in the palette which appears adjust the **Output size** to **1024 × 768** or to a larger size if possible (Fig. 16.20).
10. Render the 3D model again and if now satisfied save to a suitable file name.

Fig. 16.21 shows four renderings in the four **Type** settings.

Fig. 16.20 Selecting an **Output size** from the **ADVANCED RENDER SETTINGS** palette

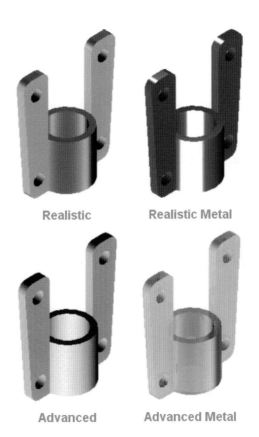

Fig. 16.21 First example – **Rendering**

Note

The limited descriptions of rendering given in these pages do not show the full value of different types of lights, materials and rendering methods. The reader is advised to experiment with the facilities available for rendering.

Second example – rendering a 3D model (Fig. 16.23)

1. Construct 3D models of the two parts of the stand and support given in the projections in Fig. 16.22 with the two parts assembled together.

Fig. 16.22 Second example – **Rendering** – projections of the two parts

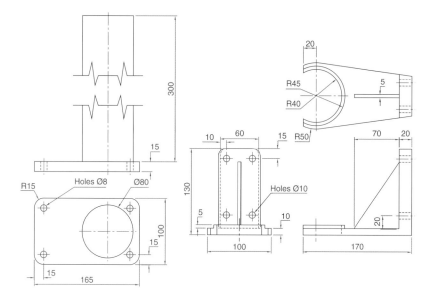

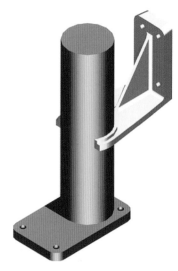

2. Place the scene in the **3D Navigate/Top** view, **Zoom** to **1** and add lighting.
3. Add different materials to the parts of the assembly and render the result.

Fig. 16.23 shows the resulting rendering.

Third example – rendering a 3D model (Fig. 16.25)

Fig. 16.24 is an exploded third angle orthographic projection of a pumping device from a machine and Fig. 16.25 is an exploded and rendered 3D model of the device.

The 3D Orbit tool

At the command line *enter* **3dorbit**. The command line shows:

Command: 3dorbit
Press ESC or ENTER to exit, or right-click to display shortcut-menu.

Fig. 16.23 Second example – **Rendering**

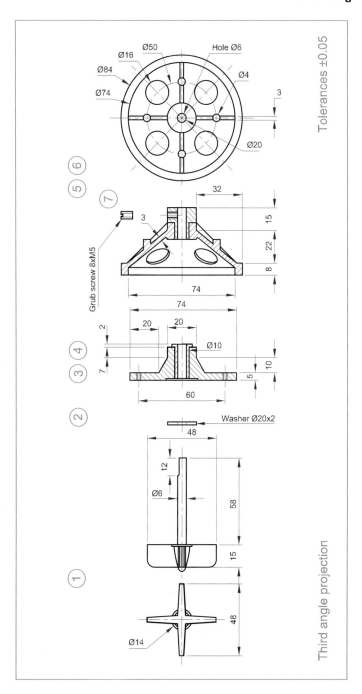

Fig. 16.24 Third example –
Rendering – exploded
orthographic drawing

Right-click anywhere on screen and the **3dorbit** *right-click* menu appears
(Fig. 16.26). *Click* **Free Orbit**. A circle and movement icon appears on
screen. The position and angle of the model can be adjusted by either
clicking in one of the four outer small circles or by *clicking* outside the
main circle and moving the mouse.

Fig. 16.25 Third example –
Rendering – exploded and
rendered 3D model

Exit		
Current Mode: Constrained Orbit		
Other Navigation Modes ▶	Constrained Orbit	1
	✔ Free Orbit	2
✔ Enable Orbit Auto Target	Continuous Orbit	3
Animation Settings ...	Adjust Distance	4
	Swivel	5
Zoom Window		
Zoom Extents	Walk	6
Zoom Previous	Fly	7
✔ Parallel	Zoom	8
Perspective	Pan	9
Reset View		
Preset Views ▶		
Named Views		
Visual Styles ▶		
Visual Aids ▶		

Fig. 16.26 The *right-click* menu of
the **3dorbit** tool

Example – 3D Orbit (Fig. 16.28)

This is another tool for the manipulation of 3D models into different positions within 3D space.

1. Open the file of the second example of rendering (Fig. 16.23).
2. Shade the model using **Visual Styles/Realistic**.
3. *Enter* **3dorbit** at the command line.
4. With the cursor outside the circle move the mouse. The 3D model
   rotates within the circle.
5. With the cursor inside the circle move the mouse. The 3D model
   rotates around the screen.
6. With the cursor inside any one of the small quadrant circles the 3D
   model can be moved vertically or horizontally as the mouse is moved
   (Fig. 16.27).

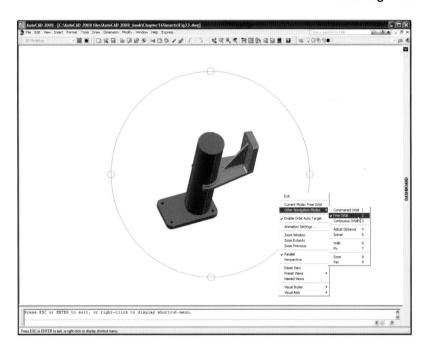

Fig. 16.27 Example – **3dorbit**

7. Fit the 3D model into a **Four: Equal** viewports setting. Note that the **Visual Styles/Realistic** mode still shows in each of the four viewports (Fig. 16.28).

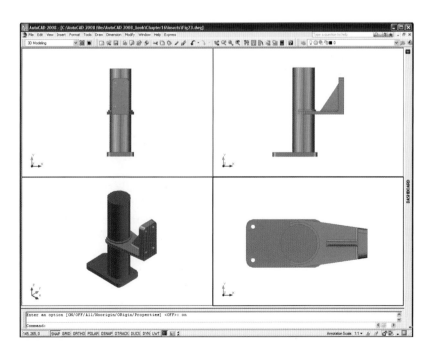

Fig. 16.28 Example – **3dorbit** the example in a **Four: Equal** viewport layout

Producing hardcopy

Printing or plotting a drawing on screen using AutoCAD 2008 can be carried out from either **Model Space** or **Paper Space**. In versions of AutoCAD before AutoCAD 2004, it was necessary to print or plot from **PSpace**.

First example – printing a single copy (Fig. 16.30)

Note

The drawing being printed in this example is in a **Visual Styles/Conceptual** shading mode.

1. With a drawing to be printed or plotted on screen *click* the **Plot** tool icon in the **Standard Annotation** toolbar. (Fig. 16.29).
2. The **Plot** dialog appears. Set the **Printer/Plotter** to a printer or plotter currently attached to the computer and the **Paper Size** to a paper size to which the printer/plotter is set.
3. *Click* the **Preview** button of the dialog and if the preview is OK, *right-click* and in the *right-click* menu which appears, *click* **Plot**. The drawing plots producing the necessary 'hardcopy' (Fig. 16.30).

Second example – multiple view copy (Fig. 16.32)

A 3D model to be printed is a **Realistic** view of a 3D model which has been constructed on three layers – **Red, Blue** and **Green** in colour. To print a multiple view copy:

1. Place the drawing in a **Four: Equal** viewports setting.
2. Make a new layer **vports** of colour cyan and make it the current layer.

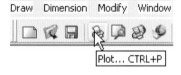

Fig. 16.29 Calling the **Plot** tool from the **Standard** toolbar

Fig. 16.30 First example – printing a single copy

3. *Click* the **Layout** button in the status bar. The drawing appears in **PSpace**. A view of the 3D model appears within a cyan-coloured viewport (Fig. 16.31).

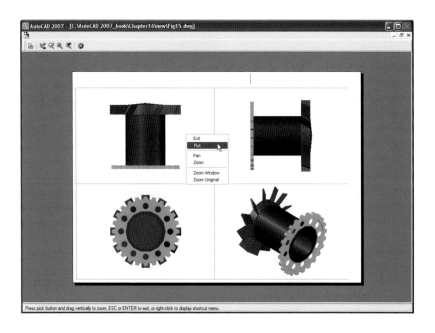

Fig. 16.31 Second example
Multiple view copy – the **Plot Preview**

4. *Click* the **Plot** tool icon in the **Standard Annotation** toolbar. Make sure the correct **Printer/Plotter** and **Paper Size** settings are selected and *click* the **Preview** button of the dialog.
5. A preview of the 3D model appears.
6. If the preview is satisfactory (Fig. 16.32), *right-click* and from the *right-click* menu *click* **Plot**. The drawing plots to produce the required four-viewport hardcopy.

Other forms of hardcopy

When working in AutoCAD 2008, several different forms of hardcopy can be printed or plotted determined by the settings in the **3D Navigate/Visual Styles** settings. As an example a single view plot preview of the same 3D model is shown in the **Hidden** shading form (Fig. 16.32).

Saving and opening 3D model drawings

3D model drawings are saved and/or opened in the same way as are 2D drawings. To save a drawing *click* **Save As...** in the **File** drop-down menu and save the drawing in the **Save Drawing As** dialog and *enter* a file name in the **File Name** field of the dialog before *clicking* the **Save** button. To open a drawing which has been saved *click* **Open...** in the **File** drop-down

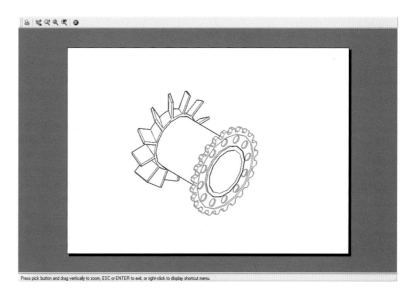

Fig. 16.32 An example of a
Hidden Style plot **Preview**

menu, and in the **Select File** dialog which appears select a file name from the file list.

There are differences between saving a 2D and a 3D drawing, in that when a 3D model drawing is shaded by using a shading mode from the **Visual Styles** control panel, the shading is saved with the drawing.

Exercises

1. A rendering of an assembled lathe tool holder is shown in Fig. 16.33. The rendering includes different materials for each part of the assembly. Working to the dimensions given in the parts orthographic drawing (Fig. 16.34), construct a 3D model drawing of the assembled lathe tool holder on several layers of different colours, add lighting and materials and render the model in an isometric view.

Fig. 16.33 Exercise 1 – a rendering

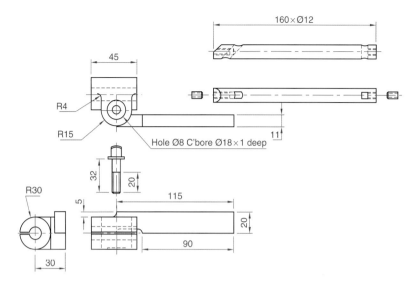

Fig. 16.34 Exercise 1 – parts drawing

Shade with **3D Visual Styles/Hidden** and print or plot a **Southwest Isometric** view of the model drawing.

2. Working to the sizes given in Fig. 16.35, construct a 3D model drawing of the drip tray from an engine. Add lighting and a suitable material, place the model in an isometric view and render (Fig. 16.36).

3. A three-view drawing of a hanging spindle bearing in third angle orthographic projection is shown in Fig. 16.37. Working to the dimensions in the drawing, construct a 3D model drawing of the bearing. Add lighting and a material and render the model.

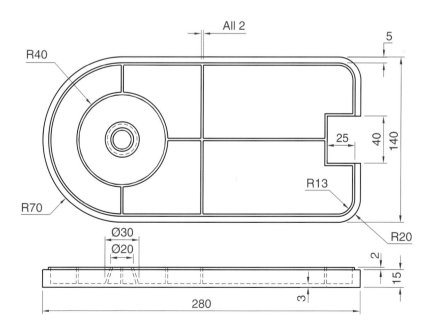

Fig. 16.35 Exercise 2 – two-view projection

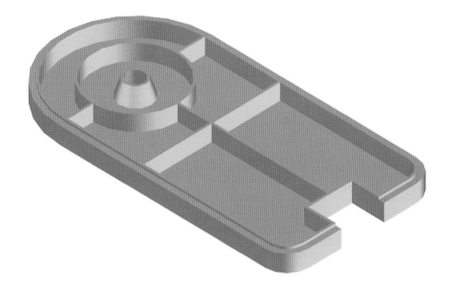

Fig. 16.36 Exercise 2

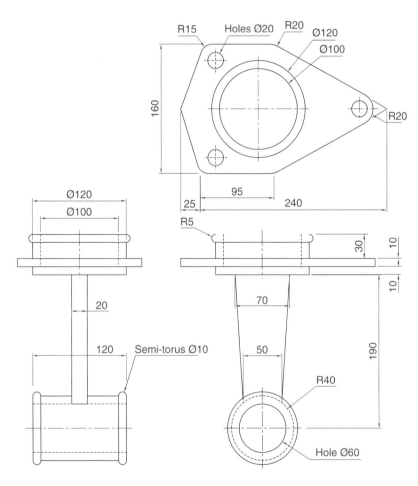

Fig. 16.37 Exercise 3

CHAPTER 17

3D space

Aims of this chapter

1. To show in examples the methods of manipulating 3D models in 3D space using tools from the **UCS** toolbars or from the command line.
2. To introduce some of the **Surfaces** tools.

3D space

So far in this book, when constructing 3D model drawings, they have been constructed on the AutoCAD 2008 coordinate system which is based upon three planes: the **XY Plane** – the screen of the computer; the **XZ Plane** at right angles; to the **XY Plane** and as if coming towards the operator of the computer; and a third plane (**YZ**) is lying at right angles to both the other two planes (Fig. 17.1).

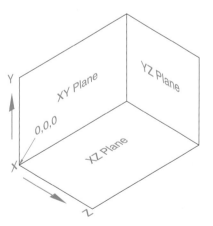

Fig. 17.1 The 3D space planes

In earlier chapters in order to view 3D objects which have been constructed on these three planes at other angles we have used views from the **3D Navigate** control panel and have indicated other methods of rotating the model in 3D space and placing the model in other viewing positions using the **Vpoint Presets** dialog and the **3dorbit** tool.

The User Coordinate System (UCS)

Fig. 17.2 The **New UCS** submenu from the **Tools** dropdown menu

Note

The **XY** plane is the basic **UCS** plane, which in terms of the ucs is known as the ***WORLD*** plane.

The **UCS** allows the operator to place the AutoCAD coordinate system in any position in 3D space using a variety of **UCS** tools (commands). Features of the **UCS** can be called either by *entering* **ucs** at the command line, by selection from the **Tools** drop-down menu (Fig. 17.2) or from the two **UCS** toolbars – **UCS** and **UCS II** (Fig. 17.3).

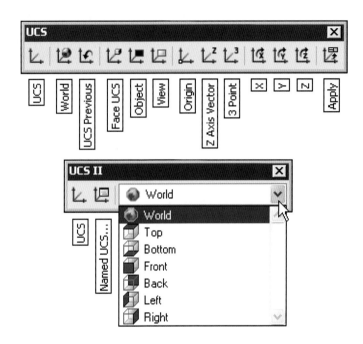

Fig. 17.3 The tools from the two **UCS** toolbars

If **ucs** is *entered* at the command line, it shows:

> **Command** *enter* **ucs** *right-click*
> **Current ucs name:** *WORLD*
> **Enter an option [New/Move/orthoGraphic/Prev/Restore/Save/Del/**
> **Apply/?/World] <World>:** *enter* **n** (New) *right-click*
> **Specify origin of UCS or [ZAxis/3point/OBject/Face/View/X/Y/Z]**
> **<0,0,0>:**

And from these prompt lines a selection can be made.

The variable UCSFOLLOW

UCS planes can be set from either of the two **UCS** toolbars (Figs 17.2 and 17.3). For the UCS to operate from the command line, the variable **UCS-FOLLOW** must first be set on as follows:

Command: *enter* **ucsfollow** *right-click*
Enter new value for UCSFOLLOW <0>: *enter* **1** *right-click*
Command:

The UCS icon

The **UCS** icon which indicates the direction of the three coordinate axes **X, Y** and **Z** is by default showing in the AutoCAD drawing area as arrows pointing in the directions of the axes. When working in 2D, only the **X** and **Y** axes are showing, but when the drawing area is in a 3D view all three coordinate arrows are showing, except when the model is in the **XY** plane. The icon can be turned off as follows:

Command: *enter* **ucsicon** *right-click*
Enter an option [ON/OFF/Noorigin/ORigin/Properties] <ON>:

To turn the icon off, *enter* **off** in response to the prompt line and the icon disappears from the screen.

The appearance of the icon can be changed by *entering* **p** (Properties) in response to the prompt line. The **UCS Icon** dialog appears in which changes can be made to the shape, line width and colour of the icon if wished.

Types of UCS icon

The shape of the icon can be varied partly when changes are made in the **UCS Icon** dialog but also according to whether the AutoCAD drawing area is in 2D, 3D or Paper Space (Fig. 17.4).

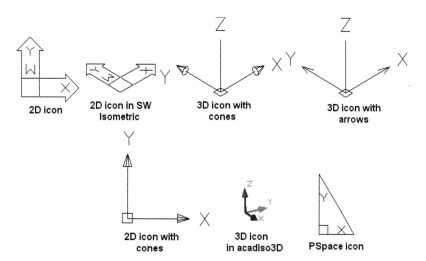

Fig. 17.4 Types of **UCS** icon

Examples of changing planes using the UCS

First example – changing UCS planes (Fig. 17.6)

1. Set **UCSFOLLOW** to **1** (ON).
2. Place the screen in **3D Navigate/Front** and **Zoom** to **1**.

3. Construct the pline outline in Fig. 17.5 and extrude to a height of **120**.
4. Set **UCSFOLLOW** to **1**.
5. Place in the **3D Navigate/Southwest Isometric** view and **Zoom** to **1**.
6. With the **Fillet** tool, fillet corners to a radius of **20**.

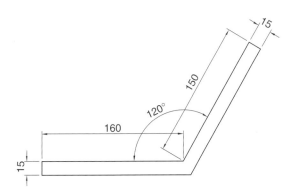

Fig. 17.5 First example –
Changing UCS planes – pline
for extrusion

7. At the command line:

> **Command:** *enter* **ucs** *right-click*
> **Current ucs name: *WORLD***
> **Enter an option [New/Move/orthoGraphic/Prev/Restore/Save/Del/**
>   **Apply/?/World] <World>:** *enter* **n** (New) *right-click*
> **Specify origin of new UCS or [ZAxis/3point/OBject/Face/View/X/**
>   **Y/Z/]:** *enter* **f** (Face) *right-click*
> **Select face of solid object:** *pick* the sloping face – its outline high-
>   lights
> **Enter an option [Next/Xflip/Yflip] <accept>:** *right-click*
> **Command:**

And the 3D model changes its plane so that the sloping face is now on the new UCS plane. **Zoom** to **1**.

8. On this new UCS, construct four cylinders of radius 7.5 and height − 15 (note the minus) and subtract them from the face.
9. *Enter* **ucs** at the command line again and *right-click* to place the model in the ***WORLD* UCS**.
10. Place four cylinders of the same radius and height into position in the base of the model and subtract them from the model.
11. Place the 3D model in the **3D Navigate/Southwest Isometric** view and set in the **Visual Styles/Hidden** format (Fig. 17.6).

Second example – UCS (Fig. 17.9)

The 3D model for this example is a steam venting valve from a machine, the two-view third angle projection of which is shown (Fig. 17.7).

1. Make sure that **UCSFOLLOW** is set to **1**.
2. The **UCS** plane is the ***WORLD*** plane. Construct the **120** square plate at the base of the central portion of the valve. Construct five

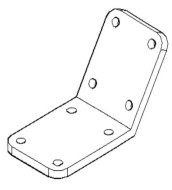

Fig. 17.6 First example –
changing UCS planes

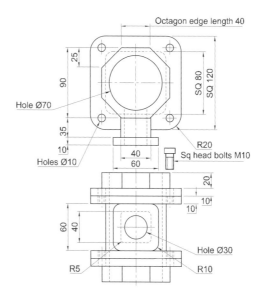

Fig. 17.7 Second example – **UCS** – The orthographic projection of a steam venting valve

Fig. 17.8 Second example – **UCS** – step 11 + rendering

Fig. 17.9 Second example – **UCS** – steps 12 and 13 + rendering

cylinders for the holes in the plate. Subtract the five cylinders from the base plate.

3. Construct the central part of the valve – a filleted **80** square extrusion with a central hole.
4. Place the models in the **UCS orthoGonal/Front** plane.
5. With the **Move** tool, move the central portion vertically up by **10**.
6. With the **Copy** tool, copy the base up to the top of the central portion.
7. With the **Union** tool form a single 3D model of the three parts.
8. Make the layer **Construction** current.
9. Place the model in the **UCS *WORLD*** plane. Construct the separate top part of the valve – a plate forming a union with a hexagonal plate and with holes matching those of the other parts.
10. Place the scene so far in the **UCS/orthoGonal/Front** plane and move the parts of the top into their correct positions relative to each other and with **Union** and **Subtract** tools, complete the part. This will be made easier if the layer **0** is turned off.
11. Turn layer **0** back on and move the top into its correct position relative to the main part of the valve. Then with the **Mirror** tool, mirror the top to produce the bottom of the assembly (Fig. 17.8).
12. While in the ***FRONT*** UCS construct the three parts of a 3D model of the extrusion to the main body.
13. In the **UCS *WORLD*** move the parts into their correct position relative to each other and with **Union** form a union of the two filleted rectangular extrusions and the main body. Then with **Subtract**, subtract the cylinder from the whole (Fig. 17.9).
14. In the **UCS *FRONT*** plane, construct one of the bolts as shown in Fig. 17.10, forming a solid of revolution from a pline. Then add a head to the bolt and with **Union** add it to the screw.

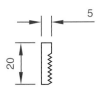

Fig. 17.10 Second example –
UCS – pline for the bolt

Fig. 17.11 Second example –
UCS

Fig. 17.12 Third example –
UCS – outline for 3D model

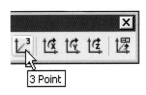

Fig. 17.13 The **3 Point UCS** icon
in the **UCS** toolbar

15. With the **Copy** tool, copy the bolt seven times to give eight bolts. With **Move**, and working in the **UCS** *WORLD* and *FRONT* planes, move the bolts into their correct positions relative to the 3D model.
16. Add suitable lighting and attach materials to all parts of the assembly and render the model.
17. Save the model to a suitable file name.
18. Finally move all the parts away from each other to form an exploded view of the assembly (Fig. 17.11).

Third example – UCS (Fig. 17.15)

1. Set **UCSFOLLOW** to **1**.
2. Place the drawing area in the **UCS FRONT** view.
3. Construct the outline in Fig 17.12 and extrude to a height of **120**.
4. Either *click* the **3 Point UCS** tool icon in the **UCS** toolbar (Fig. 17.13) or at the command line:

> **Command:** *enter* ucs *right-click*
> **Current ucs name:** *RIGHT*
> **Enter an option [prompts]:** *enter* **n** (New) *right-click*
> **Specify origin of UCS or [prompts]:** *enter* **3** (3point) *right-click*
> **Specify new origin point:** *pick*
> **Specify point on positive portion of X-axis:** *pick*
> **Specify point on positive-Y portion of UCS XY plane:** *enter* **.xy** *right-click*
> of *pick* (**need Z**): *enter* **−1** (Note the minus sign) *right-click*
> **Regenerating model**.
> **Command:**

Fig. 17.14 shows the **UCS** points and the model regenerates in this new 3point plane. Fig. 17.14 shows the **UCS** points.

5. On the face of the model construct a rectangle **80 × 50** central to the face of the front of the model, fillet its corners to a radius of **10** and extrude to a height of **10**.
6. Place the model in the **3D Navigate/Southwest Isometric** view and fillet the back edge of the second extrusion to a radius of **10**.

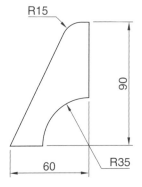

R15

90

60

R35

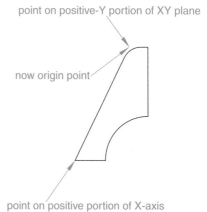

point on positive-Y portion of XY plane

now origin point

point on positive portion of X-axis

Fig. 17.14 Third example – **UCS** – the three UCS points

7. Subtract the second extrusion from the first.
8. Add lights and a suitable material and render the model (Fig. 17.15).

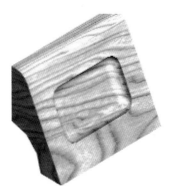

Fig. 17.15 Third example – **UCS**

Fourth example – UCS (Fig. 17.17)

1. With the last example still on screen, place the model in the **UCS** *WORLD* view.
2. *Click* the **Z Axis Vector UCS** tool icon in the **UCS** toolbar (Fig. 17.16).
   The command line shows:

   Command:_ucs
   Current ucs name: *WORLD*
   Enter an option [prompts] <World>: _zaxis
   Specify a new origin point: *enter* **40,60** *right-click*
   Specify point on positive portion of Z-axis <40,60,0>: *enter* **.xy** *right-click*
   of *enter* **170,220** *right-click* (**need Z**): *enter* **1** *right-click*
   Regenerating model.
   Command:

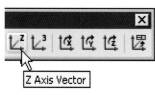

Z Axis Vector

Fig. 17.16 The **Z Axis Vector UCS** icon in the **UCS** toolbar

3. Render the model in its new **UCS** plane (Fig. 17.17).

Fig. 17.17 Fourth example – **UCS**

Saving UCS views

If a number of different **UCS** planes are used in connection with the construction of a 3D model, each can be saved to a different name and recalled when required. To save the UCS plane in which a 3D model drawing is being constructed, either *click* the **UCS** tool icon in the **UCS** toolbar (Fig. 17.18) or *enter* **ucs** at the command line:

> **Command:_ucs**
> **Current ucs name: NW Isometric**
> **Enter an option [prompts]:** *enters* **s** (Save) *right-click*
> **Enter name to save current UCS or [?]:** *enter* **SW Isometric** *right-click*
> **Regenerating drawing**.
> **Command:**

Fig. 17.18 The **UCS** icon in the **UCS** toolbar

Now *click* the **Named UCS...** tool icon in the **UCS II** toolbar (Fig. 17.19) and the **UCS** dialog appears (Fig. 17.20) showing the names of the views saved in the current drawing.

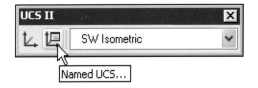

Fig. 17.19 The **Named UCS...** tool icon in the **UCS II** toolbar

Constructing 2D objects in 3D space

In previous chapters of this book we have seen examples of 2D objects constructed with the **Polyline, Line, Circle** and other 2D tools to form the

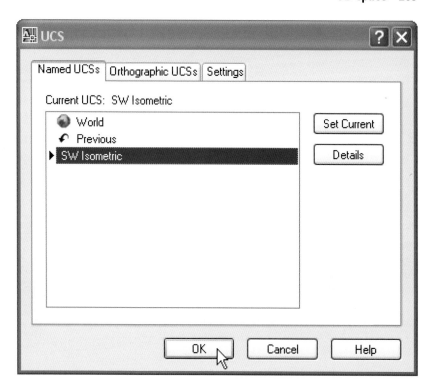

Fig. 17.20 The **UCS** dialog

outlines for extrusions and solids of revolution. These outlines have been drawn on planes set either from the **3D Views** submenu of the **Views** drop-down menu, or in **UCS** planes such as the **UCS** *RIGHT*, *FRONT* and *LEFT* planes.

First example – 2D outlines in 3D space (Fig. 17.23)

1. Construct a **3point UCS** to the following points:

   Origin point: 80,90
   X-axis point: 290,150
   Positive-Y point: .xy of **80,90**
   (**needZ**): *enter* **1**.

2. On this **3point UCS** construct a 2D drawing of the plate to the dimensions given in Fig. 17.21, using the **Polyline, Ellipse** and **Circle** tools.
3. Save the **UCS** plane in the **UCS** dialog to the name **3point**.
4. Place the drawing area in the **3D Navigate/Southwest Isometric** view (Fig. 17.22).
5. With the **Region** tool form regions of the six parts of the drawing and with the **Subtract** tool, subtract the circles and ellipse from the main outline.
6. Extrude the region to a height of **10** (Fig. 17.23).

Fig. 17.21 First example – **2D outlines in 3D space**

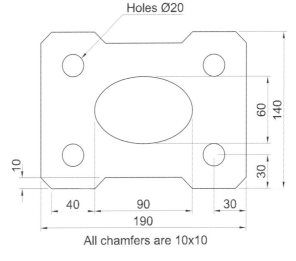

Holes Ø20

All chamfers are 10x10

Fig. 17.22 First example – **2D outlines in 3D space** – The outline in a SW Isometric view

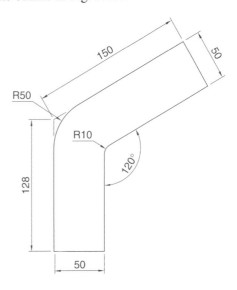

Fig. 17.23 First example – **2D outlines in 3D space**

Second example – 2D outlines in 3D space (Fig. 17.26)

1. Place the drawing area in the **UCS *FRONT*** view, **Zoom** to **1** and construct the outline in Fig. 17.24.

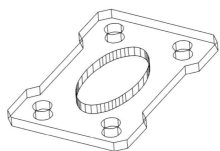

R50

R10

150

50

120°

128

50

Fig. 17.24 Second example – **2D outlines in 3D space** – outline to be extruded

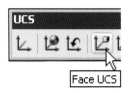

Fig. 17.25 The **Face UCS** icon from the **UCS** toolbar

2. Extrude the outline to a height of **150**.
3. Place in the **3D Navigate/Southwest Isometric** view and **Zoom** to **1**.
4. *Click* the **Face UCS** tool icon in the **UCS** toolbar (Fig. 17.25) and place the 3D model in the ucs plane shown in Fig. 17.26, selecting the sloping face of the extrusion for the plane and again **Zoom** to **1**.
5. With the **Circle** tool draw five circles as shown in Fig. 17.26.

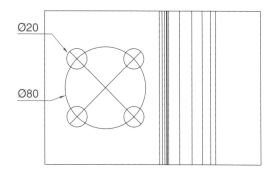

Fig. 17.26 Second example – **2D outlines in 3D space** – the circles in the new UCS face

6. Form a region from the five circles and with **Union** form a union of the regions.
7. Extrude the region to a height of **−60** (note the minus) – higher than the width of the sloping part of the 3D model.
8. Place the model in the **3D Navigate/Southwest Isometric** view and subtract the extruded region from the model.
9. With the **Fillet** tool, fillet the upper corners of the slope of the main extrusion to a radius of **30**.
10. Place the model in another **UCS FACE** plane and construct a filleted pline of sides **80** and **50**, filleted to a radius of **20**. Extrude to a height of **−60** and subtract the extrusion from the 3D model.
11. Place in the **3D Navigate/Southwest Isometric** view; add lighting and attach a material and render (Fig. 17.27).

The Surfaces tools

The construction of 3D surfaces has already been dealt with – see pages 210 to 211 and 248 to 250. In this chapter examples of the construction of 3D surfaces constructed with the tools **Edgesurf**, **Rulesurf** and **Tabsurf** will be described.

Surface meshes

Surface meshes are controlled by the set variables **Surftab1** and **Surftab2**. These variables are set as follows:

At the command line:

Fig. 17.27 Second example – **2D outlines in 3D space**

Command: *enter* **surftab1** *right-click*
Enter new value for SURFTAB1 <6>: *enter* **24** *right-click*
Command:

The Edgesurf tool (Fig. 17.30)

1. Make a new layer colour **magenta**. Make that layer current.
2. Place the drawing area in the **3D Navigate/Right** view. **Zoom** to **1**.
3. Construct the polyline to the sizes and shape as shown in Fig. 17.28.
4. Place the drawing area in the **3D Navigate/Top** view. **Zoom** to **1**.
5. Copy the pline to the right by **250**.

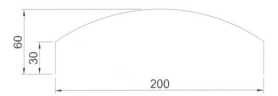

Fig. 17.28 Example – **Edgesurf** – pline outline

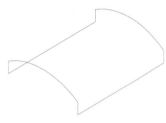

Fig. 17.29 Example – **Edgesurf** – adding lines joining the plines

6. Place the drawing in the **3D Navigate/Southwest Isometric** view. **Zoom** to **1**.
7. With the **Line** tool, draw lines between the ends of the two plines using the **endpoint** osnap (Fig. 17.29). Note that if polylines are drawn they will not be accurate at this stage.
8. Set **SURFTAB1** to **32** and **SURFTAB2** to **64**.
9. At the command line:

Command: *enter* **edgesurf** *right-click*
Current wire frame density: SURFTAB1 = 32SURFTAB2 = 64
Select object 1 for surface edge: *pick* one of the lines (or plines)
Select object 2 for surface edge: *pick* the next adjacent line (or pline)
Select object 3 for surface edge: *pick* the next adjacent line (or pline)
Select object 4 for surface edge: *pick* the last line (or pline)
Command:

The result is shown in Fig. 17.30.

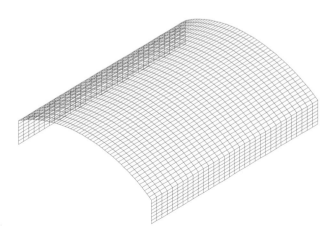

Fig. 17.30 Example – **Edgesurf**

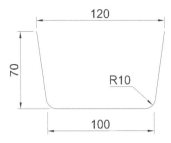

Fig. 17.31 Example – **Rulesurf** – pline outline

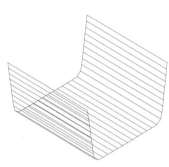

Fig. 17.32 Example – **Rulesurf**

The Rulesurf tool (Fig. 17.32)

1. Make a new layer colour **blue** and make the layer current.
2. In the **3D Navigate/Front** view construct the pline as shown in Fig. 17.31.
3. In the **3D Navigate/Top** view, **Zoom** to **1** and copy the pline to a vertical distance of **120**.
4. Place in the **3D Navigate/Southwest Isometric** view and **Zoom** to **1**.
5. Set **SURFTAB1** to **32**.
6. At the command line:

   Command: *enter* **rulesurf** *right-click*
   Current wire frame density: SURFTAB1 = 32
   Select first defining curve: *pick* one of the plines
   Select second defining curve: *pick* the other pline
   Command:

The result is given in Fig. 17.32.

The Tabsurf tool (Fig. 17.33)

1. Make a new layer of colour **blue** and make the layer current.
2. Set **SURFTAB1** to **2**.
3. In the **3D Navigate/Top** view construct a hexagon of edge length **35**.
4. In the **3D Navigate/Front** view and in the centre of the hexagon construct a pline of height **100**.
5. Place the drawing in the **3D Navigate/Southwest Isometric** view.
6. At the command line:

   Command: *enter* **tabsurf** *right-click*
   Current wire frame density: SURFTAB1 = 2
   Select objects for path curve: *pick* the hexagon
   Select object for direction vector: *pick* the pline
   Command:

The result is shown in Fig. 17.33.

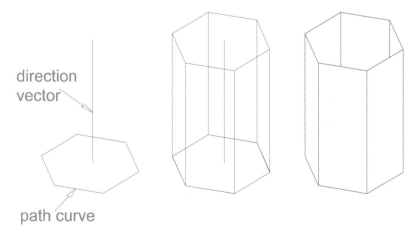

direction vector

path curve

Fig. 17.33 Example – **Tabsurf**

Revision notes

1. The **UCS** (User Coordinate System) tools can be called from the two toolbars **UCS** and **UCS II** or from sub-menus from the **Tools** drop-down menu or by *entering* **ucs** at the command line.
2. The variable **UCSFOLLOW** must first be set on (to 1) before operations of the UCS can be brought into action.
3. There are several types of **UCS** icon – 2D (different types), 3D (different types), Pspace.
4. The position of the plane in 3D space on which a drawing is being constructed can be varied using tools from the **UCS**.
5. The different planes on which drawings are constructed in 3D space can be saved in the **UCS** dialog.
6. The tools **Edgesurf, Rulesurf** and **Tabsurf** can be used to construct surfaces in addition to surfaces which can be constructed from plines and lines using the **Extrude** tool.

Exercises

1. Fig. 17.34 is a two-view projection of an angle bracket in which two pins are placed in holes in each of the arms of the bracket.
    Construct a 3D model of the bracket and its pins.
    Add lighting to the scene and materials to the parts of the model and render (Fig. 17.35).

Fig. 17.34 Exercise 1 – details of the shapes and sizes

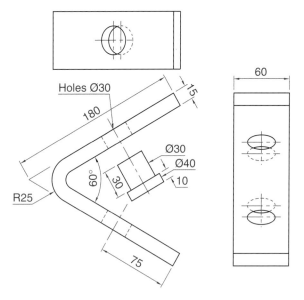

Fig. 17.35 Exercise 1 – a rendering

2. The two-view projection (Fig. 17.36) shows a stand consisting of two hexagonal prisms. Circular holes have been cut right through each face of the smaller hexagonal prism and rectangular holes with rounded ends have been cut right through the faces of the larger.

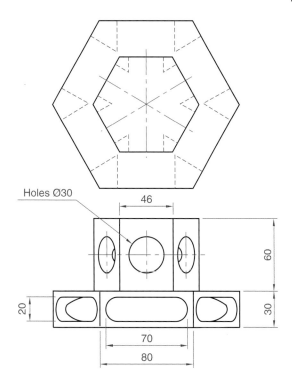

Holes Ø30   46   60   20   70   30   80

Fig. 17.36 Exercise 2 – details of
the shapes and sizes

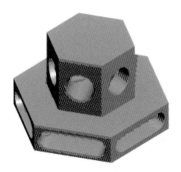

Fig. 17.37 Exercise 2 – a rendering

Construct a 3D model of the stand. When completed add suitable lighting to the scene. Then add a material to the model and render (Fig. 17.37).

3. The two-view projection in Fig. 17.38 shows a ducting pipe. Construct
a 3D model drawing of the pipe. Place in a **Southeast Isometric** view,
add lighting to the scene and a material to the model and render.

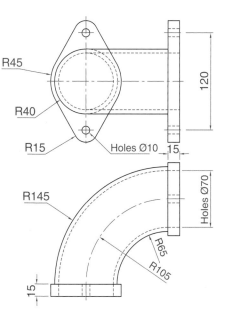

R45   R40   R15   Holes Ø10   15   120   Holes Ø70   R145   R65   R105   15

Fig. 17.38 Exercise 3 – details of
the shapes and sizes

4. A point marking device is shown in two two-view projections in Fig. 17.39. The device is composed of three parts – a base, an arm and a pin. Construct a 3D model of the assembled device and add appropriate materials to each part. Then add lighting to the scene and render in a **SW Isometric** view (Fig. 17.40).

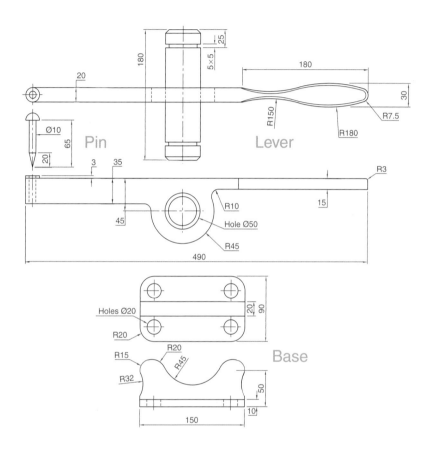

Fig. 17.39 Exercise 4 – details of shapes and sizes

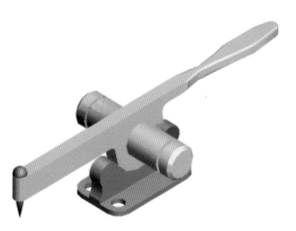

Fig. 17.40 Exercise 4 – a rendering

Fig. 17.41 Exercise 5 – a rendering

Fig. 17.42 Exercise 5 – two-view drawing

Fig. 17.43 Exercise 6

5. Fig. 17.41 shows the rendering of a 3D model drawing of the connecting device shown in the orthographic projection in Fig. 17.42. Construct the 3D model drawing of the device and add a suitable lighting to the scene.

  Then place in a **Southwest Isometric** view, add a material to the model and render.

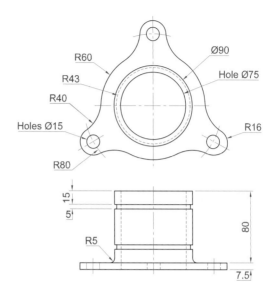

6. A fork connector and its rod are shown in a two-view projection in Fig. 17.43. Construct a 3D model drawing of the connector with its rod in position. Then add lighting to the scene, place in an **Isometric** viewing position, add materials to the model and render.

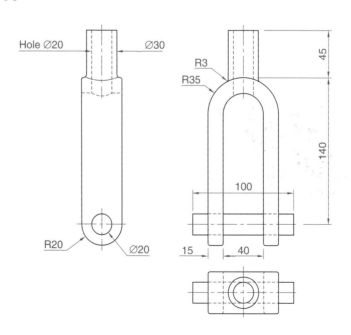

7. An orthographic projection of the parts of a lathe steady are given in Fig. 17.44. From the dimensions shown in the drawing, construct an assembled 3D model of the lathe steady.

When the 3D model has been completed, add suitable lighting and materials and render the model Fig. 17.45.

Fig. 17.44 Exercise 7 – details

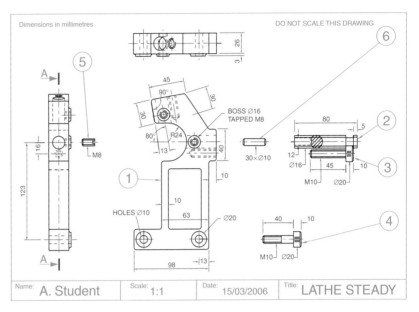

Dimensions in millimetres

DO NOT SCALE THIS DRAWING

BOSS Ø16
TAPPED M8

30×Ø10

HOLES Ø10

| Name: A. Student | Scale: 1:1 | Date: 15/03/2006 | Title: LATHE STEADY |

8. Fig. 17.46 shows in the **3D Navigate Southwest Isometric** view a semi-circle of radius **25** constructed in the **3D Navigate/Top** view on a layer of colour **magenta**, with a semicircle of radius **75** constructed in the **3D Navigate/Front** view with its left-hand end centred on the circle.

Fig. 17.47 shows a surface constructed from the two semicircles in a **Visual Styles/Realistic** mode. Construct the surface.

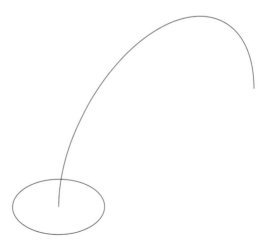

Fig. 17.45 Exercise 7 – a rendering

Fig. 17.46 Exercise 8 – the circle and semicircle

Fig. 17.47 Exercise 8

CHAPTER 18

Editing 3D solid models

Fig. 18.1 The toolbars menu

Aims of this chapter

1. To introduce the use of tools from the **Solid Editing** toolbar.
2. To give examples of the use of the tools from the **Solid Editing** toolbar.
3. To show examples of a variety of 3D solid and 3D surface models.

The Solid Editing tools

The **Solid Editing** tools can be called from the **Solid Editing** toolbar. *Right-click* on any toolbar on the screen and the toolbars menu appears (Fig. 18.1). *Click* **Solid Editing** in the menu and the **Solid Editing** toolbar appears on screen (Fig. 18.2).

Examples of the results of using some of the tools from the **Solid Editing** toolbar are shown in this chapter. These tools are of value if the design of a 3D solid model requires to be changed (edited), although some have a value in constructing solids which cannot easily be constructed using other tools.

First example – Extrude faces tool (Fig. 18.5)

1. Set **ISOLINES** to 24.
2. In the **3D Navigate/Right** view construct a cylinder of radius **30** and height **30** (Fig. 18.3).
3. In the **3D Navigate/Front** view construct the pline as in Fig. 18.3. Mirror the pline to the other end of the cylinder.
4. In the **3D Navigate/Top** view move the pline to lie central to the cylinder.
5. Place the screen in the **3D Navigate/Southwest Isometric** view.
6. *Click* the **Extrude faces** tool icon in the **Solid Editing** toolbar (Fig. 18.4). The command line shows:

Command: _solidedit
Solids editing automatic checking: SOLIDCHECK=1

Fig. 18.2 The **Solid Editing** toolbar

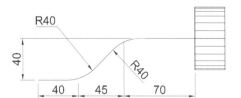

Fig. 18.3 First example – **Extrude faces tool** – first stages

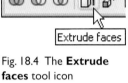

Extrude faces

Fig. 18.4 The **Extrude faces tool** icon

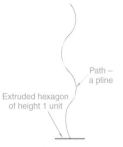

Original cylinder

After extruding faces along paths

Fig. 18.5 First example – **Extrude faces tool**

Enter a solids editing option [Face/Edge/Body/Undo/eXit] <eXit>: _face
Enter a face editing option.
[Extrude/Move/Rotate/Offset/Taper/Delete/Copy/coLor/mAterial/Undo/eXit] <eXit>: _extrude
Select faces or [Undo/Remove]: *pick* a face **2 faces found.**
Select faces or [Undo/Remove/ALL]: *enter* **r** *right-click*
Remove faces or [Undo/Add/ALL]: 2 faces found, 1 removed.
Remove faces or [Undo/Add/ALL]: *right-click*
Specify height of extrusion or [Path]: *enter* **p** *right-click*
Select extrusion path: *pick* the path
Path was moved to the center of the profile.
Solid validation started.
Solid validation completed.

7. Repeat the operation using the view at the other end of the cylinder.
8. Render the resulting edited 3D model (Fig. 18.5).

Notes

1. Note the prompt line which includes the statement **SOLIDCHECK=1**. If the variable **SOLIDCHECK** is set on (to **1**) the prompt lines include the lines **SOLIDCHECK=1, Solid validation started** and **Solid validation completed**. If set to **0** these two lines do not show.
2. When a face is *picked* other faces become highlighted; using the **Remove** option of the line **Select faces or [Undo/Remove/ALL]** allows faces which are not to be extruded to be removed from the operation of the tool.

Second example – Extrude faces tool (Fig. 18.7)

1. Construct a hexagonal extrusion just **1** unit high in the **UCS 3D Navigate/Top** view.
2. Change to the **3D Navigate/Front** view and construct the curved pline as in Fig. 18.6.
3. Back in the **3D Navigate/Top** view, move the pline to lie central to the extrusion.
4. Place in the **3D Navigate/Southwest Isometric** view and extrude the top face of the extrusion along the path of the curved pline.
5. Add lighting and a material to the model and render (Fig. 18.7).

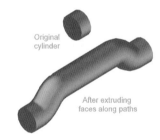

Path – a pline

Extruded hexagon of height 1 unit

Fig. 18.6 Second example – **Extrude faces tool** – pline for path

Fig. 18.7 Second example –
Extrude faces tool

Note

This example shows that a face of a 3D solid model can be extruded along any suitable path curve. If the polygon on which the extrusion had been based had been turned into a region, no extrusion could have taken place. The polygon had to be extruded to give a face to a 3D solid.

Third example – Move faces tool (Fig. 18.9)

1. Construct the 3D solid drawing shown in the left-hand drawing of Fig. 18.9 from three boxes which have been united using the **Union** tool.
2. *Click* on the **Move faces** tool in the **Solid Editing** toolbar (Fig. 18.8). The command line shows:

   Command: _solidedit
   [prompts] _face
   Enter a face editing option.
   [prompts]: _move
   Select faces or [Undo/Remove]: *pick* face **1 face found.**
   Select faces or [Undo/Remove/ALL]: *right-click*
   Specify a base point or displacement: *pick*
   Specify a second point of displacement: *pick*
   [further prompts]:

And the *picked* face is moved – right-hand drawing of Fig. 18.9.

Fig. 18.8 The **Move faces** tool
icon

Fig. 18.9 Third example – **Move faces tool**

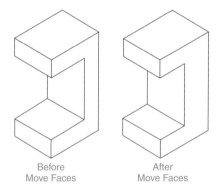

Before
Move Faces

After
Move Faces

Fourth example – Offset faces (Fig. 18.11)

1. Construct the 3D solid drawing shown in the left-hand drawing of Fig. 18.11 from a hexagonal extrusion and a cylinder which have been united using the **Union** tool.
2. *Click* on the **Offset faces** tool icon in the **Solid Editing** toolbar (Fig. 18.10). The command line shows:

   Command:_solidedit
   [prompts]:_face

Fig. 18.10 The **Offset faces** tool icon

[prompts]
[prompts]:_offset
Select faces or [Undo/Remove]: *pick* the bottom face of the 3D model **2 faces found**.
Select faces or [Undo/Remove/All]: *enter* **r** *right-click*
Select faces or [Undo/Remove/All]: *pick* highlighted faces other than the bottom face **2 faces found, 1 removed**.
Select faces or [Undo/Remove/All]: *right-click*
Specify the offset distance: *enter* **30** *right-click*

3. Repeat, offsetting the upper face of the cylinder by **50** and the right-hand face of the lower extrusion by **15**.

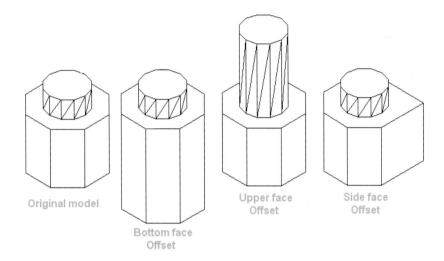

Original model

Bottom face
Offset

Upper face
Offset

Side face
Offset

Fig. 18.11 Fourth example –
Offset faces tool

Fifth example – Taper faces tool (Fig. 18.12)

1. Construct the 3D model as in the left-hand drawing of Fig. 18.12. Place in the **3D Navigate/Southwest Isometric** view.
2. Call **Taper faces**. The command line shows:

Command:_solidedit
[prompts]:_face
[prompts]
[prompts]:_taper
Select faces or [Undo/Remove]: *pick* the upper face of the base **2 faces found**.
Select faces or [Undo/Remove/All]: *enter* **r** *right-click*
Select faces or [Undo/Remove/All]: *pick* highlighted faces other than the upper face **2 faces found, 1 removed**.
Select faces or [Undo/Remove/All]: *right-click*
Specify the base point: *pick* a point on left-hand edge of the face
Specify another point along the axis of tapering: *pick* a point on the right-hand edge of the face
Specify the taper angle: *enter* **10** *right-click*

And the selected face tapers as indicated in the right-hand drawing (Fig. 18.12).

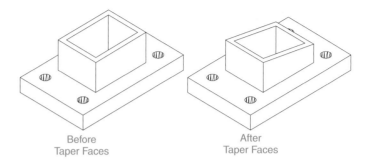

Fig. 18.12 Fifth example – **Taper faces tool**

Before
Taper Faces

After
Taper Faces

Fig. 18.13 The **Copy faces** tool icon from the **Solid Editing** toolbar

Sixth example – Copy faces tool (Fig. 18.15)

1. Construct a 3D model to the sizes as given in Fig. 18.14.
2. *Click* on the **Copy faces** tool in the **Solid Editing** toolbar (Fig. 18.13). The command line shows:

Command:_solidedit
[prompts]:_face
[prompts]
[prompts]:_copy
Select faces or [Undo/Remove]: *pick* the upper face of the solid model **2 faces found.**
Select faces or [Undo/Remove/All]: *enter* r *right-click*
Select faces or [Undo/Remove/All]: *pick* highlighted face not to be copied **2 faces found, 1 removed.**
Select faces or [Undo/Remove/All]: *right-click*
Specify a base point or displacement: *pick* anywhere on the high-lighted face
Specify a second point of displacement: *pick* a point some 50 units above the face

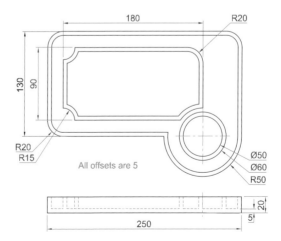

Fig. 18.14 Sixth example – **Copy faces tool** – details of the 3D solid model

Fig. 18.15 Sixth example – **Copy faces tool**

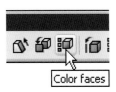

Color faces

Fig. 18.16 The **Color faces** tool icon from the **Solid Editing** toolbar

3. Add lights and a material to the 3D model and its copied face and render (Fig. 18.15).

Seventh example – Color faces tool (Fig. 18.18)

1. Construct a 3D model of the wheel to the sizes as shown in Fig. 18.17.
2. *Click* the **Color faces** tool icon in the **Solid Editing** toolbar (Fig. 18.16). The command line shows:

Command:_solidedit
[prompts]:_face
[prompts]
[prompts]:_color
Select faces or [Undo/Remove]: *pick* the inner face of the wheel **2 faces found**.
Select faces or [Undo/Remove/All]: *enter* **r** *right-click*
Select faces or [Undo/Remove/All]: *pick* highlighted faces other than the required face **2 faces found, 1 removed**.
Enter new color <ByLayer>: *enter* **1** (which is red) *right-click*

3. Add lights and a material to the edited 3D model and render (Fig. 18.18).

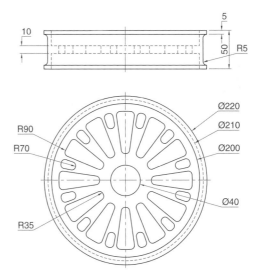

Fig. 18.17 Seventh example – **Color faces tool** – details of the 3D model

Examples of more 3D models

These 3D models can be constructed in the **acadiso3D.dwt** screen. The descriptions of the stages needed to construct these 3D models have been reduced from those given in earlier pages, in the hope that readers have already acquired a reasonable skill in the construction of such drawings.

Fig. 18.18 Seventh example –
Color faces tool

Fig. 18.19 First example of 3D
models

First example (Fig. 18.19)

1. **3D Navigate/Front** view. Construct the three extrusions for the back panel and the two extruding panels to the details given in Fig. 18.20.
2. **3D Navigate/Top** view. Move the two panels to the front of the body and union the three extrusions. Construct the extrusions for the projecting parts holding the pin.
3. **3D Navigate/Front** view. Move the two extrusions into position and union them to the back.
4. **3D Navigate/Top** view. Construct two cylinders for the pin and its head.
5. **3D Navigate/Top** view. Move the head to the pin and union the two cylinders.
6. **3D Navigate/Front** view. Move the pin into its position in the holder. Add lights and materials.
7. **3D Navigate/Southwest Isometric** view. Render. Adjust lighting and materials as necessary (Fig. 18.19).

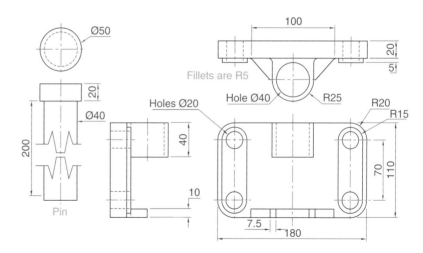

Fig. 18.20 First example 3D
models – details of sizes and
shapes

8. In the **Visual Styles** control panel select **3D Wireframe**.
9. Press and hold the **Ctrl** key. The **Selecting Subobjects on Solids** warning window (Fig. 18.21) appears. *Click* its **Close** button. Then while still holding the **Ctrl** key down *pick* the top centre point of the back of the holder. The command line shows:

Command:
** STRETCH **
Specify stretch point or [Base point/Undo/eXit]: *pick* a point to the rear of the holder
Command:

The 3D model can again be rendered and then appears as shown in Fig. 18.22.

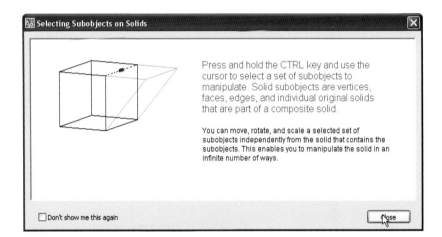

Fig. 18.21 The **Selecting Subobjects on Solids** warning window

Fig. 18.22 The stretched first example

Note

When using this method of holding down the **Ctrl** key with a 3D model on screen, while the **Return** key of the keyboard is pressed repeatedly, the command line shows:

** MOVE **
Specify move point or [Base point/Undo/eXit]:
** ROTATE **
Specify rotation angle or [Base point/Undo/Reference/eXit]:
** SCALE **
Specify scale factor or [Base point/Undo/Reference/eXit]:
** MIRROR **
Specify second point or [Base point/Undo/eXit]:

This Allows the operator to use any of these modify commands on the 3D model.

Second example (Fig. 18.24)

1. **3D Navigate/Top**. Construct polyline outlines for the body extrusion and the solids of revolution for the two end parts (Fig. 18.23). Extrude the body and subtract its hole and using the **Revolve** tool form the two end solids of revolution.

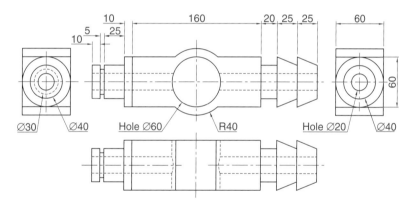

Fig. 18.23 Second example – dimensions

2. **3D Navigate/Right**. Move the two solids of revolution into their correct positions relative to the body and union the three parts. Construct a cylinder for the hole through the model.
3. **3D Navigate/Front**. Move the cylinder to its correct position and subtract from the model.
4. **3D Navigate/Top**. Add lighting and a material.
5. Render (Fig. 18.24).

Third example (Fig. 18.26)

1. **3D Navigate/Front**. Construct the three plines needed for the extrusions of each part of the model (details Fig. 18.25). Extrude to the given heights. Subtract the hole from the **20** high extrusion.

Fig. 18.24 Second example of 3D models

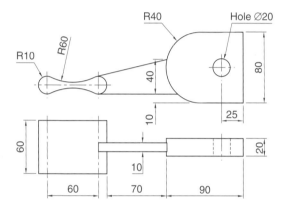

Fig. 18.25 Third example of 3D models – details of shapes and sizes

2. **3D Navigate/Top**. Move the **60** extrusion and the **10** extrusion into their correct positions relative to the **20** extrusion. With **Union** form a single 3D model from the three extrusions.
3. Add suitable lighting and a material to the model.
4. **3D Navigate/Southwest Isometric**. Render (Fig. 18.26).

Fig. 18.26 Third example of 3D models

Fourth example (Fig. 18.27)

1. **3D Navigate/Front**. Construct the polyline – left-hand drawing of Fig. 18.27.
2. With the **Revsurf** tool form a surface of revolution from the pline.
3. **3D Navigate/Top**. Add suitable lighting and a coloured glasslike material.
4. **3D Navigate/Southwest Isometric**. Render (right-hand illustration of Fig. 18.27).

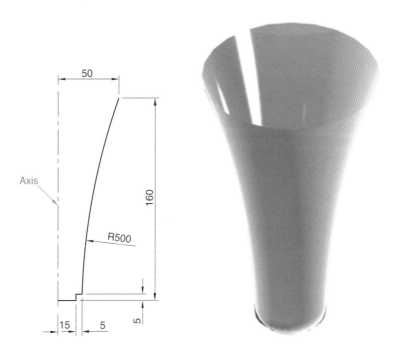

Fig. 18.27 Fourth example of 3D models

Exercises

1. Construct suitable polylines to sizes of your own discretion in order to form the two surfaces to form the box shape shown in Fig. 18.28 with the aid of the **Rulesurf** tool.

   Add lighting and a material and render the surfaces so formed.

   Construct another three **Edgesurf** surfaces to form a lid for the box. Place the surface in a position above the box, add a material and render (Fig. 18.29).
2. Working to the dimensions given in the orthographic projections of the three parts of this 3D model (Fig. 18.31), construct the assembled part as shown in the rendered 3D model in Fig. 18.30.

   Add suitable lighting and materials, place in one of the isometric viewing position and render the model.
3. Construct the 3D model shown in the rendering in Fig. 18.32 from the details given in the parts drawing in Fig. 18.33.

Fig. 18.28 Exercise 1 – first part

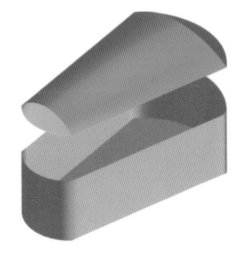

Fig. 18.29 Exercise 1 – second part

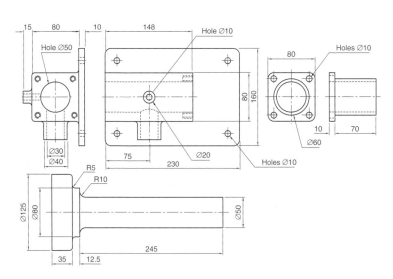

Fig. 18.30 Exercise 2

Fig. 18.31 Exercsie 2 – details of shapes and sizes

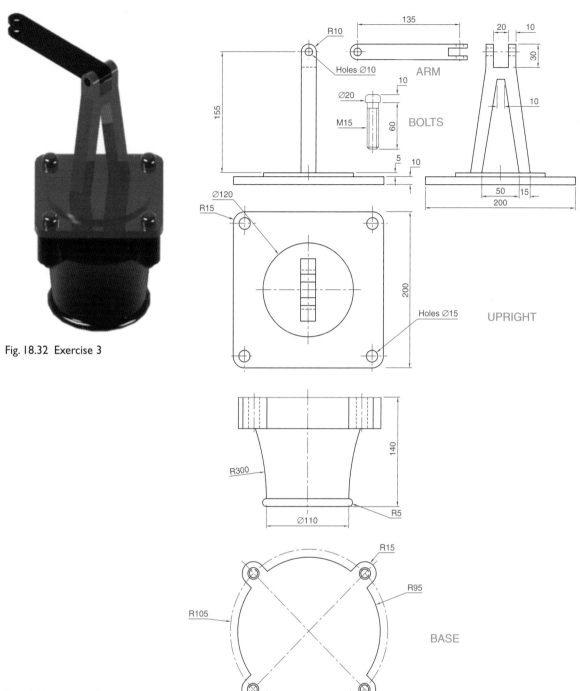

Fig. 18.32 Exercise 3

Fig. 18.33 Exercise 3 – the parts
drawing

4. A more difficult exercise.

A rendered 3D model of the parts of an assembly are shown in Fig. 18.37.

Working to the details given in the three orthographic projections Figs 18.34, 18.35 and 18.36, construct the two parts of the 3D model, place them in suitable positions relative to each other, add lighting and materials and render the model.

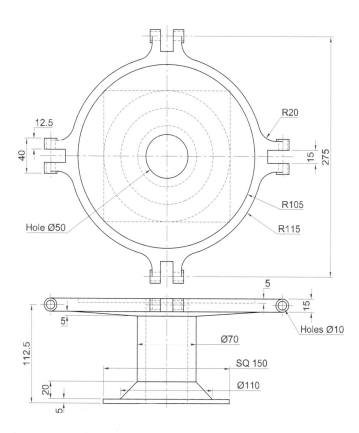

Fig. 18.34 Exercise 4 – first orthographic projection

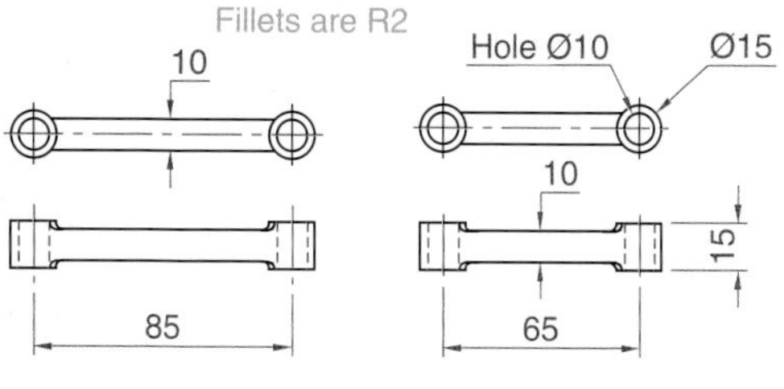

Fig. 18.35 Exercise 4 – second orthographic projection

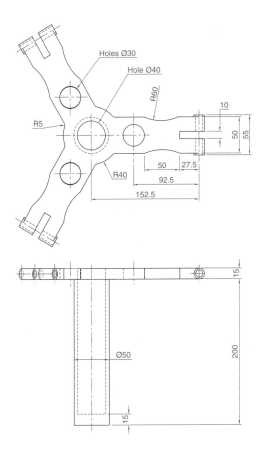

Fig. 18.36 Exercise 4 – third
orthographic projection

Fig. 18.37 Exercise 4

CHAPTER 19

Other features of 3D modelling

Aims of this chapter

1. To give a further example of placing raster images in an AutoCAD drawing.
2. To give examples of methods of printing or plotting not given in previous chapters.
3. To give examples of polygonal viewports.

Raster images in AutoCAD drawings

Example – Raster image in a drawing (Fig. 19.5)

This example shows the raster file **12.bmp** of the 3D model constructed to the details given in the drawing in Fig. 19.1.

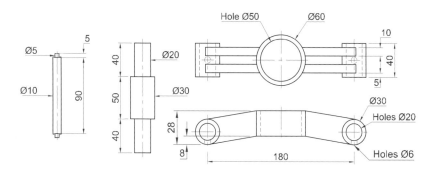

Fig. 19.1 Example – **Raster image in a drawing** – details

Raster images are graphics images such as those taken from files ending with the file extensions *.**bmp**; *.**pcx**; *.**tif** and the like. The types of graphics files which can be inserted into AutoCAD drawings can be seen by first *clicking* on **Raster Image Reference...** in the **Insert** dropdown menu (Fig. 19.2), which brings the **Select Image File** dialog (Fig. 19.3) on screen. In the dialog *click* the arrow to the right of the **Files of type** field and the popup list which appears lists the types of graphics files which can be inserted into AutoCAD drawings. Such

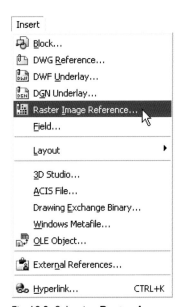

Fig. 19.2 Selecting **Raster Image Reference...** from the **Insert** dropdown menu

graphics files can be used to describe in 3D the details shown in 2D by a technical drawing.

1. Construct the 3D model to the shapes and sizes given in Fig. 19.1 working in four layers each of a different colour.
2. Place in the **SW Isometric** view.
3. Shade the 3D model using **Realistic** shading from **Visual Styles**.
4. **Zoom** the shaded model to a suitable size and press the **Print Scr** key of the keyboard.
5. Open the Windows **Paint** application and *click* **Edit** in the menu bar, followed by another *click* on **Paste** in the drop-down menu. The whole AutoCAD screen which includes the shaded 3D assembled model appears.
6. *Click* the **Select** tool icon in the toolbar of **Paint** and *window* the 3D model. Then *click* **Copy** in the **Edit** drop-down menu.
7. *Click* **New** in the **File** drop-down menu, followed by a *click* on **No** in the warning window which appears.
8. *Click* **Paste** in the **Edit** drop-down menu. The shaded 3D model appears. *Click* **Save As...** from the **File** drop-down menu and save the bitmap to a suitable file name – in this example – **12.bmp**.
9. Open the orthographic projection drawing in AutoCAD.
10. Open the **Select Image File** dialog and from the **Look in** field select the raster file **12.bmp** from the file list (Fig. 19.3). Another dialog (**Image**) opens (Fig. 19.4) showing the name of the raster image file. *Click* the **OK** button of the dialog and a series of prompts appear at the command line requesting position and scale of the image. *Enter* appropriate responses to these prompts and the image appears in position in the orthographic drawing (Fig. 19.5).

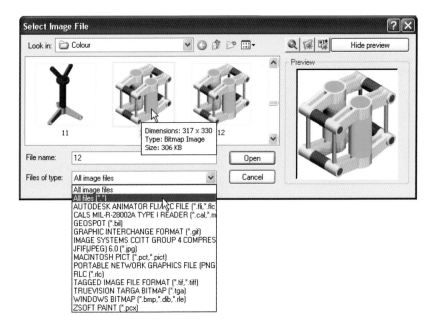

Fig. 19.3 The **Select Image File** dialog

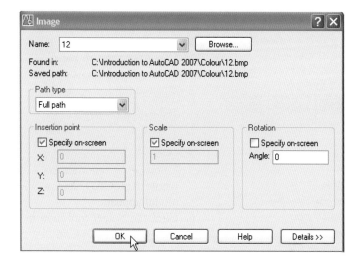

Fig. 19.4 Example – **Raster image in a drawing – the Image** dialog

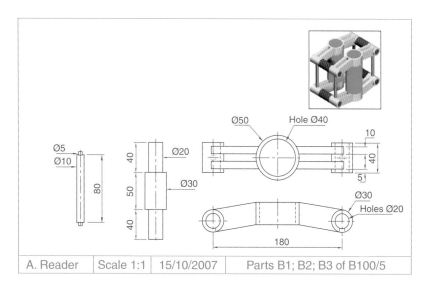

Fig. 19.5 Example – **Raster image in a drawing**

Notes

1. It will normally be necessary to *enter* a scale in response to the prompt lines otherwise the raster image may appear very small on screen. If it does it can be zoomed anyway.
2. Place the image in position in the drawing area. In Fig. 19.5 the orthographic projections have been placed within a margin and a title block has been added.

Printing/Plotting

Hardcopy (prints or plots on paper) from a variety of AutoCAD drawings of 3D models can be obtained. Some of this variety has already been shown on pages 272 to 274 in Chapter 16.

First example – Printing/Plotting (Fig. 19.8)

If an attempt is made to print a multiple viewport screen with all viewport drawings appearing in the plot, only the current viewport will be printed. To print or plot all viewports:

1. Open a four-viewport screen of the assembled 3D model shown in the first example (page 315).
2. Make a new layer **vports** of colour **yellow**. Make this layer current.
3. *Right-click* on the **Layout1** tab and *click* **Rename** in the menu which appears. *Enter* a new name in the **Layout1** tab (Fig. 19.6).

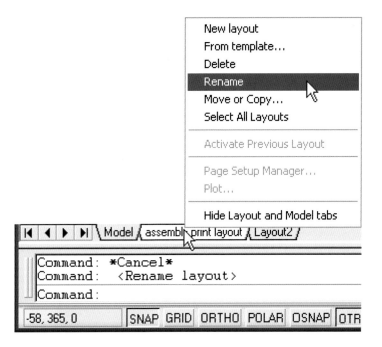

Fig. 19.6 First example
Printing/Plotting – renaming
the **Layout1** tab

4. *Click* the renamed **Layout** tab. The screen changes to a **PSpace** layout.
5. The Paper Space layout appears with the current viewport outlined in **yellow** (the colour of the **vports** layer). Using the **Erase** tool, erase the viewport with a *click* on its boundary line. The viewport and its contents disappear.
6. At the command line:

   Command: *enter* **mv** (Mview) *right-click*
   MVIEW
   Specify corner of viewport or [ON/OFF/Shadeplot/Lock/Object/ Polygonal/Restore/2/3/4]: *enter* **4** *right-click*
   Specify first corner of viewport or [Fit] <Fit>: *right-click*
   Regenerating model.
   Command:

And four viewports reappear with the 3D model drawing in each viewport.

7. *Click* the **PAPER** button in the status bar to turn it to **MODEL**. With a *click* in each viewport in turn and using the **3D Navigate** settings set viewports in **Front, Right, Top** and **Southwest/Isometric** views.
8. Turn the layer **vports** off with a *click* on its **Turn a layer On or Off** icon.
9. *Click* the **Plot** tool icon in the **Standard New** toolbar (Fig. 19.7). A **Plot** dialog appears.
10. Check that the printer/plotter is correct and the paper size is also correct.
11. *Click* the **Preview** button. The full preview of the plot appears (Fig. 19.8).

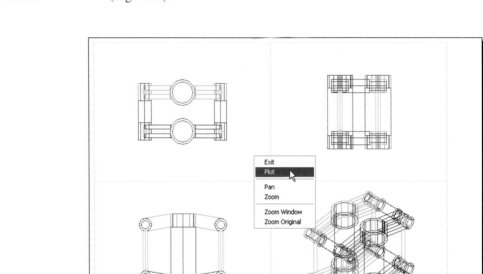

Fig. 19.7 The **Plot** tool icon from the **Standard New** toolbar

Fig. 19.8 First example – **Printing/Plotting**

12. *Right-click* anywhere in the drawing and *click* on **Plot** in the *right-click* menu which then appears.
13. The drawing plots (or prints).

Second example – Printing/Plotting (Fig. 19.9)

1. Open the orthographic drawing with its raster image (Fig. 19.5).
2. While still in **Model Space** *click* the **Plot** tool icon. The **Plot** dialog appears. Check that the required printer/plotter and paper size have been chosen.
3. *Click* the **Preview** button.
4. If satisfied with the preview (Fig. 19.9), *right-click* and in the menu which appears *click* the name **Plot**. The drawing plots.

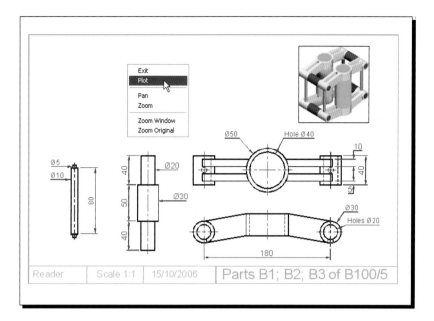

Fig. 19.9 Second example –
Printing/Plotting

Third example – Printing/Plotting (Fig. 19.10)

1. Open the 3D model drawing of the assembly shown in Fig. 19.8 in a single **Southwest/Isometric** view.
2. While in **MSpace**, *click* the **Plot** tool icon. The **Plot** dialog appears.
3. Check that the plotter device and sheet sizes are correct. *Click* the **Preview** button.
4. If satisfied with the preview (Fig. 19.10) *right-click* and *click* on **Plot** in the menu which appears. The drawing plots.

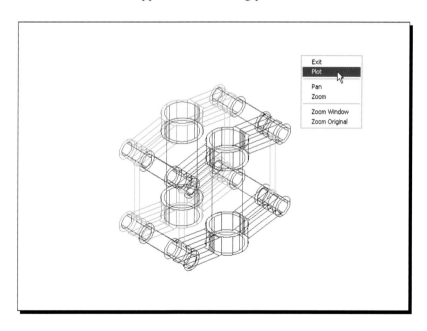

Fig. 19.10 Third example –
Printing/Plotting

Polygonal viewports (Fig. 19.11)

The example to illustrate the construction of polygonal viewports is based upon exercise 7 (page 323). When the 3D model for this assignment has been completed in **Model Space:**

1. Make a new layer of colour **yellow** and make this layer current.
2. *Click* the **Layout1** tab.
3. Erase the viewport with a *click* on its bounding line. The outline and its contents are erased.
4. At the command line:

   Command: *enter* **mv** *right-click*
   [prompts]: *enter* **4** *right-click*
   [prompts]: *right-click*
   Regenerating model.
   Command:

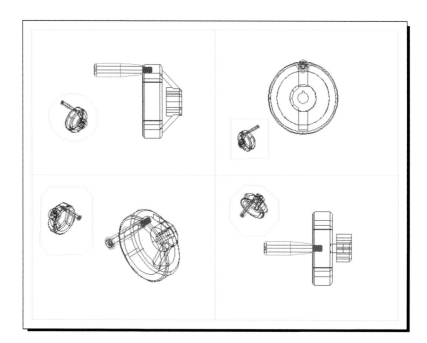

Fig. 19.11 **Polygonal viewports –** plot preview

And the model appears in a four-viewport layout.

6. *Click* the **PAPER** button in the status bar to turn it to **MODEL**. With a *click* in each viewport in turn and using the **3D Navigate** settings set viewports in **Front, Right, Top** and **Southwest/Isometric** views.
7. **Zoom** each viewport to **All**.
8. *Click* the **MODEL** button to turn back to **PAPER**.
9. Enter **mv** at the command line, which shows:

   Command: *enter* **mv** *right-click*
   MVIEW

[**prompts**]: *enter* **p** (Polygonal) *right-click*

Specify start point: In the top-right viewport *pick* one corner of a square

Specify next point or [Arc/Close/Length/Undo]: *pick* next corner for the square

Specify next point or [Arc/Close/Length/Undo]: *pick* next corner for the square

Specify next point or [Arc/Close/Length/Undo]: *enter* **c** (Close) *right-click*

Regenerating model.

Command:

And a square viewport outline appears in the top-right viewport within which is a copy of the model.

10. Repeat in each of the viewports with different shapes of polygonal viewport outlines (Fig. 19.11).
11. *Click* the **PAPER** button to change to **MODEL**.
12. In each of the polygonal viewports make a different isometric view. In the bottom-right viewport change the view using the **3D Orbit** tool.
13. Turn the layer **Yellow** off. The viewport borders disappear.
14. *Click* the **Plot** icon. Make plot settings in the **Plot** dialog. *Click* on the **Preview** button of the **Plot** dialog. The **Preview** appears (Fig. 19.12). If satisfied with the preview, *right-click* and in the menu which appears *click* **Plot**. The drawing plots.

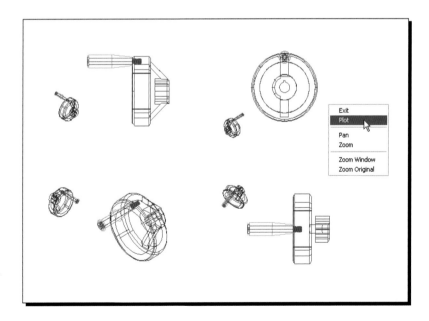

Fig. 19.12 **Polygonal viewports –** plot preview after turning the layer **Yellow** off

Exercises

1. Fig. 19.13 shows a polyline for each of the four objects from which the surface shown in Fig. 19.14 was obtained. Construct the surface and shade with **Realistic** shading.

Fig. 19.13 Exercise 1 – the pline for each of the four objects

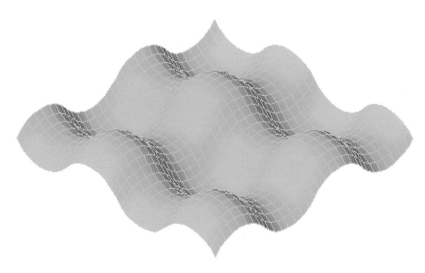

Fig. 19.14 Exercise 1

2. Working to the sizes given in Fig. 19.16, construct an assembled 3D model drawing of the spindle in its two holders and render (Fig. 19.15).

Fig. 19.15 Exercise 2

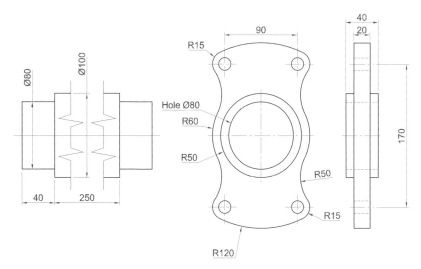

Fig. 19.16 Exercise 2 – details of shapes and sizes

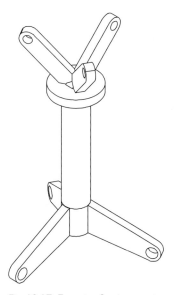

Fig. 19.17 Exercise 3 – isometric drawing

3. A partial front view of a stand is shown in an isometric drawing (Fig. 19.17). From the details given in the drawing in Fig. 19.18, construct a 3D model drawing of the stand.

Using appropriate lighting and material, render the 3D model which has been constructed.

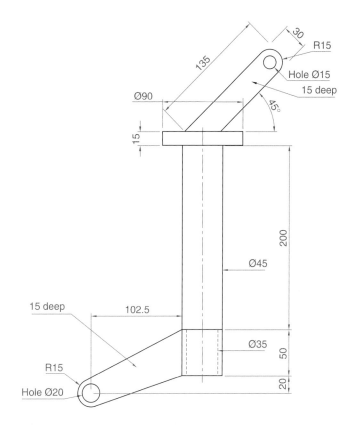

Fig. 19.18 Exercise 3

4. Construct an assembled 3D model drawing, working to the details given in Fig. 19.19.

When the drawing has been constructed disassemble the parts as shown in the given isometric drawing (Fig. 19.20).

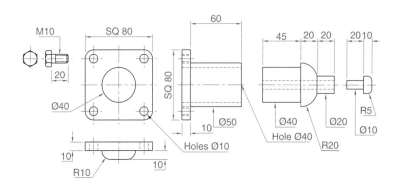

Fig. 19.19 Exercise 4 – details of shapes and sizes

Fig. 19.20 Exercise 4 – an exploded isometric drawing

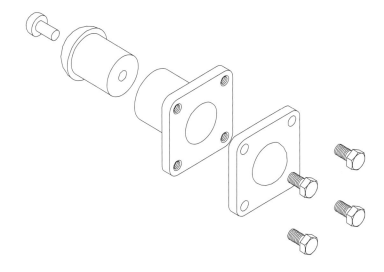

Fig. 19.21 Exercise 5

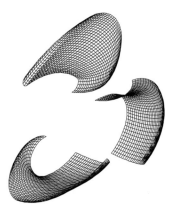

Fig. 19.22 Exercise 5 – surfaces separated

Fig. 19.23 Exercise 5 – objects for edgesurf surface model

5. The surface model for this exercise was constructed from three edgesurf surfaces, working to the suggested objects for the surface as shown in Fig. 19.23. The sizes of the outlines of the objects in each case are left to your discretion. Fig. 19.21 shows the completed surface model. Fig. 19.22 shows the three surfaces of the model separated from each other.

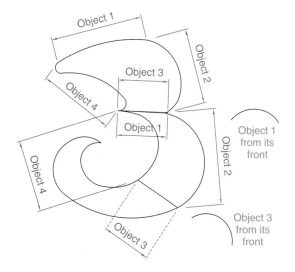

6. Working to the details shown in Fig. 19.24, construct an assembled 3D model, with the parts in their correct positions relative to each other. Then separate the parts as shown in the isometric drawing in Fig. 19.25. When the 3D model is complete add suitable lighting and materials and render the result.

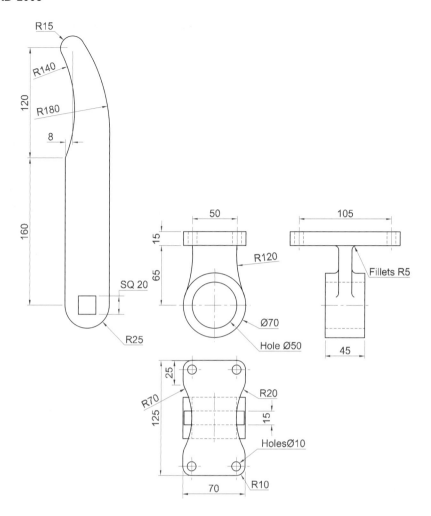

Fig. 19.24 Exercise 6 – details drawing

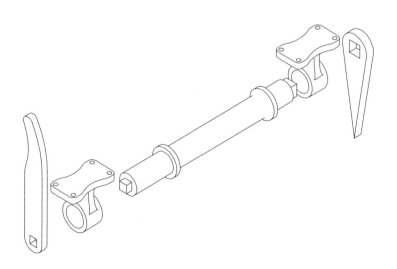

Fig. 19.25 Exercise 6 – exploded isometric drawing

7. Working to the details shown in Fig. 19.26, construct a 3D model of the parts of the wheel with its handle.

Two rendered 3D models of the rotating handle are shown in Fig. 19.27, one with its parts assembled and the other with the parts in an exploded position relative to each other.

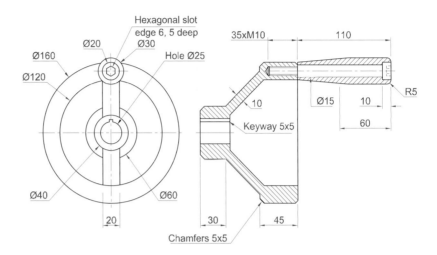

Fig. 19.26 Exercise 7 – details drawing

Fig. 19.27 Exercise 7 – renderings

CHAPTER 20

Internet tools and Help

Aim of this chapter

The purpose of this chapter is to introduce the tools which are available in AutoCAD 2008 which make use of facilities available on the World Wide Web (www).

Emailing drawings

As with any other files which are composed of data, AutoCAD drawings can be sent by email as attachments. If a problem of security of the drawings is involved they can be encapsulated with a password as the drawings are saved prior to being attached in an email. To encrypt a drawing with a password, *click* **Tools** in the **Save Drawing As** dialog and from the popup list which appears *click* **Security Options...** (Fig. 20.1). Then in the **Security Options** dialog which appears (Fig. 20.2) *enter* a password in the **Password or phrase to open this drawing** field. After *entering* a password *click* the **OK** button and *enter* the password in the **Confirm Password** dialog which appears. The drawing then cannot be opened until the password is *entered* in the **Password** dialog which appears when an attempt is made to open the drawing by the person receiving the email (Fig. 20.3).

There are many reasons why drawings may require to be password encapsulated in order to protect confidentiality of the contents of drawings.

Creating a web page (Fig. 20.5)

To create a webpage which includes AutoCAD drawings *left-click* **Publish to Web...** from the **File** drop-down menu. A series of ten **Publish to Web** dialogs appear, the third of which is shown in Fig. 20.4. After making

Fig. 20.1 Selecting **Security Options...** in the **Save Drawing As** dialog

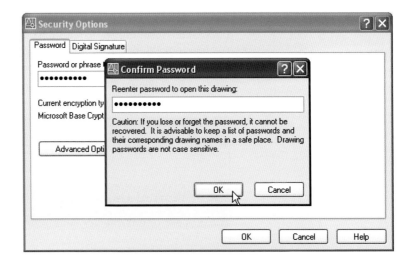

Fig. 20.2 *Entering* and confirming a password in the **Security Options** dialog

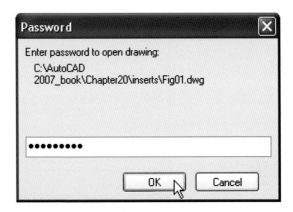

Fig. 20.3 The **Password** dialog appearing when a password-encrypted drawing is about to be opened

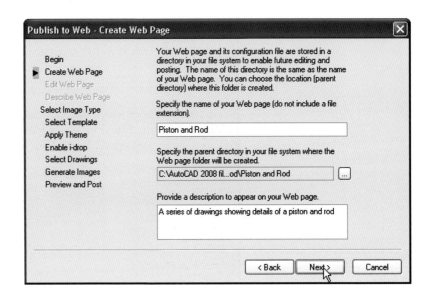

Fig. 20.4 One of the **Publish to Web** dialogs

entries in the dialogs which come on screen after each **Next** button is *clicked*, the resulting webpage such as that shown in Fig. 20.5 will be seen (which, in the dialog **Enable i-drop**, can be posted on the Web). A *double-click* in any of the thumbnail views in this webpage and another page appears showing the selected drawing in full (Fig. 20.6).

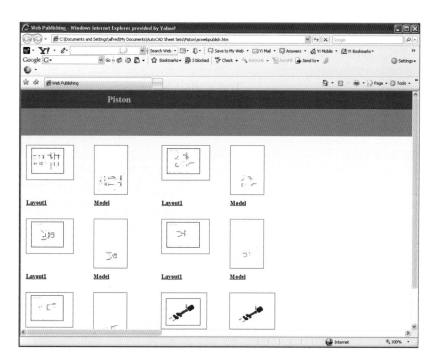

Fig. 20.5 The webpage resulting from completing the **Publish to Web** series of dialogs

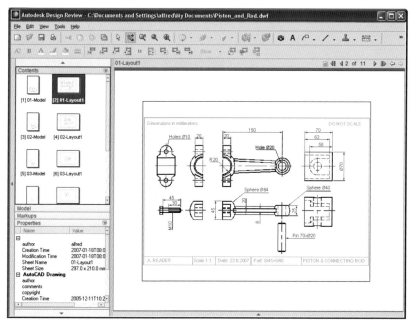

Fig. 20.6 The DWF file opened in an **Autodesk Design Review** window

In this example the drawings are the same as those which were included in a **DWF** file for the set of drawings shown in the sheet set for Exercise 1 of Chapter 11 (page 184). The drawings are shown in Fig. 20.6 in an **Autodesk Design Review** window.

The eTransmit tool

Click **eTransmit...** in the **File** drop-down menu and the **Create Transmittal** dialog appears (Fig. 20.7). The transmittal shown in this example is the drawing on screen at the time. Fill in details as necessary and *click* the **Transmittal Setups...** button and a **zip** file is formed from the drawing file by making settings in the next dialog to appear (Fig. 20.8). This **zip** file is easier and quicker to email than the drawing file. The AutoCAD drawing can be obtained by unzipping the **zip** file at the receiving end.

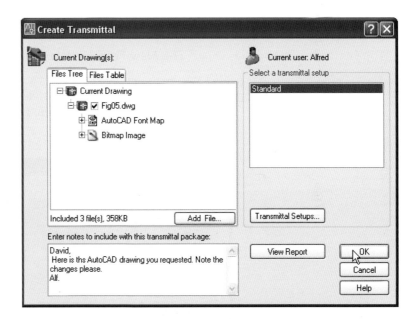

Fig. 20.7 The **Create Transmittal** dialog

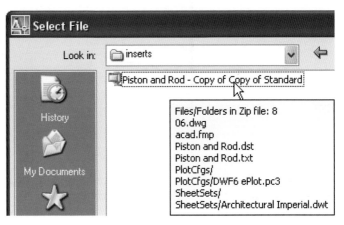

Fig. 20.8 The **zip** file created from the **Create Transmittal** dialog

Help

Fig. 20.9 shows the **Help** drop-down menu. Apart from the standard Windows **Help** feature, other features are shown in the menu.

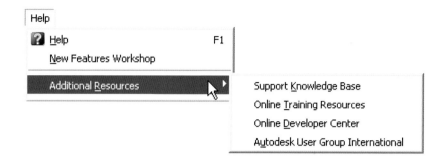

Fig. 20.9 The **Help** drop-down menu

The New Features Workshop

Click this option in the menu and a series of explanatory illustrated notes can be selected from lists in the window which appears. Fig. 20.10 shows the window explaining **Photometric Lights**.

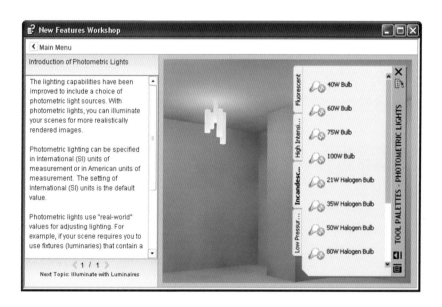

Fig. 20.10 One of the windows from the **New Features Workshop**

Additional Resources

A *click* on any one of the **Additional Resources** brings up an Autodesk webpage. Fig. 20.11 shows part of the webpage brought to screen with a *click* on **Support Knowledge Base**.

Fig. 20.11 The **Support Knowledge Base** webpage

The InfoCenter

Another **Help** system has been included in AutoCAD 2008. It is situated at the top right-hand corner of the AutoCAD 2008 window in the **Info-Center** (Fig. 20.12).

Fig. 20.12 The **InfoCenter**

Enter a request in the **InfoCenter** field, followed by *clicking* the **InfoCenter** icon and a menu appears offering choices from which a selection may be made. (Fig. 20.13).

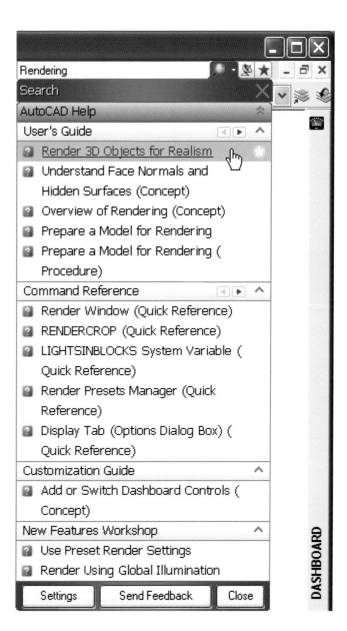

Fig. 20.13 *Entering* a request in the
InfoCenter field, followed by a
click on the **InfoCenter** icon

Click the **Communication Center** icon and another menu appears
from which choices may be made (Fig. 20.14).

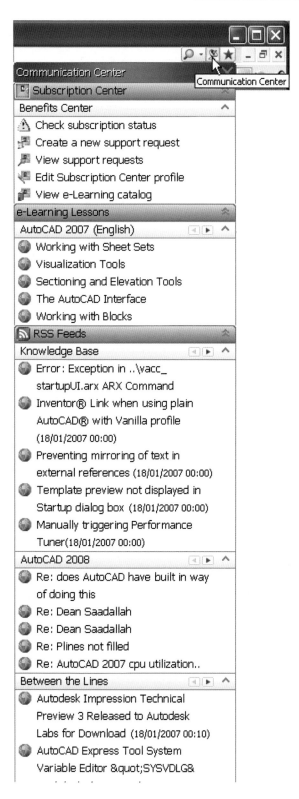

Fig. 20.14 The **Communication Center** menu

CHAPTER 21

Design and AutoCAD 2008

Ten reasons for using AutoCAD

1. A CAD software package such as AutoCAD 2008 can be used to produce any form of technical drawing.
2. Technical drawings can be produced much more speedily using AutoCAD than when working manually – probably as much as ten times as quickly when used by skilled AutoCAD operators.
3. Drawing with AutoCAD is less tedious than drawing manually – features such as hatching, lettering, adding notes, etc. are easier, quicker and indeed more accurate.
4. Drawings or parts of drawings can be moved, copied, scaled, rotated, mirrored and inserted into other drawings without having to redraw.
5. AutoCAD drawings can be saved to a file system without necessarily having to print the drawing. This can save the need for large drawing storage areas.
6. The same drawing or part of a drawing need never be drawn twice, because it can be copied or inserted into other drawings with ease. A basic rule when working with AutoCAD is: ***Never draw the same feature twice***.
7. New details can be added to drawings or be changed within drawings without having to mechanically erase the old detail.
8. Dimensions can be added to drawings with accuracy reducing the possibility of making errors.
9. Drawings can be plotted or printed to any scale without having to redraw.
10. Drawings can be exchanged between computers and/or emailed around the world without having to physically send the drawing.

The place of AutoCAD 2008 in designing

The contents of this book are designed to help only those who have a limited (or no) knowledge of and skills in the construction of technical drawings using AutoCAD 2008. However it needs to be recognised that the impact of modern computing on the methods of designing in industry has been immense. Such features as analysis of stresses, shear forces, bending forces and the like can be carried out more quickly and accurately using computing methods. The storage of data connected with a design and the ability to recover the data speedily are carried out much easier using computing methods than prior to the introduction of computing.

AutoCAD 2008 can play an important part in the design process because technical drawings of all types are necessary for achieving well-designed artefacts whether it be an engineering component, a machine, a building, an electronics circuit or any other design project.

In particular, 2D drawings, which can be constructed in AutoCAD 2008, are still of great value in modern industry. AutoCAD 2008 can also be used to produce excellent and accurate 3D models, which can be rendered to produce photographic-like images of a suggested design. Although not dealt with in this book, data from 3D models constructed in AutoCAD 2008 can be taken for use in computer-aided machining (CAM).

At all stages in the design process, either 2D or 3D drawings (or both) can play an important part in aiding those engaged in designing to assist in assessing the results of their work at various stages. It is in the design process that drawings constructed in AutoCAD 2008 play an important part.

In the simplified design process chart shown in Fig. 21.1 an asterisk (*) has been shown against those features where the use of AutoCAD 2008 can be regarded as being of value.

A design chart (Fig. 21.1)

The simplified design chart in Fig. 21.1 shows the following features:

Design brief: A design brief is a necessary feature of the design process. It can be in the form of a statement, but it is usually much more. A design brief can be a written report which not only includes a statement made

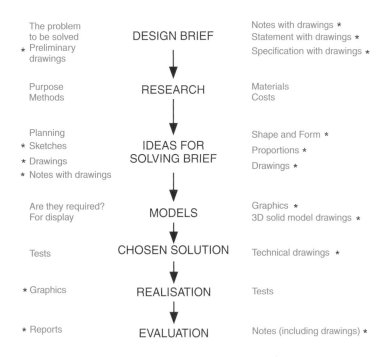

Fig. 21.1 A simplified design chart

of the problem which the design is assumed to be solving, but includes preliminary notes and drawings describing difficulties which may be encountered in solving the design and may include charts, drawings, costings, etc. to emphasise some of the needs in solving the problem for which the design is being made.

Research: The need to research the various problems which may arise when designing is often much more demanding than that shown in the chart (Fig. 21.1). For example the materials being used may require extensive research as to costing, stress analysis, electrical conductivity, difficulties in machining or in constructional techniques and other such features.

Ideas for solving the brief: This is where technical and other drawings and sketches play an important part in designing. It is only after research that designers can ensure the brief will be fulfilled.

Models: These may be constructed models in materials representing the actual materials which have been chosen for the design, but in addition 3D solid model drawings, such as those which can be constructed in AutoCAD 2008, can be of value. Some models may also be made in the materials from which the final design is to be made so as to allow testing of the materials in the design situation.

Chosen solution: This is where the use of drawings constructed in AutoCAD 2008 are of great value. 2D and 3D drawings come into play here. It is from such drawings that the final design will be manufactured.

Realisation: The design is made. There may be a need to manufacture a number of the designs in order to enable evaluation of the design to be fully assessed.

Evaluation: The manufactured design is tested in situations such as it is liable to be placed in use. Evaluation will include reports and notes which could include drawings with suggestions for amendments to the working drawings from which the design was realised.

Enhancements in AutoCAD 2008

AutoCAD 2008 contains major enhancements over previous releases, when working in either a **2D** or a **3D** environment. Please note that not all the enhancements in AutoCAD 2008 are described in this introductory book. Among the more important enhancements are the following:

1. The introduction of a 64-bit software edition of AutoCAD 2008 as well as a 32-bit edition.
2. The introduction of a new workspace – **2D Drafting & Annotation**.
3. Major changes to the **DASHBOARD** with the introduction of new control panels.
4. Control panels now include **2D Draw, 3D Make, 2D Navigate, Light, Visual Styles, Materials, Render, Layers, Annotation Scaling, Text, Dimensions, Multi-leaders, Tables, 3D Navigate, Object Properties** and **Block Attributes**.
5. Multiple copies added to the **Copy** command.
6. Changes to methods of constructing sheet sets.

7. New commands and set variables added.
8. Drawings constructed in **MicroStation V8** can be imported and exported into and from AutoCAD.
9. Some new dimension commands, including a new command **DIMBREAK** with which dimension lines can be broken as they cross features in a drawing.
10. Other enhancements in dimensioning.
11. Enhancements in **Mtext**.
12. Enhanced settings available in the **Layer Settings** dialog of the **Layer Properties Manager**.
13. Some new commands and new system variables introduced.
14. New **Help** features in an **InfoCenter** (top right-hand corner of AutoCAD 2008 window).
15. Changes to methods of rendering 3D solid model drawings, with the introduction of new tools, new methods of lighting, adding materials, shading and rendering. Changes in methods of applying materials and lighting, including sun lighting.
16. Enhanced **Materials** palette allowing easier viewing and editing of materials.
17. Many new materials added to the **Textures** folder.
18. A new command **- render** (the hyphen [-] must be included) allowing use of the command line to set rendering presets.
19. Photometric lighting introduced akin to wattage in electric lights.
20. Of the new control panels, two have not been included in examples in previous chapters – **Annotation Scaling** and **Multi-leaders**. Simple examples of the use of tools from these control panels are given below.

Annotation scaling

Annotation scaling has many uses. This example shows only one of its many uses.

1. The drawing in Fig. 21.2 shows a scale **1:30** view of the front view of a bungalow in **Model Space** in a **Paper Space** window.
2. *Click* the down-pointing arrow at the right-hand end of the status bar and, in the menu which appears, note that the drawing has been constructed to a scale of **1:30** (Fig. 21.2).
3. *Click* **1:50** in the Annotation Scaling menu and the front view changes to show a scale **1:50** front view (Fig. 21.3).

Multileaders

There are a variety of uses for mutlileaders. This example shows one such use. The drawing in which multileaders are to be included is shown in Fig. 21.4.

1. In the **Multileaders** control panel *click* the **Multileader Style Manager** icon (Fig. 21.5). The dialog appears (Fig. 21.6).

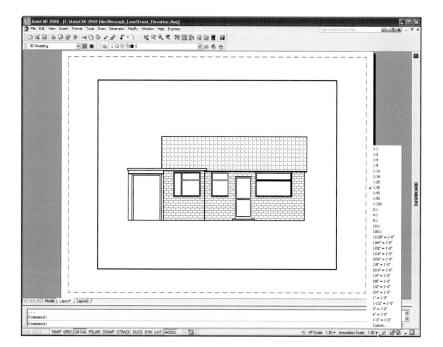

Fig. 21.2 First example –
Annotation Scaling. The front
view of a bungalow drawn to a
scale of **1:30**

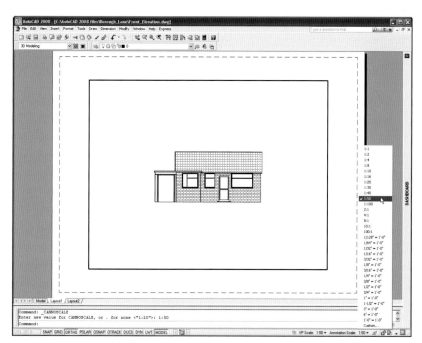

Fig. 21.3 First example –
Annotation Scaling. The front
view scaled to **1:50**

2. In the dialog make entries as shown in Figs 21.6, 21.7 and 21.8.
3. *Click* **Multileader** icon in the control panel.
4. In the drawing, in response to prompts at the command line, add multi-leaders one after the other to the drawing in Fig. 21.4, numbering the parts **1** to **4**. See Fig. 21.9.

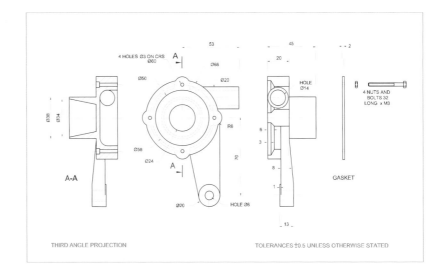

Fig. 21.4 Second example –
Multileaders. The drawing to
which multileaders are to be
added

Fig. 21.5 Second example –
Multileaders. The **Multileader
Style Manager** icon in the
Multileaders control panel

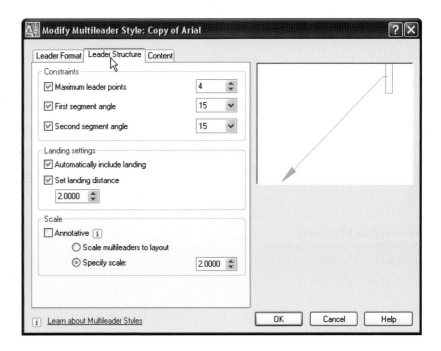

Fig. 21.6 Second example –
Multileaders. Settings in the
Leader Structure part of the
dialog

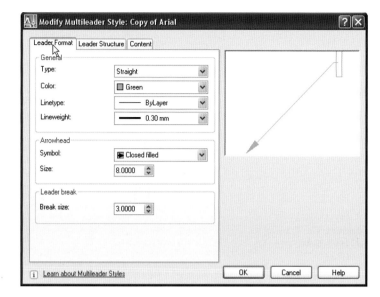

Fig. 21.7 Second example –
Multileaders. Settings in the
Leader Format part of the
dialog

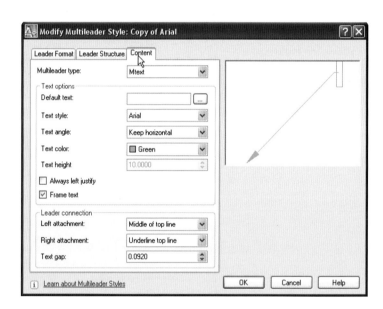

Fig. 21.8 Second example –
Multileaders. Settings in the
Content part of the dialog

System requirements for running AutoCAD 2008

Note

There are two editions of AutoCAD 2008 – 32-bit and 64-bit editions.

Operating system: Windows XP Professional, Windows XP Professional
(x64 Edition), Windows XP Home Edition, Windows 2000 or Windows
Vista 32 bit, Windows Vista 64 bit.

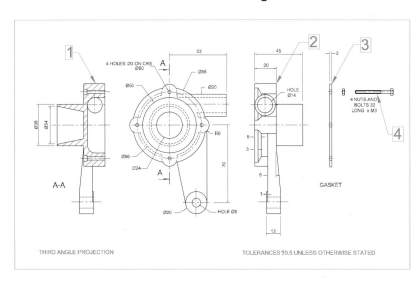

Fig. 21.9 Second example –
Multileaders

Microsoft Internet Explorer 7.0.

Processor: Pentium III 800 Mhz.

RAM: At least 128 MB.

Monitor screen: 1024 × 768 VGA with True Colour as a minimum.

Hard disk: A minimum of 300 MB.

Graphics card: An AutoCAD certified graphics card. Details can be found
on the webpage **AutoCAD Certified Hardware XML Database**.

APPENDIX A

Printing/Plotting

Introduction

Some suggestions for printing/plotting of AutoCAD drawings have already been given (pages 272 to 274). Plotters or printers can be selected from a wide range and are used for printing or plotting drawings constructed in AutoCAD 2008. The example given here has been from a print using one of the default printers connected to the computer used by the author. However if another plotter or printer is connected to the computer, its driver can be set by first opening the Windows **Control Panel** and with a *double-click* on the **Autodesk Plotter Manager** icon the **Plotters** dialogs appears (Fig. A.1).

Fig. A.1 The **Plotters** window

Double-click on the **Add, remove or change plotter properties** icon and the **Plotter Configuration Editor** dialog appears. Add settings as required in the first of the dialogs from this editor (Fig. A.2). There are several more dialogs in the series in which selections will need to be made before completing the setting up of a printer or plotter for the printing of AutoCAD drawings.

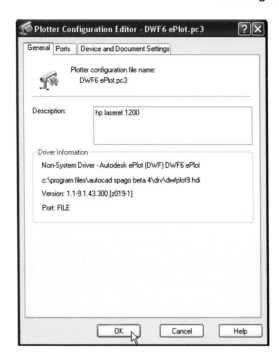

Fig. A.2 The first of the series of
Plotter Configuration Editor
dialogs

Notes

1. AutoCAD drawings can be printed from the default printers already installed in the Windows system of the computer on which AutoCAD 2008 is loaded.
2. Plots or prints from drawings constructed in AutoCAD 2008 can be made from either Model Space or Paper Space.

An example of a printout

1. Either select **Plot...** with a *click* on its tool icon in the **Standard** toolbar (Fig. A.3) or from the **File** drop-down menu. The **Plot** dialog appears (Fig. A.4).

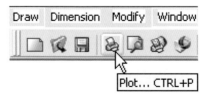

Fig. A.3 The **Plot** tool icon in the
Standard toolbar

2. There are two parts in the **Plot** dialog. Fig. A.4 shows both the parts. A *click* on the arrow at the bottom right-hand corner of the dialog closes to reveal only the left-hand part and vice versa.
3. Select an appropriate printer or plotter from the **Printer/plotter** list. In this example this is a colour printer. Then select the correct paper size

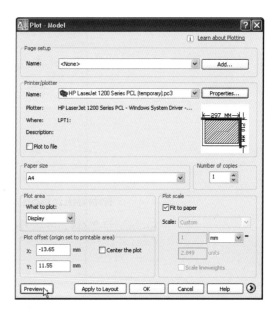

Fig. A.4 The **Plot** dialog

from the **Paper size** popup list. Then select what is to be printed/plotted from the **What to plot** popup list – in the example shown this is **Display**. Make sure the **Landscape** button is showing a dot (on). *Click* the **Properties** button and in the **Custom Properties** dialog (not shown) set **Orientation** to **Landscape** (dot in radio button). Then *click* the **Preview** button of the **Plot** dialog.

4. A preview of the drawing to be printed/plotted appears (Fig. A.5). If satisfied with the preview, *right-click* and from the menu which appears *click* **Plot**. If not satisfied *click* **Exit**. The preview disappears and the **Plot** dialog reappears. Make changes as required from an inspection of the preview and carry on in this manner until a plot can be made.

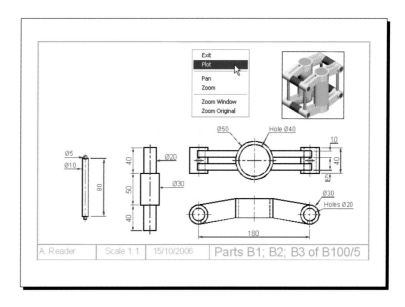

Fig. A.5 The **Plot Preview**
window with its *right-click* menu

List of tools

Introduction

AutoCAD 2008 allows the use of over 300 tools. Some operators prefer using the word "commands", although command as an alternative to tool is not in common use today. The majority of these tools are described in this list. Many of the tools described here have not been used in this book, because this book is an introductory text designed to initiate readers into the basic methods of using AutoCAD 2008. It is hoped the list will encourage readers to experiment with those tools not described in the book. The abbreviations for tools which can be abbreviated are included in brackets after the tool name. Tool names can be *entered* in upper or lower case.

A list of 2D tools is followed by a listing of 3D tools. Internet tools are described at the end of this listing.

2D tools

About – Brings the **About AutoCAD** bitmap on screen
Appload – Brings the **Load/Unload Applications** dialog to screen
Adcenter (dc) – Brings the **DesignCenter** palette on screen
Align (al) – Aligns objects between chosen points
Arc (a) – Creates an arc
Area – States in square units the area selected from a number of points
Array (ar) – Creates **Rectangular** or **Polar** arrays in 2D
Ase – Brings the **dbConnect Manager** on screen
Attdef – Brings the **Attribute Definition** dialog on screen
Attedit – Allows editing of attributes from the Command line
Audit – Checks and fixes any errors in a drawing
Autopublish – Creates a **DWF** file for the drawing on screen
Bhatch (h) – Brings the **Boundary Hatch** dialog on screen
Block – Brings the **Block Definition** dialog on screen
Bmake (b) – Brings the **Block Definition** dialog on screen
Bmpout – Brings the **Create Raster File** dialog
Boundary (bo) – Brings the **Boundary Creation** dialog on screen
Break (br) – Breaks an object into parts
Cal – Calculates mathematical expressions
Chamfer (cha) – Creates a chamfer between two entities

Chprop (ch) – Brings the **Properties** window on screen

Circle (c) – Creates a circle

Copytolayer – Copies objects from one layer to another

Copy (co) – Creates a single or multiple copies of selected entities

Copyclip (Ctrl+C) – Copies a drawing, or part of a drawing, for inserting into a document from another application

Copylink – Forms a link between an AutoCAD drawing and its appearance in another application such as a word-processing package

Customize – Brings the **Customize** dialog to screen, allowing the customisation of toolbars, palettes, etc.

Dashboard – Brings the **DASHBOARD** to screen

Dashboardclose – Closes the **DASHBOARD**

Dblist – Creates a database list in a Text window for every entity in a drawing

Ddattdef (at) – Brings the **Attribute Definition** dialog to screen

Ddatte (ate) – Edits individual attribute values

Ddatext – Brings the **Attribute Extraction** dialog on screen

Ddcolor (col) – Brings the **Select Color** dialog on screen

Ddedit (ed) – The **Text Formatting** dialog box appears on selecting text

Ddim (d) – Brings the **Dimension Style Manager** dialog box on screen

Ddinsert (i) – Brings the **Insert** dialog on screen

Ddmodify – Brings the **Properties** window on screen

Ddosnap (os) – Brings the **Drafting Settings** dialog on screen

Ddptype – Brings the **Point Style** dialog on screen

Ddrmodes (rm) – Brings the **Drafting Settings** dialog on screen

Dd units (un) – Brings the **Drawing Units** dialog on screen

Ddview (v) – Brings the **View** dialog on screen

Del – Allows a file (or any file) to be deleted

Dgnexport – Creates a **MicroStation V8 dgn** file from the drawing on screen

Dgnimport – Allows a **MicroStation V8 dgn** file to be imported as an AutoCAD dwg file

Dim – Starts a session of dimensioning

Dimension tools – The **Dimension** toolbar contains the following tools – **Linear, Aligned, Arc Length, Ordinate, Radius, Jogged, Diameter, Angular, Quick Dimension, Baseline, Continue, Quick Leader, Tolerance, Center Mark, Dimension Edit, Dimension Edit Text, Update** and **Dimension Style**

Dim1 – Allows the addition of a single dimension to a drawing

Dist (di) – Measures the distance between two points in coordinate units

Distantlight – Creates a distant light

Divide (div) – Divides an entity into equal parts

Donut (do) – Creates a donut

Dsviewer – Brings the **Aerial View** window on screen

Dtext (dt) – Creates dynamic text. Text appears in drawing area as it is *entered*

Dxbin – Brings the **Select DXB File** dialog on screen

Dxfin – Brings the **Select File** dialog on screen

Dxfout – Brings the **Save Drawing As** dialog on screen

Ellipse (el) – Creates an ellipse

Erase (e) – Erases selected entities from a drawing

Exit – Ends a drawing session and closes AutoCAD 2008

Explode (x) – Explodes a block or group into its various entities

Explorer – Brings the Windows **Explorer** on screen

Export (exp) – Brings the **Export Data** dialog on screen

Extend (ex) – To extend an entity to another

Fillet (f) – Creates a fillet between two entities

Filter – Brings the **Object Selection Filters** dialog on screen

Gradient – Brings the **Hatch and Gradient** dialog on screen

Group (g) – Brings the **Object Grouping** dialog on screen

Hatch – Allows hatching by the *entry* responses to prompts

Hatchedit (he) – Allows editing of associative hatching

Help – Brings the **AutoCAD 2008 Help: User Documentation** dialog on screen

Hide (hi) – To hide hidden lines in 3D models

Id – Identifies a point on screen in coordinate units

Imageadjust (iad) – Allows adjustment of images

Imageattach (iat) – Brings the **Select Image File** dialog on screen

Imageclip – Allows clipping of images

Import – Brings the **Import File** dialog on screen

Insert (i) – Brings the **Insert** dialog on screen

Insertobj – Brings the **Insert Object** dialog on screen

Isoplane (Ctrl/E) – Sets the isoplane when constructing an isometric drawing

Join (j) – Joins lines which are in line with each other or arcs which are from the same centre point

Laycur – Changes layer of selected objects to current layer

Laydel – Deletes and purges a layer with its contents

Layer (la) – Brings the **Layer Properties Manager** dialog on screen

Layout – Allows editing of layouts

Lengthen (len) – Lengthens an entity on screen

Limits – Sets the drawing limits in coordinate units

Line (l) – Creates a line

Linetype (lt) – Brings the **Linetype Manager** dialog on screen

List (li) – Lists in a text window details of any entity or group of entities selected

Load – Brings the **Select Shape File** dialog on screen

Ltscale (lts) – Allows the linetype scale to be adjusted

Measure (me) – Allows measured intervals to be placed along entities

Menu – Brings the **Select Menu File** dialog on screen

Menuload – Brings the **Menu Customization** dialog on screen

Mirror (mi) – Creates an identical mirror image of selected entities

Mledit – Brings the **Multiline Edit Tools** dialog on screen

Mline (ml) – Creates mlines

Mlstyle – Brings the **Multiline Styles** dialog on screen

Move (m) – Allows selected entities to be moved

Mslide – Brings the **Create Slide File** dialog on screen

Mspace (ms) – When in PSpace changes to MSpace

Mtext (mt or t) – Brings the **Multiline Text Editor** on screen

Mview (mv) – To make settings of viewports in Paper Space

Mvsetup – Allows drawing specifications to be set up

New (Ctrl+N) – Brings the **Select template** dialog on screen

Notepad – For editing files from the Windows 95 **Notepad**

Offset (o) – Offsets selected entity by a stated distance

Oops – Cancels the effect of using **Erase**

Open – Brings the **Select File** dialog on screen

Options – Brings the **Options** dialog to screen

Ortho – Allows ortho to be set ON/OFF

Osnap (os) – Brings the **Drafting Settings** dialog to screen

Pagesetup – Brings either the **Page Setup Model** or **Page Setup-Layout1** dialog to screen for setting print/plot parameters

Pan (p) – *Drags* a drawing in any direction

Pbrush – Brings Windows **Paint** on screen

Pedit (pe) – Allows editing of polylines. One of the options is **Multiple** allowing continuous editing of polylines without closing the command

Pline (pl) – Creates a polyline

Plot (Ctrl+P) – Brings the **Plot** dialog to screen

Point (po) – Allows a point to be placed on screen

Polygon (pol) – Creates a polygon

Polyline (pl) – Creates a polyline

Preferences (pr) – Brings the **Options** dialog on screen

Preview (pre) – Brings the print/plot preview box on screen

Properties – Brings the **Properties** palette on screen

Psfill – Allows polylines to be filled with patterns

Psout – Brings the **Create Postscript File** dialog on screen

Purge (pu) – Purges unwanted data from a drawing before saving to file

Qsave – Saves the drawing file to its current name in AutoCAD 2008

Quickcalc (qc) – Brings the **QUICKCALC** palette to screen

Quit – Ends a drawing session and closes down AutoCAD 2008

Ray – A construction line from a point

Recover – Brings the **Select File** dialog on screen to allow recovery of selected drawings as necessary

Recoverall – Repairs damaged drawing

Rectang (rec) – Creates a pline rectangle

Redefine – If an AutoCAD command name has been turned off by **Undefine**, **Redefine** turns the command name back on

Redo – Cancels the last **Undo**

Redraw (r) – Redraws the contents of the AutoCAD 2008 drawing area

Redrawall (ra) – Redraws the whole of a drawing

Regen (re) – Regenerates the contents of the AutoCAD 2008 drawing area

Regenall (rea) – Regenerates the whole of a drawing

Region (reg) – Creates a region from an area within a boundary

Rename (ren) – Brings the **Rename** dialog on screen

Replay – Brings the **Replay** dialog on screen from which bitmap image files can be selected

Revcloud – Forms a cloud-like outline around objects in a drawing to which attention needs to be drawn

Save (Ctrl+S) – Brings the **Save Drawing** As dialog box on screen

Saveas – Brings the **Save Drawing** As dialog box on screen

Saveimg – Brings the **Save Image** dialog on screen

Scale (sc) – Allows selected entities to be scaled in size – smaller or larger

Script (scr) – Brings the **Select Script File** dialog on screen

Setvar (set) – Can be used to bring a list of the settings of set variables into an AutoCAD Text window

Shape – Inserts an already loaded shape into a drawing

Shell – Allows MS-DOS commands to be entered

Sketch – Allows freehand sketching

Solid (so) – Creates a filled outline in triangular parts

Spell (sp) – Brings the **Check Spelling** dialog on screen

Spline (spl) – Creates a spline curve through selected points

Splinedit (spe) – Allows the editing of a spline curve

Stats – Brings the **Statistics** dialog on screen

Status – Shows the status (particularly memory use) in a Text window

Stretch (s) – Allows selected entities to be stretched

Style (st) – Brings the **Text Style** dialog on screen

Tablet (ta) – Allows a tablet to be used with a pointing device

Tbconfig – Brings the **Customize** dialog on screen to allow configuration of a toolbar

Text – Allows text from the Command line to be entered into a drawing

Thickness (th) – Sets the thickness for the Elevation command

Tilemode – Allows settings to enable Paper Space

Tolerance – Brings the **Geometric Tolerance** dialog on screen

Toolbar (to) – Brings the **Toolbars** dialog on screen

Trim (tr) – Allows entities to be trimmed up to other entities

Type – Types the contents of a named file to screen

UCS – Allows selection of **UCS** (User Coordinate System) facilites

Undefine – Suppresses an AutoCAD command name

Undo (u) (Ctrl+Z) – Undoes the last action of a tool

View – Brings the **View** dialog on screen

Vplayer – Controls the visibility of layers in Paperspace

Vports – Brings the **Viewports** dialog on screen

Vslide – Brings the **Select Slide File** dialog on screen

Wblock (w) – Brings the **Create Drawing File** dialog on screen

Wmfin – Brings the **Import WMF File** dialog on screen

Wipeout – Forms a polygonal outline within which all crossed parts of objects are erased

Wmfopts – Brings the **Import Options** dialog on screen

Wmfout – Brings the **Create WMF** dialog on screen

Xattach (xa) – Brings the **Select Reference File** dialog on screen

Xline – Creates a construction line
Xref (xr) – Brings the **Xref Manager** dialog on screen
Zoom (z) – Brings the zoom tool into action

3D tools

3darray – Creates an array of 3D models in 3D space
3dface (3f) – Creates a 3- or 4-sided 3D mesh behind which other features can be hidden
3dmesh – Creates a 3D mesh in 3D space
3dcorbit – Allows methods of manipulating 3D models on screen
3ddistance – Allows the controlling of the distance of 3D models from the operator
3dfly – Allows walkthroughs in any 3D plane
3dforbit – Controls the viewing of 3D models without constraint
3dmove – Shows a 3D move icon
3dorbit (3do) – Allows a continuous movement and other methods of manipulation of 3D models on screen
3dorbitctr – Allows further and a variety of other methods of manipulation of 3D models on screen
3dpan – Allows the panning of 3D models vertically and horizontally on screen
3drotate – Displays a 3D rotate icon
3dsin – Brings the **3D Studio File Import** dialog on screen
3dsout – Brings the **3D Studio Output File** dialog on screen
3ddwf – Brings up the **Export 3D DWF** dialog
3dwalk – Starts walk mode in 3D
anipath – Opens the **Motion Path Animation** dialog
Align – Allows selected entities to be aligned to selected points in 3D space
Ameconvert – Converts AME solid models (from Release 12) into AutoCAD 2000 solid models
Box – Creates a 3D solid box
Cone – Creates a 3D model of a cone
convertoldlights – Converts lighting from previous releases to AutoCAD 2008 lighting
convertoldmaterials – Converts materials from previous releases to AutoCAD 2008 materials
convtosolid – Converts plines and circles with thickness to 3D solids
convtosurface – Converts objects to surfaces
Cylinder – Creates a 3D cylinder
Dducs (uc) – Brings the **UCS** dialog on screen
Edgesurf – Creates a 3D mesh surface from four adjoining edges
Extrude (ext) – Extrudes a closed polyline
Flatshot – Creates flattened view
Freepoint – Point light created without settings
Freespot – Spot light created without settings
Helix – Constructs a helix

Interfere – Creates an interference solid from selection of several solids

Intersect (in) – Creates an intersection solid from a group of solids

Light – Brings the **Lights** dialog on screen

Lightlist – Opens the **Lights in Model Space** palette

Loft – Activates the **Loft** command

Materials – Opens the **Materials** palette

Matlib – Brings the **Materials Library** dialog on screen

Mirror3d – Mirrors 3D models in 3D space in selected directions

Mview (mv) – When in PSpace brings in MSpace objects

Pface – Allows the construction of a 3D mesh through a number of selected vertices

Plan – Allows a drawing in 3D space to be seen in plan (UCS World)

Planesurf – Creates a planar surface

Pointlight – Creates a **Point** light

Pspace (ps) – Changes MSpace to PSpace

Pyramid – Creates a pyramid

Renderpresets – Opens the **Render Presets Manager** dialog

Renderwin – Opens the **Render** window

Revolve (rev) – Forms a solid of revolution from outlines

Revsurf – Creates a solid of revolution from a pline

Rmat – Brings the **Materials** dialog on screen

Rpref (rpr) – Brings the **Rendering Preferences** dialog on screen

Rulesurf – Creates a 3D mesh between two entities

Scene – Brings the **Scenes** dialog on screen

Section (sec) – Creates a section plane in a 3D model

Shade (sha) – Shades a selected 3D model

Slice (sl) – Allows a 3D model to be cut into several parts

Solprof – Creates a profile from a 3D solid model drawing

Sphere – Creates a 3D solid model sphere

Spotlight – Creates a spotlight

Stlout – Saves a 3D model drawing in ASCII or binary format

Sunproperties – Opens the **Sun** palette

Sunstudywizard – Creates a sun study through a wizard

Torus (tor) – Allows a 3D torus to be created

Ucs – Allows settings of the UCS plane

-render – Can be used to make rendering settings from the command line. Note the hyphen (-) must preceed **render**

Sweep – Creates a 3D model from a 2D outline along a path

Tabsurf – Creates a 3D solid from an outline and a direction vector

Ucs – Allows settings of the UCS plane

Union (uni) – Unites 3D solids into a single solid

View – Creates view settings for 3D models

Visualstyles – Opens the **Visual Styles** palette

Vpoint – Allows viewing positions to be set from x,y,z entries

Vports – Brings the **Viewports** dialog on screen

Wedge (we) – Creates a 3D solid in the shape of a wedge

Xedges – Creates a 3D wireframe for a 3D solid

Internet tools

Browse the Web – Brings **Autodesk home page** from the Internet on screen

Etransmit – Brings the **Create Transmittal** dialog to screen

Publish – Brings the **Publish to Web** dialog to screen

APPENDIX C

Some of the set variables

Introduction

AutoCAD 2008 is controlled by a large number of variables (over 460 in number), the settings of many of which are determined when making entries in dialogs. Others have to be set at the command line. Some are read-only variables which depend upon the configuration of AutoCAD 2008 when it originally loaded into a computer (default values).

A list of those set variables follows which are of interest in that they often require setting by *entering* figures or letters at the command line. To set a variable, enter its name at the command line and respond to the prompts which arise.

To see all set variables, *enter* **set** (or **setvar**) at the command line:

> **Command:** *enter* **set** *right-click*
> **SETVAR Enter variable name or ?:** *enter* ?
> **Enter variable name to list <*>:** *right-click*

And a Text window opens showing a first window with a list of the first of the variables. To continue with the list press the **Return** key when prompted and at each press of the **Return** key another window opens.

To see the settings for each set variable *enter* the name of the variable at the command line, followed by pressing the **F1** key which brings up the **Help** screen, *click* the search tab, followed by *entering* set variables in the **Ask** field. From the list then displayed the various settings of all set variables can be read.

Some of the set variables

ANGDIR – Sets angle direction. **0** counterclockwise; **1** clockwise
APERTURE – Sets size of pick box in pixels
AUTODWFPUBLISH – Sets **Autopublish** on or off
BLIPMODE – Set to **1** marker blips show; set to **0** no blips
COMMANDLINE – Opens the command line palette
COMMANDLINEHIDE – Closes the command line palette
COPYMODE – Sets whether **Copy** repeats

Note

DIM variables – There are over 70 variables for setting dimensioning, but most are in any case set in the **Dimension Style** dialog or as dimensioningproceeds. However one series of the **Dim** variables may be of interest.

DMBLOCK – Sets a name for the block drawn for an operator's own arrowheads. These are drawn in unit sizes and saved as required

DIMBLK1 – Operator's arrowhead for first end of line

DIMBLK2 – Operator's arrowhead for other end of line

DRAGMODE – Set to **0** no dragging; set to **1** dragging on; set to **2** automatic dragging

DRAG1 – Sets regeneration drag sampling. Initial value is 10

DRAG2 – Sets fast dragging regeneration rate. Initial value is 25

FILEDIA – Set to **0** disables **Open** and **Save As** dialogs; set to **1** enables these dialogs

FILLMODE – Set to **0** hatched areas are filled with hatching. Set to **0** hatched areas are not filled. Set to **0** and plines are not filled.

GRIPS – Set to **1** and grips show. Set to **0** and grips do not show.

LIGHTINGUNITS – Set to **1** (international) or **2** (USA) for photometric lighting to function

MBUTTONPAN – Set to **0** no *right-click* menu with the Intellimouse. Set to **1** Intellimouse *right-click* menu on

MIRRTEXT – Set to **0** text direction is retained; set to **1** text is mirrored

PELLIPSE – Set to **0** creates true ellipses; set to **1** polyline ellipses

PICKBOX – Sets selection pick box height in pixels

PICKDRAG – Set to **0** selection windows picked by two corners; set to **1** selection windows are dragged from corner to corner.

RASTERPREVIEW – Set to **0** raster preview images not created with drawing. Set to **1** preview image created

SHORTCUTMENU – For controlling how *right-click* menus show: **0** all disabled; **1** default menus only; **2** edit mode menus; **4** command mode menus; **8** command mode menus when options are currently available. Adding the figures enables more than one option

SURFTAB1 – Sets mesh density in the M direction for surfaces generated by the **Surfaces** tools

SURFTAB2 – Sets mesh density in the N direction for surfaces generated by the **Surfaces** tools

TEXTFILL – Set to **0** True Type text shows as outlines only; set to **1** True Type text is filled

TILEMODE – Set to **0** Paper Space enabled; set to **1** tiled viewports in Model Space

TOOLTIPS – Set to **0** no tool tips; set to **1** tool tips enabled

TPSTATE – Set to **0** and the Tool Palettes window is inactive. Set to **1** and the Tool Palettes window is active

TRIMMODE – Set to **0** edges not trimmed when **Chamfer** and **Fillet** are used; set to **1** edges are trimmed

UCSFOLLOW – Set to **0** new UCS settings do not take effect; set to **1** UCS settings follow requested settings

UCSICON – Set **OFF** UCS icon does not show; set to **ON** it shows

Index